Creating Economic Stability Amid Global Uncertainty

Enrique Murillo · Paolo Riccardo Morganti ·
Javier Moreno Espinosa
Editors

Creating Economic Stability Amid Global Uncertainty

Post-Pandemic Recovery in Mexico's Emerging Economy

palgrave
macmillan

Editors
Enrique Murillo
Universidad Panamericana
Mexico City, Mexico

Paolo Riccardo Morganti
Universidad Panamericana
Mexico City, Mexico

Javier Moreno Espinosa
Universidad Panamericana
Mexico City, Mexico

ISBN 978-3-031-41385-8 ISBN 978-3-031-41386-5 (eBook)
https://doi.org/10.1007/978-3-031-41386-5

This Palgrave Macmillan imprint is published by the registered company Springer Nature Switzerland AG
The registered company address is: Gewerbestrasse 11, 6330 Cham, Switzerland

Preface

When we decided the theme for the Call for Chapters of this book, in October of 2021, we as Editors had some misgivings as to whether another research volume about the effects of the COVID-19 pandemic was needed or relevant, as some of us had already contributed to two previous books on the same topic. In the Fall of 2021 there was some guarded optimism that with the increasing availability of vaccines and boosters, the virus could finally be brought under control, and businesses could at long last transit to "a recovery stage of indeterminate duration." However, the first weeks of 2022 would soon disprove these optimistic notions.

We felt that the phase of recovery deserved an analysis of its own, as the challenges that businesses are about to face to rebuild their market presence will require a novel set of theories. As an example, several authors felt that working habits have changed permanently since after the pandemic, with workers now expecting their employers to concede flexible schedules. While some firms embraced this trend and took advantage of it to cut fixed costs, others are trying to resist it and to convince their staff to return to office. Such frictions are one of the main challenges for businesses during the phase of rebuilding and are probably going to transform corporate culture in the foreseeable future. We felt this trend required a fresh perspective, and for this reason we welcomed research on the topic.

To understand the deeper forces at play during this recovery, as editors we agreed that we needed perspectives that transcend the scope of individual disciplines. For this reason, we encouraged participation of authors from diverse backgrounds. We were pleasantly surprised by the number and the quality of the submissions. As editors, we observed an emerging narrative that we endeavoured to shape within this book. At the same time, we are well aware that no single volume, even with a multidisciplinary perspective, can hope to fully describe the intricate interplay of economic, organizational and societal dynamics in the wake of the COVID-19 pandemic. Thus we hope that this collection of studies will stimulate further reflection, debate and scholarly research on one of the most difficult periods in modern economic history.

Mexico City, Mexico
June 2023

Enrique Murillo
Paolo Riccardo Morganti
Javier Moreno Espinosa

Contents

Notes on Contributors

Connie Atristain-Suárez is a full-time Professor and Researcher at the Universidad Panamericana and Director of the Ph.D. program in Business Science. Her interest and professional and teaching experience include the areas of Competitiveness, Strategic Planning and Business Management and Development. She has taught training courses to senior executives and has carried out more than 25 management development programs on relevant topics of current importance, not only for the academic world but also for the business sector. Her research includes the measurement and modeling of competitiveness, theoretical and empirical models of micro- and macro-competitiveness, cluster competitiveness, FBFs' competitiveness, strategy and operational efficiency in small and medium enterprises (SMEs).

Suhey Ayala-Ramírez is a Research Professor at the University of Guadalajara, where she earned her Ph.D. in Education, and is a member of the National System of Researchers in Mexico. She is Leader of the Academic Group: Food System and Knowledge Management and a specialist in issues related to the processes of adding value to tacit knowledge and the use of information and communication technologies in economic activities and informal educational innovation, management of non-formal learning and learning ecosystems.

Jaime Humberto Beltrán-Godoy is a Research Professor at the Faculty of Economics and Business of the Universidad Anahuac México and a member of the National System of Researchers. He has a Ph.D. in Administrative Sciences from EGADE Business School, Tecnológico de Monterrey. Master's degree in Engineering with a Specialty in Quality and Productivity and a Bachelor's degree in Industrial Engineering from the Tecnológico de Monterrey. His research interests lie in value creation in organizations, behavioral finance and financial inclusion.

J. Lee Brown III is a Professor of Management and the founding Dean of the College of Graduate and Continuing Studies at Coastal Carolina University in the USA. He earned his Ph.D. in Strategic Management and International Business at the Strome College of Business at Old Dominion University. His recent work has focused on the impact of healthcare-related technology implementation on healthcare delivery, as well as national and regional determinants of entrepreneurial failures. His scholarly work has been published in outlets such as *Health Information and Technology, Entrepreneurship Theory and Practice*, and the *Journal of International Business Studies*. It has also been presented at prestigious conferences, such as the Strategic Management Society, Academy Health ARM, the Academy of International Business, the Academy of Management, and the Conference on Corporate Governance and Global Financial Crisis at the University of Pennsylvania Wharton School of Business.

Yvette Mucharraz y Cano earned her Doctorate in Social Sciences and her Master of Arts in Interdisciplinary Studies at Royal Roads University in Canada. She holds the position of Human Resources Management Associate Professor and serves as Director of the Women in Senior Management Research Centre at IPADE Business School. She is the author of several publications including Harvard Business Review, Geoforum, Kaustubham Human Resources Management and Labour Relations Journal in India, Forbes, Business Insider and Medium, among others. She has participated in consultancy projects and as an international lecturer in: Canada, United Kingdom, United States, Italy, Switzerland, Germany, Ecuador, Peru and Chile. She is an active member of the International Coaching Federation and formerly in the Association for Talent Development. She is a certified coach in Leadership Development, Team Development, 360 Feedback/Evaluation and Talent Development. Her research and scholarly interests are focused on human resources, gender studies, organizational resilience and crisis communication.

Víctor Manuel Castillo-Girón is a Research Professor at the University of Guadalajara; member of the National System of Researchers, Mexico. He has a Ph.D. in the Economics of Agricultural, Agrifood and Rural Development from l'École Nationale Supérieure d'Agriculture, Montpellier, France. He is specialist in topics related to organizational theory; knowledge management; regional development and sustainability; food policy and economics; leadership and management skills; and research methodology.

Cecilia Y. Cuellar is a Ph.D. Candidate in Economics at the Universidad Autónoma de Nuevo León (UANL), earned a Master in Industrial Economics (UANL, 2019) and a B.A. in International Affairs (UANL, 2017). She has served as Adjunct Professor (Lecturer) at UANL and at the Tecnológico de Monterrey. She is the winner of the "Consuelo Meyer L'eppe Award" for the best Master's Thesis (2020) and for the Best Graduate Research Paper (2021, 2022). Her work has been published in national and international academic journals. She is currently Junior Research Analyst at the Hibbs Institute for Business and Economic Research at the University of Texas at Tyler. Her research areas are Labor Economics, Gender Economics and Applied Economics.

Karla Cuilty-Esquivel earned her Master's degree in Economics from El Colegio de México, México. She is Senior Researcher of Center for Research on Women in Senior Management at IPADE Business School. She has coordinated three books about Women and Leadership development, five research papers with themes related to women's inclusion and decent work, four female cases. Her research interests include women in careers STEM (Science, Technology, Engineering and Mathematics), gender stereotypes and women on boards. Her professional activities include roles as Manager of Impact Assessment Analysis and Coordinator of the Observatories for Transparency and Accountability on Gender Mainstreaming for the Mexican Government.

Diana Dávila-Ruiz earned her Doctorate in Business Administration from the Grenoble École de Management in France, and is a Senior Professor of Marketing at the School of Business, Anáhuac University. Her expertise lies in examining corporate brands. She is the Editor-in-Chief of the *Anáhuac Journal*, and a founding partner of Ambassador Brands where opinions of top marketers in México evaluate top brands that represent México positively. His lecturing focuses on marketing, women's leadership and championing equality worldwide; she teaches in undergraduate programs, M.B.A. and Executive M.B.A. Before joining academia, she worked for multinational companies such as Procter and Gamble, Johnson and Johnson, and served as Marketing and Public Relations Director for Steelcase Co. in Latam.

Lorena DelaTorre-Diaz is a doctoral student in Business Sciences at Universidad Panamericana. She has a degree with honors in Business Administration and Finance from Universidad Panamericana and obtained the Master's degree in Finance at the Universidad del Valle de Atemajac. She has performed as a treasury manager, financial analyst and the administrative manager of a family business. She has been a Lecturer at Universidad Panamericana since 2008, in courses of Financial Analysis, Financial Mathematics, Financial Investment Systems, Economic Engineering, Technological Tools and Advanced Excel. Her research areas are social mobility, inequality, microcredits and micro and small enterprises.

Javier Moreno Espinosa is a Research Professor at the School of Economics and Business Administration at the Universidad Panamericana. He has a Ph.D. in Strategic Management and Development Policies from Anahuac University and is a member of the National System of Researchers level candidate in Mexico; his research areas are focused on Economic Theory, Public Finance, Artificial Intelligence and Text Mining applied, in the area of social sciences.

Santiago García-Álvarez received his Ph.D. in Organizational Governance and Culture at the Universidad of Navarra (Spain), and his doctoral dissertation was entitled "Management Policy Elements in Henry Mintzberg." He also received his Master's degree in Science and Operations Research at Georgia Institute of Technology, and his Bachelor's degree with honors in Industrial Engineering at Universidad Panamericana (México). He has been in several directive positions since 2003, and currently, he is President of Universidad Panamericana at Mexico City's Campus. Dr. García teaches Government and Public Policy at Government and Economics School in the Master's program, and Business and Management in the Bachelor's program. His main publications discuss directive management, leadership and organizational performance among other topics.

Gabriela García-Cano is a graduate in Business Administration from Universidad Panamericana, where she joined the program for Young

Researchers at the School of Economics and Business Administration. She worked as a Research Assistant for Dr. Paolo Morganti for two years. Currently, she is a digital Key Account Manager at the online retailer Mercado Libre.

Andrée Marie López-Fernández is a Professor and Researcher at the School of Economics and Business Administration at the Universidad Panamericana. She obtained a Ph.D. in Administrative Sciences from the EGADE Business School, and her research areas of interest include corporate social responsibility, social media and viral marketing, governance, leadership, and consumer behavior. The latter has resulted in the presentation of her work at International Conferences and publications in *International Refereed Journals*, as well as a couple of books and book chapters. She is an Associate Editor for *Emerald Emerging Markets Case Studies Journal*, and has been conferred as a member of the Mexican National System of Researchers by CONACYT.

Antonieta Martínez-Velasco is a Researcher and Professor at the School of Engineering, Universidad Panamericana. She is a member of the Mexican National System of Researchers. She has a Master's degree in Computer Science from the Instituto Politécnico Nacional, and Ph.D. in Engineering from the Universidad Panamericana. Her area of specialization is Artificial Intelligence applied to Engineering, Health Sciences and Social Sciences.

Leovardo Mata Mata is a Professor-Researcher at the Faculty of Economics and Business at Universidad Anáhuac México, has a Ph.D. in Financial Sciences from the EGADE Business School at the Tecnológico de Monterrey and is a member of the National System of Researchers Level-I in Mexico; his research areas are Economic Theory, Numerical Analysis, Earth Sciences and Interdisciplinary Quantitative Tools applicable to the area of Social Sciences.

Jorge O. Moreno has a Ph.D. and M.A. in Economics from the University of Chicago (2007 and 2010, respectively), a Master in Economics from El Colegio de México (2002) and a B.A. in Economics at the Universidad Autónoma de Nuevo León (UANL, 1999). He served as Deputy Director in the Ministry of Public Finance in Mexico, Economist JPA in the Human Development Sector at the World Bank, Visiting Researcher at the General Directorate for the Analysis of the Financial System of the Banco of Mexico, Adjunct Professor at El Colegio de

Mexico, Lecturer at the University of Chicago and Professor at the ITAM School of Business. He has published multiple books, chapters, papers, reviews and received multiple prizes nationally and internationally for his research work and academic career, including the prestigious "Wayne C. Booth Award for Excellence in Teaching (2010)" at the University of Chicago, the "FUNSALUD-GSK National Award on Biomedical Research in Health Economics" (2015) and the "IMEF-EY International Award in Financial Research (2022)," among other honors. He is currently a Professor and Researcher at the Faculty of Economics, UANL. His research areas are Human Capital (Education, Health and Labor), Financial Economics and Developmental Economics.

Paolo Riccardo Morganti is a Professor of Economics at the Universidad Panamericana, School of Economics and Business Administration. He has a Ph.D. in Economics from the New York University (USA). His research is focused on Industrial Organization and Microeconomic Theory. He has conducted studies where he analyzes firms' conducts in imperfectly competitive markets with product differentiation. His work has appeared in *Quantitative Economics, Journal of Economics, Análisis Económico* and *Revista Mexicana de Economía y Finanzas*.

Enrique Murillo is Professor of Marketing at Universidad Panamericana in Mexico City. His research focuses on Internal Branding, examining the drivers of employees' positive attitudes toward the service brand, a prerequisite for brand-aligned service encounters. In pursuit of this topic, he has conducted studies in various organizations in Latin America, including restaurants, airlines, universities, fashion retailers, drugstore chains and ride-sharing platforms. His work has appeared in top-ranked journals including *Journal of Service Management, Journal of Product & Brand Management*, *International Journal of Contemporary Hospitality Management* and *Journal of Business Research* among others.

Maria E. Ramos has Master in Education at Universidad Valle de México and a B.A. in Economics at the Universidad Autónoma de Nuevo León (UANL). She also has completed several diplomats in Stock Market, Statistics, Applied Mathematics, Economic Competition and Project Evaluation. Her professional experience includes working for the Ministry of Public Finance in Mexico, the National Institute of Statistics and Geography (INEGI) and working as Adjunct Professor for several universities in Mexico. She is currently an Assistant Professor at the Faculty of Public

Administration and Accounting, UANL. Her research areas are Labor Economics, Corporate Finance and Applied Economics.

Jose Luis Rivas is a Tenured Professor at ITAM in Mexico City where he teaches global strategy and leadership. He held different executive positions at ADO Mobility where he was also a board member before joining academia. He holds a Ph.D. from IE Business School and an M.B.A. from Northwestern University. His research focuses on boards, top managers and IPOs. He has published academic articles, book chapters, business cases and a book on corporate governance in Mexico. He is Vice President of the Ibero-American Academy of Management, editorial board member of the journal *Corporate Governance: An International Review*, and a board member of the International Corporate Governance Society.

Salvador Rivas-Aceves has a Ph.D. in Economic Sciences, a Master's degree in Economic Sciences, a Bachelor's degree in Economics by the Universidad Autónoma Metropolitana, México and a specialty in Anthropology by the Universidad Panamericana. He is an Economics, Finance and Politics Analyst and, since 2006, he has been a Research Professor. He was Chief of the Economics Academy at the School of Economics and Business Administration during 2013–2105. From 2015 to 2019, he was the Academic Dean as well as Research Dean of the Government and Economics School at the Universidad Panamericana. Since 2020, he has been the Research Dean at the School of Economics and Business Administration. He has published research on Economic Growth, Technological Change, Financial Regulation and Risk Analysis on the Financial Sector in several scientific papers, books and chapters in scientific books since 2005. He is a member of the National Research System of Mexico since 2010.

Ricardo Murcio Rodríguez earned his Ph.D. and Master's degrees, both, in Organizational Governance and Culture from University of Navarra, Spain, and his M.B.A. from IPADE Business School, México. He is Guest Professor at the Organizational Behavior Department. He is author of the book "Human Centered Leadership" edited by the University of Navarra and co-author in several books. He is board member and consultant in some families' companies and is Personal Coach for career and life planning. His professional activities include Corporate Director, Academic Director, Human Resources Manager, Learning and Development Manager, Human Resources Project Executive and Professor. His research interests are focus on Artificial Intelligence and the future of Management, Humanistic Management and Organizational Behavoir.

Antonia Terán-Bustamante is a Researcher and Professor at the School of Economics and Business Administration at the Universidad Panamericana and is a member of the Mexican National System of Researchers by CONACYT. She has a Ph.D. in Administration Sciences and Master's in Administration International Business from the Universidad Nacional Autónoma de México (UNAM). Her research is focused on Human Capital, Competitiveness, Innovation and Entrepreneurship.

List of Figures

List of Tables

PART I

Human, Economic and Technological Levers

CHAPTER 1

Looking Back at 2022: A Recovery or a Protracted Crisis?

Enrique Murillo and Salvador Rivas-Aceves

An Uncommonly Turbulent Year

The events of 2022 finally put to rest any lingering hopes that the global economy will at some point return to pre-COVID-19 levels. The year witnessed an alarming succession of macroeconomic shocks, starting with the rapid spread of the highly contagious Omicron variant; the inflation caused by cumulative supply chain disruptions and pent-up consumer demand; the war in Ukraine, which started in February, and had an immediate impact on the global supply of food and fuel; the record-breaking heat waves in the Spring, that affected Argentina, Australia, India, Pakistan, Spain, France, the UK, Japan, China, and the United States; these combined shocks contributed to economic and business volatility (Alexander et al., 2022). By October of 2022, the news were

E. Murillo · S. Rivas-Aceves (✉)
Facultad de Ciencias Económicas y Empresariales, Universidad Panamericana, Mexico City, Mexico
e-mail: srivasa@up.edu.mx

E. Murillo
e-mail: emurillo@up.edu.mx

E. Murillo et al. (eds.), *Creating Economic Stability Amid Global Uncertainty*, https://doi.org/10.1007/978-3-031-41386-5_1

dominated by widespread fears of a global recession, as central banks, led by the Federal Reserve in the United States, aggressively hiked interest rates to contain rising prices (Tooze, 2022). In the same month, the IMF's *World Economic Output* report forecasted that global growth would drop from 6.0% in 2021 to just 3.2 in 2022 (International Monetary Fund, 2022). In sum, the year will probably go down in history as one of the most volatile periods in the global economy.

The news from the airline industry, in the Spring and Summer of 2022, provide a useful glimpse of the challenges that organizations are facing in this new period. As travel demand surged after the Great Confinement. Unchecked by high fares, both airlines and airports faced severe staff shortages caused by the layoffs and early retirements implemented during the long months of the pandemic (Katz & Sider, 2022). The airline industry is characterized by substantial training requirements, not only for pilots and cabin crews, but also for ground personnel, such as mechanics, aircraft handlers, customs and immigration officers, security personnel, etc. Hence, even though all airlines were hiring by mid-2021, getting new employees to proficiency levels is going to take time. Furthermore, airlines encountered a tight labor market, with people demanding better wages and working conditions. By the fall, signing bonuses had become commonplace, especially for pilots (Arnold, 2021).

Air travel is a complex system which requires a high level of synchronization; delays in any part of the system inevitably spill over to other parts. When airlines have chronic staff shortages, passengers take longer to check in and also face delays to get their luggage back when they reach their destination. When not enough employees are available in security screening checkpoints, long lines form and some passengers may miss their flights. When customs and immigration facilities are filled to overflowing, passengers are sometimes asked to wait for hours inside aircraft, instead of disembarking (Sider, 2022).

This adverse situation has been further complicated by external environmental contingencies. The Summer months in the United States were plagued by bad weather, which caused severe disruption to flight operations (Sider, 2022). In addition, the BA.5 Omicron variant became dominant in May, which caused many airline employees to call in with symptoms, thus needing to isolate. Lacking replacements, airlines were often forced to cancel flights, causing even more congestion at airports.

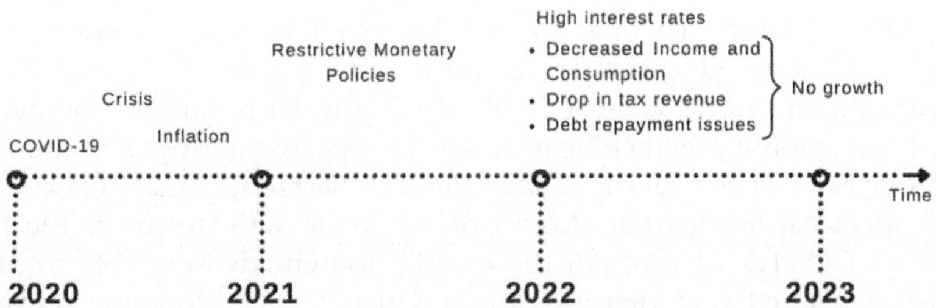

Fig. 1.1 A timeline of key macroeconomic problems stemming from the pandemic (*Source* Authors)

Many of these disruptions so prominently displayed by the airline industry were also reflected in less visible manufacturing and service organizations, as they attempted to pivot to the rebuilding and recovery stage after the pandemic. Normal operations were hampered by employee absenteeism, needed inputs were delayed by supply chain disruptions, and even short-term planning was rendered difficult by wage and price inflation. Economic causes and consequences during the pandemic in previous years are well characterized by Dávila-Aragón and Rivas-Aceves (2021), and López-Fernández and Terán-Bustamante (2022). Indeed, high inflation appears to be the most severe and long-lasting damage stemming from the COVID-19 lockdowns, along with the increases in interest rates that central banks are implementing to bring it under control. However, other macroeconomic issues are also becoming grounds for concern, as displayed in the timeline in Fig. 1.1. The next section offers a more detailed analysis.

The World Economy After The Pandemic

Supply-Side Factors as the Main Cause of Post-COVID-19 Inflation

World inflation continues to increase and the monetary policy that is being applied to bring it under control is the standard increase in the interest rate. It appears that most economies, and especially central banks, have yet to grasp that the main cause of inflation after the COVID-19 pandemic is not excessive market demand, but rather a problem of supply, see Cerrato and Gitti (2022), Shapiro (2022) and Binici et al. (2022).

While it is true that most households maintained their income level, and even increased their savings during the pandemic (World Bank, 2023), the strongest cause of inflation is the large number of micro, small and medium-sized companies that disappeared during the economic closures (Gourinchas et al., 2022; Sánchez Serrano, 2022). Of course, with the total and partial closure of economic activities from the first wave of COVID-19 through the fourth, households were able to save, which generated a sudden increase in demand once economic activities were resumed. This, in and of itself, caused strong inflationary pressures. Nonetheless, many of the companies that went bankrupt were engaged in the production of intermediate goods and services (Gourinchas et al., 2022; Ramani et al., 2022; Rivas-Aceves & Mawaad Morales, 2022; Sodhi & Tang, 2021). Therefore, the input supply chain suffered a disruption, causing a precipitous drop in the rate of production of final goods, usually produced by big companies.

The automobile market is a clear example, as the availability of new vehicles has been limited by shortages in the supply of semiconductors, both from supply chain disruptions and from skyrocketing demand for consumer electronics during the lockdowns (Boranova et al., 2022; Ramani et al., 2022). In consequence, it is the scarcity of products in the market that is causing inflationary processes in most economies.

Ineffectiveness of Restrictive Monetary Policy

During 2022 worldwide, the annual rate of inflation has continued to grow globally (see Table 1.1). Such persistently high levels of inflation suggest that conventional monetary policy is not being effective, and the continuous increases in interest rates are not stopping consumption. As an example, the European Union reached 8.1% in inflation on average; nonetheless, Poland draws the attention for its high inflation rate.

In order to bring inflation under control, most of the analyzed economies have repeatedly increased interest rates. In ordinary times, it is normal to find interest rates between 1 and 1.5% in developed countries, while for developing countries between 2.5 and 3%, when there are no inflation pressures. However, by the end of 2022, central banks around the world had taken very energetic positions in terms of monetary policy, with interest rates reaching two digits levels, around 10–11%, with yet little impact on inflation.

Table 1.1 Inflation rate for selected countries in 2022

Country	*Inflation rate*
South Korea	5.9
India	6.7
Canada	6.8
United Kingdom	7.9
Mexico	7.9
Germany	7.9
United States	8.2
Spain	8.4
Brazil	9.3
Greece	9.6
Colombia	10.2
Chile	11.6
Russia	13.5
Poland	14.3
Ukraine	20.18
Turkey	72.3
Argentina	72.4
Venezuela	220.8

Source Own elaboration with World Bank data (Ha et al., 2021)

Unintended Consequences of Restrictive Monetary Policy

Not only have interest rates hikes failed to check inflation, they are currently strangling companies because credits have become more expensive. This means that companies cannot invest to expand their productive capacity and, therefore, that the market supply does not grow, see Chen et al. (2021).

Furthermore, the spike of interest rates has discouraged investment and consumption, despite the economic recovery. Direct investment has been affected the most because market conditions are highly volatile, companies lack any economic certainty, while also facing the high cost of credit. These are the biggest obstacles to boosting supply.

In addition, an even bigger problem is being generated. The restrictive monetary policy is causing a drop in tax collection, leading to public debt payment issues in several countries around the world. During 2022, countries, such as Brazil, Belize, Ecuador, Argentina, Kenya, Sri Lanka, Pakistan, Lebanon, Ethiopia, Zambia, El Salvador, among others, have shown great payment difficulties. Several have restructured their public debt, according to data from the International Monetary Fund (2022). Most of the countries have based their economic recovery on the expectations placed on the external market, but the current problem is systemic, and is affecting nearly all regions of the world. The international markets have lost confidence due to the adjustment in inflation, reduced growth expectations, and the change in monetary policy, but above all because the central banks claimed that inflation would be a temporary phenomenon, which has not been the case thus far.

The risk represented by the low payment capacity of governments, coupled with the alarming levels of the principal economic indicators, is causing markets not to grow. Destabilization produced by radical changes in monetary policy in the short term is affecting most economies. China is one of the few countries that has maintained a stable monetary policy, which has helped to foster investment thus promoting growth. It did not lower the interest rate to near zero levels during the economic downturn, and did not raise it during the recovery, resulting in moderate inflation and a continued slowdown so far in 2022.

In sum, in order to address the supply-side factors that are the main drivers of post-pandemic inflation, unconventional monetary policy in the face of economic cycles is necessary. Because scarcity of services, and of final and intermediate goods remains, the anticyclical solution is flooding markets with production, which can only be sustained by an increasing number of companies fostered by means of low interest rates.

To reverse upward pressure on prices, it is necessary to flood the market with goods and services, that is, to increase the rate of production of inputs and final goods. It is, therefore, necessary to increase public and private investment in order to increase the number of new companies, as well as expand the installed capacity of existing ones. At the same time, it is essential to forestall the bankruptcy of companies by promoting appropriate conditions for their operation, through fiscal support, strategic alliances, regulatory certainty, security, but above all a stable economic environment. Inflation can only be tamed by vigorously boosting market supply.

The Role of Central Banks and Monetary Base Expansion

In addition to the conventional setting of higher interest rates, central banks have also acted in the same conventional way with the monetary base during this time of inflationary pressures. One of the main functions of money is to be a medium of exchange. Consequently, central banks must put a sufficient amount of money into circulation to guarantee that all goods and services produced within an economy can be marketed (Teryoshin, 2023). In other words, the value of the Gross Domestic Product must be supported by the monetary base. This relationship between the real economy and money is usually very little analyzed, and much less understood.

In economic terms, the fact that an economy grows means that there is a greater physical quantity of goods and services produced per unit of time, especially with inflation staying constant or growing at a lower rate than the economy. Growth in the Gross Domestic Product can occur either by an increase in the goods and services produced, or by an increase in prices, or by both. When an economy grows and its inflation rate is controlled, then the amount of money required to trade goods and services will increase in parallel and at the same pace as the growth rate, without generating further inflationary pressures. The latter because the income is growing, so the demand meets the supply.

But what happens when there is false growth? That is to say, when it is prices that are growing but not the physical quantity of goods and services produced in the country. Under these conditions, the amount of money necessary to market the product must also grow, because it is essential to facilitate transactions. Since the amount of goods and services produced is not growing, then neither is national income. Which implies that inflation is being supported only by the monetary base and not by an increase in economic activity.

When a central bank increases the amount of money in circulation, it generates an increase in the velocity of money, in such a way that economic agents perceive a false increase in their purchasing power. This drives them to increase their demand (Geiger et al., 2023). Therefore, inflationary pressures rise even higher. Because the objective of every central bank is to maintain the stability of the payment system, when inflation expectations exist the monetary base will immediately tend to rise. However, such an increase in money actually makes the inflation expectation come true. In other words, central banks are providing feedback to the pre-existing inflationary pressures by increasing the monetary base (Geiger et al., 2023; Teryoshin, 2023).

In Mexico, from June 2019 to October 2022, the monetary base grew 54% according to data from Mexico's central bank (Bank of Mexico, 2023). This positive trend in the quantity of money is also present in economies such as the United States, Canada and the European Union, thereby exacerbating inflation levels in these economies. Given that it has not been possible to control inflation through the internal market via interest rates, it is evident that the contraction in the monetary base may be the solution. However, public policy in most economies has been focused on providing economic relief to face the pandemic. The vast majority of this expense was financed not by economic growth, that is, higher income, but by a greater amount of printed money, as happened in the United States.

In summary, the management of interest rates coupled with the increase in the monetary base, together with the disruption of supply chains and the expansion in consumer demand, have resulted in the current phase of accelerated inflation. To complete the macroeconomic picture, the growth rate is beginning to drop in several economies.

The Weakening Recovery and the Uncertain Outlook for 2023

Economic growth at the end of 2021 showed signs of weakening, and by 2022 the economic recovery petered out. In most countries, the growth rate in 2022 dropped by about half, compared to the rate registered in 2021. When economies are not growing, effects on employment always appear. In 2021, the rebound in global economic growth was 5.8% according to World Bank numbers. This rebound began to lose strength at the end of the same year, and during 2022 there were indicators that showed that the rebound had run out of steam, (see Table 1.2).

Most of the economies are growing at slower rates; the slowdown clearly indicates fewer goods and services produced from one year to the next. This means a fall in the effective market supply, which has two important repercussions: on the one hand, an increase in the unemployment rate, and on the other, an increase in prices. Several governments are determined to achieve economic growth, most of them allocating fiscal resources in the form of economic stimulus, to such an extent that public debt is growing at faster rates than economic growth. The foregoing is always a very dangerous combination because eventually the indebtedness becomes a drag on growth, generating economic recession, which under the current conditions would likely result in a profound crisis. During this difficult year of 2022, the United States, China, the United

Table 1.2 Growth and unemployment rates for selected countries in 2022

Country	*Growth rate*	*Unemployment rate*
Brazil	3	4.8
Canada	2.7	5.1
Chile	2.1	8.4
China	2.7	5.6
European Union	2.6	6.6
France	2.2	7
Germany	1.9	3.7
Greece	1.8	11.6
Hong Kong	2.9	5.1
Italy	3.9	7.8
Japan	1.4	2.4
Mexico	3.1	3.9
South Korea	2.6	2.5
Spain	5.2	13
Turkey	1.8	10.1
United Kingdom	4.1	3.7
United States	1.9	5.2

Source Own elaboration with OECD (2023) data

Kingdom, France, Italy, India, Hong Kong, Malaysia, Brazil have considerably increased their debt as a proportion of GDP during 2022 (World Bank, 2023). As of this writing, it remains to be seen whether the Federal Reserve in the United States succeeds in bringing about a "soft-landing" during 2023, and what outcomes are achieved by central banks in other major economies.

Overview of This Book

The Call for Chapters which launched this research book in the Fall of 2021 called the current environment "a recovery stage of indeterminate duration." Such a stage has already lasted nearly two years, and as of this writing, in February of 2023, even the most optimistic observers hold no hope that 2023 will be the year of returning back to normal. Indeed, some analysts speculate that there may be no returning back to pre-pandemic levels, given the structural changes that have taken place since 2021, such as the paradigm change in inflation-targeting monetary policy (Economist, 2022 October 8), or the withdrawal from the hyperglobalization and just-in-time supply chains of the first decade of this century

(Krugman, 2022), and the current trend toward near-shoring and supply chain redesign, emphasizing security over low-cost efficiency (Economist, 2022 June 18).

National and business dynamics after the pandemic lockdowns are still a new and mostly uncharted phenomenon, which is why three years after the start of the pandemic there is still ample space for new research studies, ideally with a multidisciplinary perspective. Nearly thirty researchers answered the Call for Chapters, with both conceptual and empirical contributions, focusing on the economic, technological, and human levers that are being applied by governments, industries, firms, families, and individual employees to navigate these volatile times. Accepted chapters went through a minimum of two rounds of peer review by topic experts, in addition to editorial feedback for alignment with the objectives of the book, and an independent peer review by Palgrave Macmillan.

Given the wide scope of topics addressed, and the global reach intended by several of our contributors, this volume is organized into two parts: Part I is titled ***Human, Economic, and Technological Levers*** and comprises five chapters. To set the stage, the present opening chapter examines the state of the world economy in the aftermath of the COVID-19 pandemic. The remaining chapters examine organizational, technological, and human levers that businesses can implement to rebuild their productive activities, and the effect these measures have on individual employees. The chapters in Part I are ordered from a macro to a micro-level perspective, and since they are conceptual, the levers they propose are generalizable to both advanced and emergent economies.

While Part I intends a global reach through conceptual chapters, the studies in Part II of the book adopt a data-based strategy to examine the application of various levers in the context of an emergent economy. Under the title ***Lever Deployment in an Emergent Economy***, Part II brings together five studies which cover the full range of the economy, from macro-variables related to public finance, to micro-indicators such as the level of household incomes. As these empirical studies are based on economic and company data from Mexico, a relevant emergent economy, their findings can be judiciously generalized to other similar countries.

Chapter 2, which follows this introductory chapter, bears the title "The Effects of Flexible Workspace on Organizational Structure and Inequality: An Equilibrium Analysis." Morganti and García-Cano develop the connection between the micro-dimension of the firm, and the macroeconomic dimension of the country with emphasis on inequality, firm size and distribution, and wealth. The antecedent of this research is the Great Confinement, which made telework the only safe alternative for office workers for most of 2020, until the vaccination campaigns ramped up in early 2021. The authors posit that with the implementation of hybrid work, companies experience a friction in their communications and in the transmission of knowledge across their organizational layers. As they adapt their structures under this pressure, they induce a transformation of the entire productive system with profound effects on the economy as a whole. Using a theoretical approach, the authors attempt to predict unexpected long-term outcomes. Under the new organizational structure, an efficient management of knowledge and communications is projected to lead to more firms, but of smaller size. Following this change, companies' profitability can be expected to fall, but their differences should converge. As knowledge transmission slows down, the authors expect a fall in a country's GDP and in workers' wages. Unfortunately, the combined effects are projected to contribute to an increase in the country's inequality. Morganti and García-Cano conclude that in the post-COVID-19 era, organizational design and knowledge management are levers that need to be mastered in order to survive the new competitive environment. Indeed, these crucial organizational levers are investigated in Chapters 4 and 10 of this volume.

Chapter 3 is titled "Harnessing Middle Management Innovation for Business Recovery." Its focal lever is the human capital of the organization, specifically its middle managers, in order to enhance firm innovativeness, which is essential to navigate the uncertain post-pandemic environment. In this chapter, Brown and Rivas make a theoretical contribution grounded in the resource-based view of the firm (Barney, 1991). They advance a model which refines and extends this theory by asserting that middle management behavior is a valuable and unique resource bundle that can be leveraged to increase organizational innovation. Specifically, this model advances four managerial behaviors, questioning, observing, experimenting, and networking that are posited to have a positive impact on organizational innovativeness. Furthermore, the model proposes that three external factors will positively moderate the effect of the behaviors on innovativeness, specifically a higher population density in the region, a low level corruption in the region, and a high level of patent activity in the region. This model highlights the importance of managerial activity within the organizations. Thus, it is not just the ownership and control of valuable and rare resources that confers competitive advantage, but the development and application of said resources by the firm's middle managers.

The next chapter is a conceptual contribution focused on the issue of leading people in large organizations after the workplace changes sparked by the pandemic. Titled "Co-creating Value Through People-centered Leadership: Lessons Learned from the COVID-19 Crisis," Chapter 4 draws from organizational design theory, specifically the organizational form of adhocracy, advanced by Mintzberg. Specifically, García-Álvarez and López-Fernández examine the interaction between adhocracy and a person-centered leadership style, which is proposed as a management lever that is well-suited for the challenges faced by organizations after the pandemic forced the closure of offices and the shift to remote work. Some of those challenges have endured even after the end of mandatory confinement, with many employees resisting in 2022 a return to the office as before. Among the challenges now faced by organizations are calls for greater organizational flexibility, optimal use of technology, and the need for a leadership style that enables employees to perform their tasks and contribute their knowledge and competencies without compromising efficiency. Accordingly, García-Álvarez and López-Fernández posit that moving forward, value may be co-created as employee well-being is prioritized with the intent to build work communities; in such way that, a successful recovery is not only based on organizational flexibility, optimal technology use, and efficiency, but is driven by both business and social growth and development.

Chapter 5, titled "COVID-19: An Opportunity to Explore Hybrid Work," analyzes how, in the wake of the Great Confinement, there has been an expansion of telework, which had begun decades earlier, and a push by employees for hybrid work models to improve results for organizations and employees. Mucharraz y Cano, Dávila-Ruiz, Murcio Rodríguez, and Cuilty-Esquivel explain how the Fourth Industrial Revolution with its technological communication tools had largely made it possible for many office employees to work from home. However, the once-in-a-generation lockdowns sparked by the COVID-19 pandemic resulted in most companies and workers experiencing for the first time the benefits and challenges of working from home. Many employees perceived a reduction of work-life conflict and increased productivity. Others experienced more ambiguous results, especially for female talent. Difficulties arose from the intersection of three elements: (a) family, (b) work, and (c) school in the same place and, often at the same time. Many women professionals experienced these as conflicting demands on their attention, resulting in stress, Zoom fatigue, burnout, and mental health problems. After isolation measures were relaxed, the hybrid work scheme gained momentum. This is defined as the combination of work in and outside the office, where space, time, and home intersect as a novel combination of technological and human levers. Returning employees argued it allowed an optimal combination of face-to-face and remote working. The hybrid model seems to respond to the need for more malleable work schemes that allow for a better work-life balance. Nevertheless, there are still issues to be analyzed to successfully implement hybrid work in organizations, for example, the necessary changes in companies' operational frameworks and policies, and the effects on productivity. The post-COVID-19 era could bring changes in the preferences of customers, suppliers, and employees, as well as new forms of interactions at the social, family, and work level, where technology use will continue to increase. The described context is likely to maintain virtual and face-to-face interactions simultaneously, promoting a wider dissemination of hybrid models in the future labor market.

Part II of the book, as mentioned earlier, comprises five empirical studies that examine the application of various economic, technological, and human levers in the context of an emergent economy, drawing on country and company data from Mexico.

Chapter 6 is a macro-level investigation titled "VAT Elasticities on Imports as a Lever to Forecast Collection: Mexico 2010–2021." Moreno, Mata, and Beltrán-Godoy undertake an empirical analysis of VAT elasticities on merchandise imports using data from the Tax Administration Service in Mexico for the period 2010–2021. The objective of this research was to identify the main chapters of goods that generate the greatest tax collection for the government. Given that the VAT is the second source of income for the Mexican Treasury, identifying the sensitivity of VAT collection in generating tax revenue from particular chapters of goods can contribute to better forecasts of tax government revenue and can also suggest fiscal policy measures that are conducive to achieving increased revenue collection. Following the IMF recommendation on the elasticity methods, the authors estimate the elasticity of VAT collection on imports for each of the 99 chapters classified in the International Harmonized System of customs and trade procedures. The econometric analysis relied on vector autoregression, specifically a vector error correction

(VEC) model. The authors propose that by using the estimated elasticities, the Government can focus its surveillance and auditing resources on the 16 chapters that explain 82% of the value of imports and which display varying elasticities. By knowing the elasticity, the tax authority can forecast the expected increase in tax revenue from particular chapters that are growing, and where these expectations are not met, the authority can increase its auditing efforts with a higher probability of detecting illegal practices.

The next chapter, "Employment, Gender Gap, and the Mexican Industry: The Effect of COVID-19 on the Dynamic Structure and Recovery in the Labor Market," investigates the recovery of the national labor market after the pandemic lockdowns, using historical data from urban employment surveys in Mexico. Moreno, Cuellar, and Ramos identify consistent micro-founded time series of employment and wages from 1993:Q1 to 2021:Q4 segmented by industrial sector and gender. The research follows a neoclassical production and labor demand approach and, with these datasets, estimates a vector autoregression (VAR) model linking aggregate production and each labor market segment in the implied long-run equilibria. Model results suggest significant adverse effects on employment resulting from the pandemic lockdown, both for females and males. The estimations suggest a structural and persistent effect on employment losses, with lengthy recovery of employment levels, particularly in the male segment, and a more significant recovery rate of female employment. With respect to sectors, the results show that employment in the tertiary sector is highly reactive to the first COVID-19 shock compared to the other sectors. The secondary industrial sector shows a similar but less pronounced reaction, so all observed job losses are related to a structural change in the labor market. By contrast, primary sector employment is inelastic to the initial shock. The chapter's conclusion is that sectorial-gender employment effects present a lower forecasted response to the initial shock from the pandemic, but substantial employment losses by the fourth quarter of 2021, potentially linked to changes in the labor market structure due to the pandemic.

Chapter 8 adopts a micro-level perspective focused on household income which was severely affected in Mexico by the restrictions imposed by the government during the Great Confinement. Under the title "Access to Microfinance for Social Mobility in Mexico," De la Torre-Diaz analyzes the concept of social mobility as a dimension of the study of inequality of opportunities. Data from the National Survey of Household income and Expenses presented by INEGI shows that the confinement negatively impacted household income in 2020 by −3% compared to 2018. The distribution of household expenses was also altered affecting items such as education, which changed its proportion from 12 to 8% between the 2018 and 2020 surveys. This scenario raised the already high obstacles faced by the Mexican population regarding their expectations of upward social mobility, a phenomenon that in itself presents daunting challenges derived from the country's considerable level of inequality of opportunities. The chapter presents a conceptual model proposing the accumulation of household assets as a novel mechanism to promote social mobility, particularly during difficult times in which income-driven social mobility is challenging. An additional element in this model is the use of microcredit as the financial lever that enables households to acquire such assets. The proposed model, therefore, combines the previously mentioned relationships between asset accumulation and social mobility, and by including the positive impact of microcredits, offers a plausible program considered as a way for families to climb the socioeconomic conditions ladder, thus contributing to a reduction of inequality.

In Chapter 9, Murillo and Atristain focus on the lever of strategic planning, viewed as a recurring process, as a tool for managerial learning and decision-making when organizations are faced with substantial environmental volatility. More specifically, this study measures the impact of two brand-related marketing strategies implemented by a private university in Mexico City as part of its strategic plan devised to respond to the lengthy campus lockdown brought about by the pandemic. The strategies in question were the unveiling of an updated corporate visual identity (CVI) and a strong emphasis during the lockdown on the university brand promise of personal attention. Using an online survey, student assessments of brand promise delivery and of the new CVI were measured, with 288 usable surveys obtained. A conditional process analysis was applied to the data using the PROCESS macro for SPSS (Hayes et al., 2017). The results show that perceived brand promise delivery had a significant positive effect on the university's reputation and student brand advocacy, mediated, in both cases, by perceived brand image and student satisfaction. In addition, the new CVI moderates the relationship between brand promise delivery and brand image, so that in students who rated the CVI better, the link between brand promise delivery and brand image was significantly stronger. By measuring the impact on a key stakeholder group of two marketing strategies that were themselves nested within the general strategic plan of the university, Murillo and Atristain illustrate the cyclical nature of the strategic planning process, and how successive cycles of planning can be enriched with the knowledge gained through empirical research of relevant stakeholders, in addition to conventional control metrics.

The book closes with Chapter 10, titled "Knowledge Management and Innovation in the Furniture Industry in Mexico." This empirical study traces the application of the knowledge lever in the furniture industry in Mexico. Specifically, Castillo-Girón, Ayala-Ramírez, Martínez-Velasco, and Terán-Bustamante build a decision model that identifies the most critical processes that are required to manage knowledge and innovation in the furniture industry. The model was built with expert opinions obtained through multiple data collection instruments, namely a written questionnaire applied to four large furniture enterprises, triangulated by semi-structured interviews with a range of experts. Based on the information from these sources, a conceptual model of the industry was developed which maps the network of directed arcs between the 30 identified critical processes (e.g., protection of intellectual property, modern technologies, marketing capacity, e-commerce, etc.). The principal benefit of this model is that it allows companies in this sector to make the best decisions to innovate in new products/services, processes, sales, and marketing, as well as in the organization. This conceptual model was then estimated using Bayesian networks and Machine Learning techniques. Knowledge is a valuable asset for all companies. Hence, the ability to learn and accumulate new knowledge regarding the essence of their innovation processes is of great value to companies in the sector. The authors thereby illustrate the importance of the knowledge management lever in an industry that generates a significant number of jobs in the country and a substantial economic contribution.

Some observers might call 2022 the first year of the New Normal. The studies in this volume show that this dynamic economic and social environment carries with it numerous unresolved questions, that call for thoughtful multidisciplinary research studies. It is to be hoped that more books adopting such a perspective will be forthcoming in the following years.

References

Alexander, A., Blome, C., Schleper, M. C., & Roscoe, S. (2022). Managing the "new normal": The future of operations and supply chain management in unprecedented times. *International Journal of Operations & Production Management*. https://doi.org/10.1108/IJOPM-06-2022-0367

Arnold, K. (2021, September 22). Airline jobs were easy to fill. Not now: Increased flying demand and staff reductions are catching up. The candidate pool has shrunk. *Philadelphia Daily News*. https://www.proquest.com/newspapers/airline-jobs-were-easy-fill-not-now/docview/2575023760/se-2

Bank of Mexico. (2023). *Economic information system (SIE). Monetary base, currency in circulation and current account bank deposits*. Retrieved 3 February 2023 https://www.banxico.org.mx/SieInternet/consultarDirectorioInternetAction.do?sector=3&idCuadro=CF120&accion=consultarCuadro&locale=en

Barney, J. (1991). Firm resources and sustained COVID-19. *Journal of Management, 17*(1), 99–119.

Binici, M., Centorrino, S., Cevik, S., & Gwon, G. (2022). *Here comes the change: The role of global and domestic factors in Post-pandemic inflation in Europe* (IMF Working Papers). A001. https://www.elibrary.imf.org/view/journals/001/2022/241/article-A001-en.xml

Boranova, V., Huidrom, R., Ozturk, E. O., Stepanyan, A., Topalova, P., & Zhang, S. F. (2022). *Cars in Europe: Supply chains and spillovers during COVID-19 times* (IMF Working Papers). 006. https://doi.org/10.5089/9781616356897.001

Cerrato, A., & Gitti, G. (2022). *Inflation since COVID: Demand or supply* https://ssrn.com/abstract=4193594

Chen, R., Xie, Y., & Liu, Y. (2021). Defining, conceptualizing, and measuring organizational resilience: A multiple case study. *Sustainability, 13*(5), 2517.

Dávila-Aragón, G., & Rivas-Aceves, S. (Eds.). (2021). *The future of companies in the face of a new reality: Impact and development in Latin America*. Springer Nature.

Geiger, M., Gründler, D., & Scharler, J. (2023). Monetary policy shocks and consumer expectations in the Euro area. *Journal of International Economics, 140*, 103708. https://doi.org/10.1016/j.jinteco.2022.103708

Gourinchas, P. O., Kalemli-Özcan, Ş., Penciakova, V., & Sander, N. (2022). *Estimating SME failures in real time: An application to the COVID-19 crisis* (No. w27877). National Bureau of Economic Research. https://www.nber.org/papers/w27877

Ha, J., Kose, M. A., & Ohnsorge, F. (2021). *One-stop source: A global database of inflation* (Policy Research Working Paper 9737). World Bank, Washington, DC. Retrieved 3 February 2023 https://thedocs.worldbank.org/en/doc/1ad246272dbbc437c74323719506aa0c-0350012021/original/Inflation-data.xlsx

Hayes, A. F., Montoya, A. K., & Rockwood, N. J. (2017). The analysis of mechanisms and their contingencies: PROCESS versus structural equation modeling. *Australasian Marketing Journal (AMJ), 25*(1), 76–81.

International Monetary Fund. (2022). *World economic outlook: Countering the cost-of-living crisis.* Washington, DC. https://www.imf.org/-/media/Files/Publications/WEO/2022/October/English/text.ashx

Katz, B., & Sider, A. (2022, July 18). Air travel is broken: Here's why. Cutbacks in 2020 mean there aren't enough baggage handlers, pilots and others. When something goes wrong, it ripples through to flight delays, cancellations, long lines and lost luggage. *Wall Street Journal (Online).* https://www.proquest.com/newspapers/air-travel-is-broken-heres-why-cutbacks-2020-mean/docview/2691009351/se-2

Krugman, P. (2022, Sep 6). *The World Is Getting Less Flat*. New York Times. https://www.proquest.com/blogs-podcasts-websites/world-is-getting-lessflat/docview/2709939492/se-2

López-Fernández, A. M., & Terán-Bustamante, A. (Eds.). (2022). *Business recovery in emerging markets: Global perspectives from various sectors.* Palgrave Macmillan.

Organization for Economic Co-operation and Development (OECD). (2023). *Short-term labour market statistics* (Monthly Unemployment Rates). Retrieved 2 February 2023 https://stats.oecd.org/index.aspx?queryid=36324

Ramani, V., Ghosh, D., & Sodhi, M. S. (2022). Understanding systemic disruption from the Covid-19-induced semiconductor shortage for the auto industry. *Omega, 113*, 102720. https://doi.org/10.1016/j.omega.2022.102720

Rivas-Aceves, S., & Mawaad Morales, M. (2022). The K-shape economic recovery and a new company classification. In *Business recovery in emerging markets: Global perspectives from various sectors* (pp. 109–127). Springer International Publishing.

Sánchez Serrano, A. (2022). *A stylised model of price dynamics through the COVID-19 pandemic.* https://doi.org/10.2139/ssrn.4207739

Shapiro, A. H. (2022). How much do supply and demand drive inflation? *FRBSF Economic Letter, 15*, 1–6. https://www.frbsf.org/wp-content/uploads/sites/4/el2022-15.pdf

Sider, A. (2022, July 21). Airlines are making money again, but they can't keep up with surging travel demand; American, United are pulling back flying this year to focus on reliability. *Wall Street Journal (Online).* https://www.proquest.com/newspapers/airlines-are-making-money-again-they-cant-keep-up/docview/2692060640/se-2

Sodhi, M. S., & Tang, C. S. (2021). Supply chain management for extreme conditions: Research opportunities. *Journal of Supply Chain Management, 57*(1), 7–16. https://doi.org/10.1111/jscm.12255

Teryoshin, Y. (2023). Historical performance of rule-like monetary policy. *Journal of International Money and Finance, 130*, 102766. https://doi.org/10.1016/j.jimonfin.2022.102766

Tooze, A. (2022, October 4). The all too real risk of a global recession. *New York Times*. https://www.proquest.com/blogs-podcasts-websites/all-too-real-risk-global-recession/docview/2720788376/se-2

World Bank. (2023, January). *Global economic prospects*. Washington, DC, USA. https://doi.org/10.1586/978-1-4648-1906-3

CHAPTER 2

The Effects of Flexible Workspace on Organizational Structure and Inequality: An Equilibrium Analysis

Paolo Riccardo Morganti and Gabriela García-Cano

Introduction

As the world learns how to coexist with COVID-19, organizations face the unprecedented challenge of having to redesign their structures, pressured by the urgency to incorporate flexible workspaces into their systems. The new organization must be able to leverage the knowledge of its teams despite the frictions that remote work implies. The future impact of this transformation is still uncertain, but it is clear that it will affect multiple dimensions of society.

In the aftermath of the Great Confinement imposed by the COVID-19 pandemic, most organizations had to rush to implement forms of

P. R. Morganti (✉) · G. García-Cano
Facultad de Ciencias Económicas y Empresariales, Universidad Panamericana, Mexico City, Mexico
e-mail: pmorganti@up.edu.mx

G. García-Cano
e-mail: 0212976@up.edu.mx

E. Murillo et al. (eds.), *Creating Economic Stability Amid Global Uncertainty*, https://doi.org/10.1007/978-3-031-41386-5_2

hybrid work, where workers would perform their tasks partly from their homes and partly in the office. A study conducted by Microsoft Mexico reported that 55% of the small and medium firms in the country had already moved to this structure after the pandemic (Zamarrón, 2022). The challenge presented to the firms is to reorganize the distribution of tasks and the communications among team members and managers so that their productivity is affected as little as possible. This is going to be tough. Physical distance necessarily hampers the coordination of communication and the transmission of information. Recovery from the Great Confinement requires companies to rethink their organizational architecture, with particular emphasis on the management of communication and the transfer of knowledge, which are key levers that can lead them to emerge successfully in the post-COVID-19 world. As we model the new economy to include flexible workspaces, we need to ponder the long-term unanticipated consequences of the transformation.

In this chapter, we abstract from the psychological benefits and costs brought upon by home-office, and focus on one facet of this change and its unexplored long-term impact on the economy. We examine the use of knowledge in production systems and the ways the organizational architecture leverages it in today's process of reconstruction. We use a theoretical economic model to predict the effects of the loss of communication on macroeconomic variables of interest, such as the economy's aggregate wealth, income inequality, and the distribution of firms' size.

As of today, remote work has ambiguous and not entirely understood effects on productivity, with observers pointing to both gains (Kazi, 2021) and long-term losses (Glaeser & Cutler, 2021; Lawson & Scheid, 2020). A complete study of the problem would require disentangling productivity in all its fundamental components, and addressing each of them separately after allowing a sufficient amount of time to pass so that all adjustments have taken place in the economy.

In this work, we consider the team as the base productive unit and wonder what will happen when intra-team communications get hampered. Despite some of the perceived benefits that home-office can bring to the individual, it is clear that it introduces friction in the communications between team members, and in particular between employees and managers. Given the limited time that a manager has at disposal within a day, slower communications require a redesign in the coordination of tasks and of the whole production function, which inevitably brings long-term macroeconomic effects.

Because of the unprecedented scope of this transformation, it is not possible to rely on historical data to draw any conclusion, especially given our focus on the long horizon. As a consequence, we decide to follow a theoretical methodology constructed upon economic models to deduce the future evolution of the *Knowledge Economy* from basic principles. Despite the abstraction and the limitation of the analysis, it is possible to draw logical important insights from the model.

First, because introducing friction in a team's communication is equivalent to an increase in marginal costs, the whole economy will slow down. With a fall in GDP, all the distributed income is going to decrease as well. Second, companies need to adjust to the new form of work by reducing organizational layers and adopting more horizontally oriented structures. Third, as the internal costs increase, the firms will break down into a large number of smaller entities. We should expect the number of firms to increase, but their average size to become lower.

Finally, because the friction in communications flattens out individual differences in ability, we predict wage inequality among employees to decrease over time. The same patterns will be reflected in the inequality in managers' compensation. On the other hand, the reduction in communication costs amplifies the difference between managers and subordinates, inducing an increase in total inequality in the economy.

Because the model is based on neoclassical General Equilibrium, it is not equipped to address important questions about unemployment, which we leave to further research.

This study is structured as follows. In Sect. "Literature Review", we present a review of the literature. In Sect. "The Model Set up", we introduce the building blocks of the model. In Sect. "The Equilibrium of the Model", we define and solve the equilibrium of the model, and draw our main results. In Sect. "Discussion of the Results and Conclusions", we discuss our findings and present our conclusions.

Literature Review

Many organizations around the world have established plans for flexible workspaces and working hours. Most of the research commissioned to analyze the potential costs and benefits of this transformation has been conducted by consulting firms and has not yet been peer-reviewed. In an influential study conducted before the pandemic, Bloom et al. (2015) document a significant increase in productivity when workers of a Chinese travel agency were randomly assigned to work from home. The authors also reported increases in work satisfaction but a fall in the promotion rate. Despite the optimistic outcome, it is unclear if the same benefits could apply to organizations where creativity plays a more substantial role.

Kazekami (2018) estimates a significant increase in productivity in manufacturing and services but a fall in the transportation industry. The author also finds a negative impact coming from the stress that arises when a worker has to balance work and domestic life.

Several researchers have found that home-office can raise productivity by allowing workers to save time on lengthy commutes and transfers (Forbes Staff, 2016).

On the other hand, in the earlier phases of the pandemic, Gibbs et al. (2021) find an increase in working hours but a decline in individual productivity. Lawson and Scheid (2020) point out that, although in a majority of interviews employees stated that their perceived productivity had increased, the reality sees most people struggling with the change. Moreover, the authors warn about the loss of informal collaborations in companies.

Glaeser and Cutler (2021) warn that the real costs of remote work are going to appear in the long term. Although the individual worker can perceive benefits from home-office, teamwork will suffer. In many industries, the real value comes from creativity, which needs to be stimulated through dialogue, exchange of opinions, and information.

In a seminal article, Hayek (1945) identifies the transmission of information as the key ingredient for the success or failure of a society. Although his work was written as a criticism of the centralized mode of production of socialist systems, it became a staple of Organizational Economics, introducing a novel way to look at what happens inside a firm. This innovative perspective broke the stereotypical "black box" of the neoclassical production function, emphasizing the role of organizational design in leveraging non-traditional factors. "Knowledge hierarchies" are the ways institutions manage the communication of knowledge in a way to optimally allocate the time of their key employees.

To examine the processes of team formation, we follow the Matching literature. This body of work originates from the seminal works of Becker (1973, 1974) who proved that, when there are positive complementarities among team members,[1] the optimal matching in society should feature positive sorting. That is, society as a whole would benefit more when high-productive workers are matched together, leaving low-productive ones to join similarly efficient partners. As discussed in Kremer (1993), positive complementarities in production create heterogeneous enterprises from the macroeconomic point of view. On the other hand, each firm ends up employing very homogeneous teams of similarly skilled people. The model can explain the emergence of skewed wage distributions and capture fundamental patterns of income inequality in modern economies. Rosen (1981) illustrates how extreme cases of wage inequality may arise, where small skill differences get magnified and rewarded disproportionately, creating cases of Superstars.

Lucas (1978) adapts the model to study matches between heterogeneous managers and employees. Not only can he explain positive sorting across firms, but also the different sizes that these firms end up taking. Highly skilled managers have a larger "span of control," in the sense that they lead and manage larger companies. As above, complementarities in production induce skewed distributions of firm sizes.

Our research adopts the models of Garicano (2000) and of Garicano and Rossi-Hansberg (2004, 2006, 2012) on the emergence of a Knowledge Economy. These authors build up a novel production function from elementary bits, explicitly describing when problems or routine tasks are addressed by the lower levels of a hierarchy, or when they get passed to higher levels. Their emphasis is on the impact of information technology on the economy. Here, we take a different perspective and study the presence of friction in the communication process. Moreover, our solution approach differs from that presented by these authors. In fact, we were able to solve analytically for the equilibrium wage function under general distributions. This solution allowed us to bypass many of the restrictions imposed in the previous studies and obtain novel results.

[1] A production function exhibits positive complementarities when the marginal output of a worker is emphasized by the skills of the others.

The Model Set up

Following Garicano (2000) and Garicano and Rossi-Hansberg (2004, 2006, 2012), we model a population of heterogeneous workers, each characterized by a given level of knowledge $k \in [0,\underline{K}]$.[2] The distribution of knowledge in the economy is described by a cumulative distribution function (*cdf*) $G(k)$, with strictly positive density $g(k) > 0$.

Workers face problems, which are characterized by a level of difficulty $d \in [0,\underline{K}]$. The frequency with which a problem of difficulty d appears is described by a *cdf* $F(d)$, with positive density $f(d) > 0$.

Each agent receives one problem per period. An individual's level of knowledge indicates the maximum difficulty of problems that the agent can solve. For instance, a knowledge level of k implies that the worker can solve all problems with difficulty $d \leq k$. Problems with higher difficulty cannot be solved by that worker, who can, therefore, pass them to more specialized and knowledgeable agents in the organizational hierarchy.

This process resembles several productive structures in modern economies. From consulting firms to banks, it is common to let the less experienced employees manage the routine tasks, which are simpler but also tedious and time-consuming. Managers get called to face the most difficult problems. The organization should structure the assignment of problems across its layers so as to make the best use of the time of its workers.

The time of the agents is the most valuable resource in this model economy. To represent the scarcity of this factor, we set the maximum time available to each person to 1.[3] For simplicity, we assume that each worker in the lowest layer of the firm can only address one problem per day. The difficulty of each task is not known in advance, so the worker needs to attempt to solve it before asking for support. More formally, a worker with knowledge k faces the random variable d, which she can solve with probability $F(k) = Pr(d \leq k)$. On the other hand, with remaining probability $1 - F(k)$, the problem must be passed to a higher level of the hierarchy.

[2] Although it is possible to introduce education in the model and endogenize the level of ability, we believe that this effort goes beyond the scope of the present research.

[3] The Time Constraint could be set to 24 hours or any other amount. However, this number is irrelevant to the qualitative results of the model. Therefore, we can normalize it.

It is assumed that it does not take any time to process or solve a task. On the other hand, communications are time-consuming and are especially costly for managers, who need to coordinate and support the operations of all their subordinates. Although information technology has been able to improve the effectiveness of communications over the last decades, remote work will tax the functionality of the system. Let $c < 1$ denote the cost in time units of each communication between a manager and one of the subordinates. That is, every time a worker calls a manager for support, the manager needs to employ a fraction of time to help solve the problem, and this occurs with probability $1 - F(k_w)$. If a manager handles a team of size n of workers, all characterized by a knowledge level k_w, then the Time Constraint can be written as

$$\text{Time Constraint:} \, c * n[1 - F(k_w)] \leq 1 \qquad (2.1)$$

For simplicity, we assume that every manager leads a team of equally skilled workers. This assumption is actually a consequence of the Positive Sorting property of the model that we are going to discuss in the following pages and can be proved (see Garicano, 2000) although this requires adding a significant degree of complexity to the analysis.

To keep the analysis tractable, we further simplify the structure of firms and assume that individuals are sorted in only two possible layers within any organization. That is, individuals are either workers or managers. While each firm can have as many workers as it can handle, we impose that there is only one top manager per organization, its CEO. The model could be extended to include multiple endogenous layers, but there is no clear benefit in doing so. The qualitative results are not affected. However, the technical difficulties increase exponentially, obscuring the understanding of the results.

The output of each firm is given by the amount and by the level of the problems that it can solve. Suppose a given firm employs n workers of ability equal to k_w, and that the manager is characterized by a higher level of knowledge k_m, then the total output is equal to

$$Y(k_w, k_m, n) = n\, F(k_w) + n[F(k_m) - F(k_w)] = n\, F(k_m) \qquad (2.2)$$

That is, the manager's ability is the only determinant of this economy's output, but it can be leveraged by the number of subordinates that are employed. Because the manager's time is scarce, it would benefit from more skilled employees. Having more knowledgeable subordinates implies that a higher portion of tasks gets processed at the base of the hierarchy, and less gets passed on to the manager. In other words, having a team of more skilled workers allows the head of the company to save precious time and dedicate it to more valuable tasks.

This effect passes through the Time Constraint and creates a positive complementarity between managers' and employees' knowledge levels. From the Time Constraint equation, we get the maximum size for a team of knowledge k_w:

$$n(k_w) = \frac{1}{c[1 - F(k_w)]} \tag{2.3}$$

which we can plug into the production function to obtain

$$Y(k_w, k_m, n) = \frac{F(k_m)}{c[1 - F(k_w)]} \tag{2.4}$$

Proposition 1. There is a positive complementarity between k_w and k_m.

The proof simply requires computing the cross-partial derivative and to check that it is positive.

As usual in general equilibrium models, it is possible to normalize one of the prices, corresponding to the good that is taken as the *numeraire*. Given our focus on the wage distribution, it is convenient to normalize to 1 the price of the output of the production function, as it is homogeneous across firms (only the quantity that each firm is able to produce differs).

Let $w(k)$ denote the wage assigned to a worker of ability k. Then the profit of a firm managed by a boss of ability k_m and hiring employees of knowledge equal to k_w is

$$\pi = (k_w, k_m|c) = \frac{[F(k_m) - w(k_w)]}{c[1 - F(k_W)]} \tag{2.5}$$

The Equilibrium of the Model

Before beginning to show the solution of the model, we need to clarify the solution concept that we are going to adopt. Following the literature cited above, we focus on the Competitive Equilibrium defined as follows

Definition: The Competitive Equilibrium of the Knowledge Economy is given by:

1. A set of Workers A_W and a set of Managers A_M
2. A Wage function w: A_W x A_M → R^+ determining a monetary salary to each worker.
3. A Profit function π: A_W x A_M → R^+ determining the compensation of managers.
4. An Assignment Function m: $A_W \to A_M$, matching workers with their managers.
5. Such that
   a. Agents choose occupations that return the highest monetary value.
   b. Managers choose the skills and the number of their workers to maximize firms' profit.
   c. The Labor market clears, that is, the number of workers employed at each level of knowledge equates their supply.

In the next pages, we show how to obtain each of these elements and how to ensure that the equilibrium conditions are satisfied.

The Equilibrium Wage Function

In equilibrium, the wage function must be taken as given by the firms. Managers are only left with the freedom to choose the quality of their subordinates in order to maximize the profit of the firms. That is, the problem of a firm with a manager of ability k_m is:

$$\max_{k_w \in [0,K]} \pi(c) = \frac{[F(k_m) - w(k_w)]}{c[1 - F(k_w)]} \tag{2.6}$$

with First Order Condition (FOC)

$$w'(k_w)\frac{1 - F(k_w)}{f(k_w)} = F(k_m) - w(k_w) \tag{2.7}$$

Theorem 1: The wage for a worker of ability k_w, hired by a manager of skill k_m, is

$$w(k_w) = F(k_m)F(k_w) + w(0)[1 - F(k_w)] \tag{2.8}$$

Moreover, the wage function is increasing in k_w.

Our solution differs from the one presented by the literature because it does not require imposing specific functional restrictions to F (see Garicano & Rossi-Hansberg, 2004, 2006, 2012). Our result is, therefore, more general and robust.

Notice that the wage function does not depend on the communication costs, c. Such costs, however, have a strong impact on the sorting of workers and on the size of the firms, as we illustrate in the next section.

Finally, if we plug the wage function back into the profit, we obtain a useful simplification

$$\pi(c) = \frac{F(k_m) - w(0)}{c} \tag{2.9}$$

Assignment and Market Clearing Conditions

Defining the wage function is useful, but it does not complete the analysis as it does not specify which individuals end up working for an organization and which are going to lead the organization.

As mentioned above, because the model is based on a neoclassical General Equilibrium, it is not structured to allow for unemployment. In our setting, each individual will receive compensation. Although we recognize that unemployment plays an important role in the current transformation, we are forced to assume it away and focus on other relevant issues, such as wage inequality among workers and the hierarchical structure of firms.

To close the model, we need to equate the demand for labor to its supply. Before doing that, we must define an Assignment function that connects managers of ability k_m with workers of skill k_w.

Let $m(k_w)$ denote the knowledge of the manager that ends up being matched with workers of ability k_w. Then the property of positive complementarity between knowledge levels established in Proposition 1 allows applying the result of Becker's Marriage Model (Becker, 1973).

Proposition 2. (Becker): The equilibrium must involve positive sorting.

Positive sorting implies that higher quality managers hire higher quality workers, in a continuous fashion. That is, the function $m(k_w)$ is continuous and increasing. An implication of positive sorting is that both the set of workers and the set of managers are connected, individually. That is, the set of individuals is split into two intervals:

1. The set of workers is characterized by knowledge levels $k \in [0, k^*]$ for some endogenous threshold k^*.
2. A set of managers, with knowledge $k \in [k^*, \underline{K}]$.

The position of the marginal agent k^* allows us to monitor the job dynamics after the transformation.

We are equipped now to establish the job market clearing conditions. These conditions must continuously impose that the demand for workers of skill falling into a measurable interval must equate its supply. That is, for any $k \in [0, k^*]$, the following equations must hold:

$$\int_{m(0)}^{m(k)} n\left(m^{-1}[t]\right)dG(t) = G(k) - G(0) \tag{2.10}$$

where the left-hand side represents the demand for workers and the right-hand side the supply.

Because the equation holds continuously for any $k \in [0, k^*]$, we can differentiate it with respect to k and obtain the assignment function

$$m'(k_w) = c[1 - F(k_w)]\frac{g(k_w)}{g(m[k_w])} \tag{2.11}$$

with boundary conditions

$$m(0) = k^*$$
$$m\left(k^* = \underline{K}\right).$$

If we want to solve Eq. 2.11, we need to accept imposing some assumptions on the functional form of $g(k)$ and of $F(k)$. Because our objective is to draw qualitative results, it will be enough to assume that the $G(k)$ *and* $F(k)$ are Uniform cdfs over the interval [0,1], where $\underline{K} = 1$. We tried other specifications, but our numerical solutions on MATLAB revealed that the economic patterns did not change. Then, Eq. 1 can be simplified as $m'(k_w) = c\ [1 - k_w]$, which is solved by.

$$m(k_w) = k^* + ck_w\left[1 - \frac{k_w}{2}\right] \tag{2.12}$$

Notice that, because the function $m(k)$ is increasing, it can be inverted. That is, a manager of ability k_m is matched to a worker of ability $k_w = m^{-1}(k_m)$.

Using the second boundary condition, it is possible to pin down the marginal agent, k^*

$$k^* = \frac{1 + c - \sqrt{1 + c^2}}{c} \tag{2.13}$$

Then the only stable equilibrium must have agents with knowledge below k^* to take employed jobs at the base of a company, and agents with knowledge above the threshold to become managers. To sustain this equilibrium, the compensation functions must be consistent with this rule.

Compensations and Self-Selection

To close the equilibrium of the model we must determine the payoff functions of managers and workers, to ensure that occupational choices are consistent with individual monetary incentives. Individuals have linear utilities and are assumed to be income maximizers. Therefore, they will self-select into the occupation that delivers the highest income. To model this choice, we use an adaptation of the famous Roy model (Roy, 1951).

An individual of ability k can choose one of the following two positions:

1. be a worker, earning $w(k) = F(m[k])F(k) + w(0)[1 - F(k)]$
2. be a manager, retaining the profit of the firm $\pi\left(m^{-1}(k); k|c\right)$

To be consistent with the equilibrium, the lowest ability agents must self-select into paid jobs at firms for a salary. On the other hand, for high-ability agents, managerial rents must surpass the salaries they would obtain as employees. For the marginal agent, the jobs are indifferent. As a consequence, at the threshold k^* two conditions must be satisfied

$$C1 : w\left(k^*\right) = \pi\left(m^{-1}\left(k^*\right); k^*|c\right)$$

$$C2 : w'\left(k^*\right) < \pi'\left(m^{-1}\left(k^*\right); k^*|c\right).$$

The first condition guarantees that the marginal agent is indifferent between the two occupations. The second condition ensures that agents belonging to a left (right) neighborhood of k^* do not have incentives to self-select into managerial (subordinate) positions, which would destabilize the equilibrium.

Then, the wage that agent k^* would obtain is given by

$$w(k^*) = F(m[k^*])F(k^*) + w(0)[1 - F(k)] = F(\underline{1})F(k^*) \\ + w(0)[1 - F(k)] = F(k^*) = k^* + w(0)[1 - k^*]$$

where the last equality is obtained after we assume that k is uniformly distributed.

Moreover,

$$w'[k^*] = [1 - w(0)]F'(k^*) = 1 - w(0).$$

By construction, the manager obtains the profit of the firm, so that

$$\pi(m^{-1}(k^*); k * |c) = \pi(0; k^*|c) = \frac{F(k^*) - w(0)}{c} = \frac{k^* - w(0)}{c}$$

To compute the slope of the profit function at the threshold, we use the Envelope Theorem and obtain

$$\pi'(0; k^*|c) = 1/c.$$

For condition C1 to be satisfied, the marginal consumer can be also expressed as a function of the boundary wage $w(0)$:

$$k^* = \frac{(1 + c)w(0)}{1 + c - cw(0)} \tag{2.14}$$

We have obtained two different expressions for the marginal consumer, Eq. 2.13 and Eq. 2.14. If we equate them, we can pin down the boundary wage that sustains the equilibrium:

$$w(0) = \frac{(1 - c^2)}{c\sqrt{1 + c^2}} - \frac{1 - c}{c} > 0 \tag{2.15}$$

Finally, for condition C2 to be satisfied, the following must be true: $1 - w(0) < 1/c$. It can be proved that this condition is always satisfied when $c < 1$.

Comparative Statics

The equilibrium of this Knowledge Economy is defined by the matching function $m(k)$, the marginal consumer k^*, and the wage and profit functions. All these elements depend on the communication cost c. Endowed with a complete equilibrium solution, we can now study how these quantities vary as communication costs are allowed to increase. This exercise is meant to capture long-term adjustment dynamics in the markets, involving structural changes in the organizational form prevalent in the economy. Interestingly, although the model is quite simplistic and involves severe restrictions on its building blocks, it still provides valuable insights.

We list here the main results, and we leave all the discussions to the next section. Notice that, because of the complexity of the following expressions, it is often not possible to find analytical proof for the Propositions. However, it is not difficult to verify them directly through simple numerical techniques.

Proposition 3: The GDP of the economy falls as communication costs rise.
Proposition 4: All wages decrease as communication costs rise. However, the inequality among workers declines.
Proposition 5: The market restructures so that more firms emerge, though with smaller sizes.
Proposition 6: Firms' profits fall as c increases. However, the inequality among firms declines.
Proposition 7: The total inequality in the economy increases.

Discussion of the Results and Conclusions

The use of knowledge in an organization is a key factor for its growth. One of the main challenges of any enterprise is to design an appropriate architecture to permit information to flow. This requires addressing the number of layers that a hierarchy sets to establish, and the size of its teams. The micro-economy of this system is driven by the time it takes to communicate information from one layer to the next. Because time is a scarce resource, it is extremely precious and must be leveraged correctly.

As companies feel external pressure to incorporate flexible workspaces after the COVID-19 pandemic changed the world, they must take into account a new source of friction in their internal communications, which erodes the Time Constraint of its agents.

Although the methodology used for this study imposes strong simplifications,[4] the model is still able to deliver useful insights that are reasonably justified by intuition.

That the economy's GDP falls as communication costs increase should not be surprising. Introducing friction in communications acts as an increase in costs of production. The scarce resources employed by the economy (time) cannot be utilized as effectively, and the total output cannot but fall. Following this fact, it is natural that all incomes are negatively affected.

However, as we track the fall of each compensation, the model is able to capture some interesting patterns. Both workers' and managers' within-group inequalities fall. An increase in communication costs makes the differences in knowledge between different workers, and between different managers, less relevant. Therefore, the monetary premium for holding a marginally higher ability declines. However, the differences between workers and managers increase. Because coordination is less effective, in the new configuration of the economy, the role of the manager in collecting information and leading the teams becomes relatively more important than that of the subordinates. For this reason, the relative distance between profits and salaries in the economy will rise.

Finally, because managers can now handle less communications, the size of each team will collapse. To leverage knowledge in the most profitable way, firms will have to downsize. As partial compensation for this effect, the number of firms in the economy will increase, reducing industry concentration.

Unfortunately, the framework has a clear limitation as it cannot explain unemployment. Unemployment dynamics are going to be a clear challenge in the next phase of reconstruction and need to be addressed

[4] Among the biggest simplifications that we had to accept was the idea that organizations had only two layers. In reality, organizations are heterogeneous in the number of layers they implement, which is endogenous. Furthermore, for technical reasons, we only focused on the equilibrium of the economy, which forced us to ignore important issues of unemployment. Finally, our qualitative results were derived under the assumption that the distributions were uniform.

appropriately. Further research is needed to address this point. Additional areas of opportunity might involve the calibration of the model to allow for more precise predictions. For instance, the size of the firms is observable (Typically, it follows a Pareto or a Zipf distribution. See Axtell, 2001) and can be matched with its equilibrium counterpart to back out the true distribution F. This, in turn, would allow for a better fit of wage dynamics. A third possible extension would be to consider multi-layered organizations. In reality, when faced with the option to grow, companies might decide to grow vertically, adding new layers and bureaucratic structures.

As the world starts rebuilding after the Great Confinement, companies need to understand the levers that will allow them to bounce back and be successful in the post-COVID-19 economy. We focused on firms' organizational architecture as a mechanism to leverage knowledge inside the organization. As we observe the emergence of flexible workspaces, we analyzed the macro-implications on inequality, wages, and profits. The Knowledge Economy is a rich framework to introduce the management of information in neoclassical models. It allows for a significantly larger degree of firm heterogeneity than the traditional DSGE (Dynamic Stochastic General Equilibrium) models popular in Macroeconomics, permitting to focus on aspects of the economy that usually are bypassed for technical convenience.

Appendix

Proof of Theorem 1. It is possible to rewrite the differential equation in the following way

$$\frac{w'(kw)}{F(k_m) - w(k_w)} = -\frac{dlog\left[1 - F(k_{w)}\right]}{dk_w} \tag{A1}$$

where the left-hand side can be further simplified as

$$-\frac{dlog[F(k_m) - w(k_w)]}{dx} = -\frac{dlog\left[1 - F(k_{w)}\right]}{dk_w} \tag{A2}$$

After we remove the minus sign from both sides, we can integrate from zero to k_w.

$$log\left[\frac{F(k_m) - w(x)}{F(k_m) - w(0)}\right] = log[1 - F(k_w)] \tag{A3}$$

which, after a few manipulations, gives the expression

$$w(k_w) = F(k_m)\,F(k_w) + w(0)[1 - F(k_w)] \tag{A4}$$

Because the densities are strictly positive, the wage function is increasing.

■

Proof of Proposition 3: The wealth of the economy is defined as the output produced by all firms of the economy, that is:

$$Y(c) = \int_{0}^{k^*} n(t)F(n[t])dG(t) \tag{A5}$$

If we plug the equilibrium variables found above, we obtain a complicated expression in c:

$$Y(c) = \int_{0}^{\frac{1+c-\sqrt{1+c^2}}{c}} \frac{1}{c(1-t)}\left\{\frac{1+c-\sqrt{1+c^2}}{c} + ct\left[1 - \frac{t}{2}\right]\right\}dt \tag{A6}$$

Estimating numerically the integral using software such as MATLAB,[5] it is not difficult to see that the wealth of the economy declines with communication costs.

■

Proof of Proposition 4: After substituting the expression for the marginal consumer and for w(0), the wage function is given by

$$w(k) = k\left\{\frac{1+c-\sqrt{1+c^2}}{c} + ck\left(1 - \frac{k}{2}\right)\right\}$$

[5] The algorithm that we used is a simple Montecarlo technique. We first fix a value for c, then drew a vector t of values between 0 and the upper limit, which is itself a function of c. Then the integral is estimated as a sum of the integrand over different values of the vector t.

$$+\left\{\frac{1-c^2}{c}\sqrt{\frac{1}{1+c^2}}-\frac{1-c}{c}\right\}(1-k) \tag{A7}$$

It is possible to verify that all wages fall with *c*. We define inequality among workers as the difference between the wage received by the worker with the highest ability, *w(k*)*, and the worker with the lowest ability, *w(0)*. Simple numerical calculations using MATHEMATICA or MATLAB show that this difference decreases as communication costs increase.

■

Proof of Proposition 5: It is possible to see that the location of the marginal consumer must fall with *c*, indicating that more firms must emerge.

$$\frac{dk^*}{dc}=\frac{-1+\frac{1}{1+c^2}}{c^2}<0 \tag{A8}$$

Finally, it is immediate to check that each firm's size must fall.

$$\frac{dn}{dc}=-\frac{1}{c^2(1-k)}<0 \tag{A9}$$

■

Proof of Proposition 6: We can prove the first part of the proposition through numerical techniques, starting from the full expression of the profit $\pi\ (m^{-1}(k);\ k\mid c)=[k-w(0)]/c$ where *w(0)* was given by Eq. 2.15, which we report here for convenience:

$$w(0)=\frac{\left(1-c^2\right)}{c\sqrt{1+c^2}}-\frac{1-c}{c}>0 \tag{2.15}$$

Using MATHEMATICA,[6] we plotted the combined profit function for different fixed values of *k* above *k**, letting *c* vary in the open interval (0,1). The profit function was clearly decreasing in *c*.

[6] For reference, we used the following command line:

```
Manipulate[Plot[(km– ((−1 + c + 1/Sqrt[1 + c^2]-c^2/Sqrt[1 +
c^2])/c))/c,{c,0.1,1}], {km,(1 + c-Sqrt[1 + c^2])/c,1}].
```

We define the inequality among firms as the difference between the profit of the best firm and the profit of the marginal firm.

$$Inequality\ Profit = \pi\left(k^*; 1|c\right) - \pi(c) = \frac{1-k^*}{c} = -1 + \frac{\sqrt{1+c^2}}{c} \tag{A10}$$

Taking derivatives with respect to c gives

$$\frac{dInequality\ Profit}{dc} = -\frac{1}{c^2\sqrt{1+c^2}} < 0 \tag{A11}$$

■

Proof of Proposition 7: We define the total inequality in the economy as the difference between the profit of the best firm and the wage of the worker with bottom ability.

$$Total\ Inequality = \pi(c) - w(0) = \frac{1}{c} - w(0)\left[\frac{1+c}{c}\right] \tag{A12}$$

After plugging in the value of *w(0)* and taking derivatives, we obtain

$$\frac{dTotal\ Inequality}{dc} = \frac{1 - 2\sqrt{1+c^2} + c^2(3 - 2\sqrt{1+c^2})}{c^2(1+c^2)^{\frac{3}{2}}} \tag{A13}$$

It can be seen that, as long as $c < 1$, the derivative is positive.

■

References

Axtell, R. (2001). Zipf distribution of US firm sizes. *Science, 293*(5536), 1818–1820.

Becker, G. S. (1973). A theory of marriage: Part I. *Journal of Political Economy, 81*(4), 813–846.

Becker, G. S. (1974). A theory of marriage: Part II. *Journal of Political Economy, 82*(2, Part 2), S11–S26.

Bloom, N., Liang, J., Roberts, J., & Ying, Z. J. (2015). Does working from home work? Evidence from a Chinese experiment. *The Quarterly Journal of Economics, 130*(1), 165–218.

Forbes Staff. (2016, April 11). Home Office Aumenta 28% la Productividad de las Empresas. *Forbes*. https://www.forbes.com.mx/home-office-aumenta-28-la-productividad-de-las-empresas/

Garicano, L. (2000). Hierarchies and the organization of knowledge in production. *Journal of Political Economy, 108*(5), 874–904.

Garicano, L., & Rossi-Hansberg, E. (2004). Inequality and the organization of knowledge. *American Economic Review, 94*(2), 197–202.

Garicano, L., & Rossi-Hansberg, E. (2006). Organization and inequality in a knowledge economy. *The Quarterly Journal of Economics, 121*(4), 1383–1435.

Garicano, L., & Rossi-Hansberg, E. (2012). Organizing growth. *Journal of Economic Theory, 147*(2), 623–656.

Gibbs, M., Mengel, F., & Siemroth, C. (2021). *Work from home & productivity: Evidence from personnel & analytics data on IT professionals* (Becker Friedman Institute for Economics Working Paper [2021–56]). University of Chicago.

Glaeser, E., & Cutler, D. (2021, September 24). You may get more work done at home. But you'd have better ideas at the office. *The Washington Post*. https://www.washingtonpost.com/outlook/2021/09/24/working-home-productivity-pandemic-remote/

Hayek, F. A. (1945). The use of knowledge in society. *The American Economic Review, 35*(4), 519–530.

Kazekami, S. (2018). Does teleworking improve labor productivity. *In 27th Eurasia Business and Economics Society Conference on January 11th.*

Kazi, C. (2021, March 9). *Un Estudio Sobre la Productividad del Home Office Nos Muestra Una Realidad Sorprendente: 2 Años de Estudio*. https://www.greatplacetowork.com.bo/publicaciones/articulos/un-estudio-sobre-la-productividad-del-home-office-nos-muestra-una-realidad-sorprendente-2-anos-de-analisis

Kremer, M. (1993). The o-ring theory of economic development. *The Quarterly Journal of Economics, 108*(3), 551–575.

Lawson, T., & Scheid, B. (2020, September 10). Work-from-home productivity gains seen evaporating as pandemic grinds on. *S&P Global Market Intelligence*. https://www.spglobal.com/marketintelligence/en/news-insights/latest-news-headlines/work-from-home-productivity-gains-seen-evaporating-as-pandemic-grinds-on-60119373

Lucas, R. E., Jr. (1978). On the size distribution of business firms. *The Bell Journal of Economics, 9*(2), 508–523.

Rosen, S. (1981). The economics of superstars. *The American Economic Review, 71*(5), 845–858.

Roy, A. D. (1951). Some thoughts on the distribution of earnings. *Oxford Economic Papers, 3*(2), 135–146.

Zamarrón, I. (2022, May 24). 5 de cada 10 pymes ya operan con trabajo híbrido: Microsoft México. *Forbes Mexico*. https://www.forbes.com.mx/5-de-cada-10-pymes-ya-operan-con-trabajo-hibrido-microsoft-mexico/

CHAPTER 3

Harnessing Middle Management Innovation for Business Recovery

J. Lee Brown III and *Jose Luis Rivas*

Introduction

The recent global pandemic caused by the Coronavirus outbreak, initiated the largest contraction in global economic activity since the US Great Depression. This global catastrophe has spurred innovation and change in some industries, but several industries have been irreparably damaged, many businesses shuttered, and still many more have been placed on government life-support. In fact, many businesses across multiple industries have become too reliant on government subsidies made available through emergency initiatives, such as the stimulus provided through the United States' American Rescue Plan and the Canada Emergency Business

J. L. Brown III
Dean College of Graduate & Continuing Studies, Coastal Carolina University, Conway, SC, USA
e-mail: jbrown30@coastal.edu

J. L. Rivas (✉)
Department of Business Administration, Instituto Tecnológico Autónomo de México ITAM, Mexico City, Mexico
e-mail: jose.rivas@itam.mx

E. Murillo et al. (eds.), *Creating Economic Stability Amid Global Uncertainty*, https://doi.org/10.1007/978-3-031-41386-5_3

Account. As during previous global economic downturns, innovation will be the key to an economic turnaround for many of these businesses. Our study theorizes that middle management behavior could be the key to harnessing and leveraging organizational innovation for business success.

Within developed economies, organizational innovativeness is typically the focal strategic mandate (Porter, 1990). Due to the interconnected nature of the global economy, firms operating in developing economies are also beginning to focus on innovation (Guillen et al., 2009). Traditionally, researchers have focused on the role of the chief executive officer and top management team to understand how managers contribute to firm innovativeness (Wooldridge et al., 2008). However, research has shown that middle managers are also essential players in facilitating organizational innovation (Mollick, 2012; Wooldridge et al., 2008).

Middle managers are uniquely positioned to provide insight and contributions to the organizational innovation process (Kuratko et al., 2005). Indeed, they are essential "linchpins" in most of the strategic management process (Wooldridge & Floyd, 1990). Inside the firm, middle managers often participate in strategy creation, such as issue selling (Dutton & Ashford, 1993), processing the distribution of essential knowledge (Nonaka, 1994), leading informal strategic networks (Kodama, 2005) and playing a primary role for strategy implementation (Guth & MacMillan, 1986), championing important strategic initiatives (Huy, 2002), and mediating intra-firm tensions (Meyer, 2006). Outside the firm, middle managers can be a conduit for valuable external knowledge, such as creating strategic networks across firms (Kodama, 2005), and gathering innovative ideas from beyond the firm's boundaries and incorporating those ideas into innovative activity (Wooldridge et al., 2008).

Despite the essential role of middle managers in strategic management processes, the majority of studies have examined their role only in the US context (e.g., Guth & MacMillan, 1986; Hornsby et al., 2005; King et al., 2001; Wooldridge & Floyd, 1990). Previous resource-based view research did not consider contextual factors that might influence middle manager involvement (Sparrow & Cooper, 2014; Wooldridge et al., 2008). Thus, this study seeks to create a framework that better understands specific innovative behaviors of middle managers by considering the environmental context so that we clarify their contributions to organizational innovativeness.

Theory Development

Much of the global community was unprepared for the challenges caused by a global pandemic. In much of the developed world, governmental regimes, healthcare systems, and businesses had been enjoying a substantial time period of political stability, healthcare improvements, and economic growth. The COVID-19 pandemic exposed the precarious nature of this stage of prosperity, as businesses struggled to survive when confronted with a large-scale public health crisis compounded by the threat facing the global economic system. As the world adjusts to the societal and economic shocks caused by the global pandemic, the questions facing society are "when do we get back to normal?" and "what does this normal even look like?" These same questions are facing businesses that survived the pandemic and are hoping to rebuild after the Great Confinement.

The post-COVID-19 era will be characterized by significant amounts of uncertainty in the regulatory, economic, industrial, institutional, competitive, and market environments. A firm's managerial capability to navigate a maze of intra-organizational conflicts and a dynamic external environment will be key to business recovery in the "new normal." This human capital refers to the acquired skills, knowledge, and abilities of its people. Underlying the concept is the notion that such skills and knowledge are valuable because it can increase organizational performance, and more importantly help a firm create more economic value than its competitors. The COVID-19 pandemic caused a significant disruption in the human capital labor markets (Deng et al., 2021). Nevertheless, the more highly skilled a firm's workforce, and greater number of employees with leadership qualities and proven record of working in teams, the more likely an organization is to be flexible, have a decentralized structure and professional culture that fosters innovation, produces efficiencies, and delivers customer responsiveness. These are the building blocks of firm survival in a hyper-competitive, hyper-uncertain environment. Indeed, some scholars suggest the most successful companies, during this stage, will develop an organization of lifelong learners, where information is continually exchanged, and ideas are co-created (Takács et al., 2021).

Middle Management as a Resource

According to Penrose (1959), firms achieve competitive advantage based on organization-specific resources. Indeed, she asserts that managing firm-specific resources is critical to understanding firm growth. This was a challenge to the dominant paradigm of the early 1900s, which was so heavily influenced by neo-classical economics' focus on price, output, and demand.

Wernerfelt (1984) built on Penrose's (1959) assertion of firm heterogeneity to propose that a firm's ability to secure above-normal profits was not purely based on product-market position but on resource position barriers, implying the firms were able to achieve favorable product-market positions partially based on the resource positions held by the firm.

Barney (1991) refined and extended Wernerfelt's (1984) work and proposed that strategic factor markets were imperfect, and that strategic factor endowments differ from one another. Therefore, suggesting that even though firms have equal access to factor markets, how resources are obtained, developed, and leveraged differs. Furthermore, resources which are valuable, rare, inimitable, and non-substitutable have the potential to convey sustainable competitive advantage.

Amit and Shoemaker (1993) argue that competitive advantage is not only a function of resource heterogeneity and immobility as suggested by Barney (1991) but also from the discretionary decisions made by managers on resource creation, development, and allocation. Firm value is captured by managers' ability to identify opportunities that are not otherwise visible to its competitors (Denrell et al., 2003). This study delves on managerial capability as a resource by focusing on their individual activity—managerial behavior.

Individual Behaviors and Innovative Outcomes

People are central to the innovative process—identifying, developing, and commercializing innovative activity. In fact, Ramoglou and Tsang (2016) remind us of the importance of entrepreneurial agents and their behavior as key drivers in the innovative process. In their attempt to reconcile the arguments between the discovery approach, "the possibility of entrepreneurial profit requires the pre-existence of entrepreneurial opportunities," (Ramoglou & Tsang, 2016, p. 410) and the creation approach, "entrepreneurial opportunities are created through entrepreneurial behavior" (Ramoglou & Tsang, 2016, p. 410), they re-establish the entrepreneur as the primary driver of the innovative process. Indeed, without the possession of certain entrepreneurial proclivities, personalities, and competencies by the entrepreneurial agent, the entrepreneurial opportunity will never be achieved. Akin to this reasoning, many scholars have suggested people are born with many of the required characteristics. Personality traits have risen to be a significant determinant of entrepreneurial agency. Risk propensity is a personality trait correlated with business founding (Brandstätter, 2011). Johnson et al. (2018) found an overlap of personality traits between Mania and Entrepreneurship. Additionally, a person's mental health and well-being have been identified as a determinant of entrepreneurial propensity. Psychiatric conditions such as bipolar disorder (Machado-Vieira et al., 2017), psychiatric temperaments, and cognitive competencies (Freeman et al., 2019) have been linked to entrepreneurial activity propensity and outcomes of entrepreneurial activity.

Similarly, firm innovation requires managers to possess certain characteristics and competencies and practice specific behaviors or opportunities for innovation will not be recognized and innovation will not happen. Specifically, McGuirk et al (2015) argued that there was a specific set of behavioral competencies that managers employed in their daily work that were required for firm innovation. Bonesso et al. (2020) argue that managers must employ their cognitive, social, and emotional competencies to produce product innovation. Additionally, the very existence of middle management reduces the barriers for firm innovation (Grimpe et al., 2019). Our study's consideration of micro-level activity and firm-level outcome seeks to address the need for more boundary-spanning research to explain organizational management phenomena (Cowen et al., 2022).

Middle Managers' Innovative Behavior and Organizational Innovativeness

With detected opportunities managers develop new ways to deploy existing resources or obtain new ones to explore and exploit these opportunities. This continuous creation of new resource bundles represents a sustainable competitive advantage. In addition to middle managers' role in strategy formulation and implementation process (Guth & MacMillan, 1986; Huy, 2002), they also serve as new idea generators for the firm

(Burgelman, 1983; Kuratko et al., 2005). Managerial resources are one of the most important elements of firm success.

Due to the tensions between exploration and exploitation, the role of organizational innovativeness is not easily fulfilled. Indeed, for mid-level management, the pressure to innovate is in direct contradiction to the pressure for improving efficiency. Consequently, superior firm performance rests on the imperfect and discretionary decisions of rationally-bounded managers to develop and deploy selected resources (Smith & Tushman, 2005; Amit & Schoemaker, 1993).

As facilitators, middle managers serve as the communication conduit between top management and operating-level management; effectively communicating the firm's overall strategy to lower levels, while providing operational knowledge to upper levels. Middle managers synthesize information received from internal managerial stakeholders and external sources, such as customers and competitors to leverage opportunities for competitive exploitation and exploration. These novel ideas, whether operational intrafirm deficiencies, or environmental opportunities unearthed in the informal inter-firm strategic networks are then promoted to top management (Dutton et al., 2001).

Middle managers not only provide a conduit for communication between the front-line and top managers, but they are also the primary receptors of external information from strategic customers and competitors. Consequently, middle manager strategic activity is critical to the firm's innovation performance (Floyd & Lane, 2000; Floyd & Wooldridge, 1996). In many instances, middle management can be the catalyst of autonomous strategic initiatives by shepherding ideas generated by frontline managers into entrepreneurial opportunities (Burgelman, 1983; Dutton et al., 2001). In sum, middle management's strategic role can encompass all phases of strategy development and its successful execution, particularly with respect to organizational innovativeness.

From a resource-based perspective, we argue that this collective behavior of the firm's middle managers is a potentially valuable and rare resource bundle. Specifically, this bundle is composed of four sets of behaviors: (1) questioning, (2) observing, (3) experimenting, and (4) idea networking on the part of middle managers in pursuit of organizational innovativeness. Each innovative behavior is conceptualized to be a unique strategic contribution of middle management (Dyer et al., 2008; Floyd & Lane, 2000).

Proposition Development

Middle managers' questioning behavior. Innovation often occurs when an entrepreneur or manager questions the status quo. Drucker (1969, p. 50) famously stated that managers were categorized by those that had "the ability to do better rather than the courage to do differently." In other words, questioning the status quo is a critical catalyst to creative insights, and middle managers are uniquely positioned to do this.

Hauschildt and Konradt (2012) suggested managers need to be able to question taken-for-granted assumptions to be creative within an organization. Specifically, they argued that the act of questioning existing structures and routines was essential to innovation and creativity. Relatedly, Birkinshaw, Hamel, and Mol (2008) posited that organizational innovativeness needs "internal change agents." These actors are necessary to question existing practices, processes, structures, and to identify new trends in the organizational environments as well as needs within the organizations. Thus, we suggest the following relationship:

Proposition 1a: The overall degree of middle management's questioning behavior will be positively related to organizational innovativeness.

Middle managers' observing behavior. Intense observation may help to identify opportunities for new markets or product redesigns. A brand manager for a spray-on cooking oil saw his neighbor using the product on the bottom of his lawn mower to prevent grass clippings from adhering to the bottom of his mower (Leonard & Rapport, 1997). This astute observation of an unanticipated product usage led to a completely new consumer market with minimal product redesign of an existing product.

Within the firm, King et al. (2001) assert middle managers are the linchpin that connects top-level perspective with lower-level operational issues. In their field study of firm competencies and firm performance, they find middle manager perception and awareness of firm competencies was positively related to firm performance. Outside the firm, middle managers gather knowledge and innovative ideas from beyond the firm's boundaries and incorporate those external ideas into innovative activity (Sleptsov & Anand, 2008; Wooldridge et al., 2008). Thus, we suggest the following relationship:

Proposition 1b: The overall degree of middle management's observing behavior will be positively related to organizational innovativeness.

Middle managers' experimenting behavior. Lumpkin and Dess (1996) describe innovativeness as "… a firm's tendency to engage in and support new ideas, novelty, experimentation, and creative process that result in new products, services, or processes." Knowledge gained describes "what was" and "what is", but experimentation unlocks "what if". To see beyond the status quo of organizational processes and products, a middle manager must take risks inherent with uncertain experimentation to help identify new market opportunities or to address unexpected process needs.

March (1991) argued exploration through experimentation with alternatives may have uncertain and negative returns, suggesting managerial behavior will be self-interested and safe seeking to secure employment. However, Ahuja and Lampert (2001) asserted that when firms experiment with novel technologies (*the firm lacks prior experience*), emerging technologies (*recent or newly developed in the industry*), and pioneering technologies (*technologies that do not build on any existing technologies*), the firms can overcome capability-rigidity and create breakthrough inventions. Miller and Shamsie (2001) posited that experimentation leads to dynamic core competence development through the creation of new heuristics. Due to their intervening position within the organization, middle managers are uniquely positioned to conduct experiments that lead to new innovative insights. Thus, we suggest the following relationship:

Proposition 1c: The overall degree of middle management's experimenting behavior will be positively related to organizational innovativeness.

Middle managers' idea networking behavior. Typical middle managerial activity is networking for resource access. In contrast, idea networking is connecting differing areas of knowledge and perspective to spark creativity and innovation. The cross-fertilization of specialized knowledge increases diversity and size of technology reservoir; subsequently, new ideas are easily understood, developed, and implemented. Ahuja (2000) found direct and indirect ties had a positive impact on the level of organizational innovativeness. Knowledge sharing, scale economies, skill, and resource combinations are only a few of the benefits available in an efficient, information-rich network (Ahuja, 2000; Ahuja & Katila, 2001).

As internal intermediaries, middle managers are often centrally located within the organization's many formal and informal networks (Balogun & Johnson, 2004). Middle managers are structurally in the middle of an organization leading project teams, departments, and work groups, with codified lines of authority and communication, while also leveraging informal structures, such as peer groups and communities of practice, to better lead and manage the formal structures. As external intermediaries, middle managers often serve as the interface with otherwise disconnected actors (Floyd & Wooldridge, 1999), like senior management and customers. Therefore, when you consider middle managers sit at the nexus of information exchange their ability to influence the intra- and inter-firm network structure should influence firm innovative activity.

> *Proposition 1d: The overall degree of middle management's idea networking behavior will be positively related to organizational innovativeness.*

As shown in Fig. 3.1, we propose the collective behavior of the firm's middle managers is a strategic resource bundle that will directly impact organizational innovation. Specifically, this valuable and rare resource bundle is composed of four sets of behaviors: (1) questioning, (2) observing, (3) experimenting, and (4) idea networking on the part of middle managers in pursuit of organizational innovativeness.

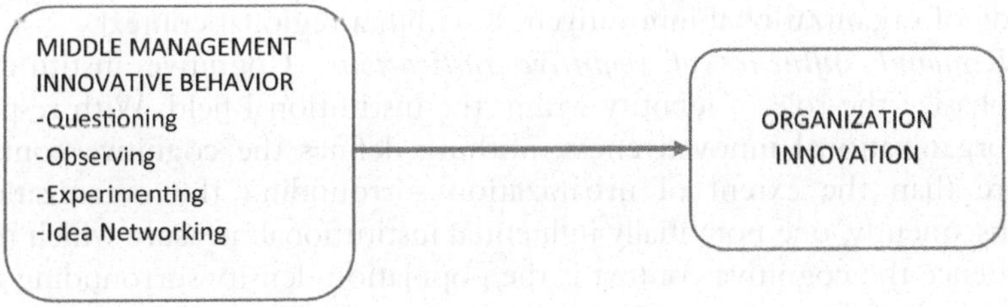

Fig. 3.1 Proposed model (*Source* Authors)

Moderating Influence of the Regional Institutional Environment

While the resource-based view emphasizes the central role of intra-organizational drivers of organizational outcomes, institutional theory argues that factors external to the organizational boundaries will likely influence organizational behaviors and outcomes (Scott, 2003). Although traditional institutional theorists focus on national institutions, Scott argues that the subnational "institutional field" has a more direct influence on organizations. In this study, we conceptualize the primary institutional field as the subnational regions which surround the organizational unit.

Indeed, organizational research studies have suggested *subnational regions* are important factors that influence organizational outcomes (Chan et al., 2010). In fact, the notion of *regional innovation systems* asserts firms located within a specific region benefit from a specific social-economic environment to support organizational innovativeness (Broekel & Brenner, 2011). Furthermore, opportunities for the creation of new products and services are identified, enacted, and exploited in a "context-dependent, social and economic process" (Dew et al., (2004, 662–663).

Scott (2003) argued that every institutional context consists of the cognitive, normative, and regulative structures and norms that provide stability and meaning to social behavior. Previous research has demonstrated that all three sets of institutions are important for understanding the institutional context for organizational activity (Judge et al., 2008). As a result, we will consider all three sets of institutional forces in this study of organizational innovativeness within a regional context.

Regional influence of cognitive institutions. Cognitive institutions emphasize the role of identity within the institutional field. With respect to organizational innovativeness, nothing defines the cognitive context more than the extent of urbanization surrounding the organization. Consequently, one potentially influential institutional measure which may influence the cognitive context is the population density surrounding the organizational unit.

Urban communities are characterized by dense populations and relatively high levels of industrialization. This leads to a concentration of resources and an "imposed" social integration, caused by more frequent interaction of diverse groups (Organization for Economic Cooperation and Development, 2011). Alternatively, rural communities are often agricultural-based economies, which require much solitary work and limited social interaction. Thus, urbanization may create a different social context for behavior to develop within a specific region.

Chabowski et al. (2010) found the urban–rural dimension reflects subcultural differences that persist even amid significant macroeconomic trends. In fact, the regional literature suggests that population density in cities generates a subculture or "a set of interconnected social networks… and the …norms and habits common [to it]" (Fischer, 1995: p544). Subsequently, the cultural norms or "ways of doing business" of managers in cities are likely to differ from their rural counterpart.

Densely populated regions may be an inherently more conducive social context for organizational innovativeness. Cities provide easy access to a diverse knowledge base; Huallachain and Lee (2011) suggest densely populated regions possess a large, more diverse population of skilled professionals, which facilitates inventiveness. Scholars have demonstrated that densely populated regions tend to emphasize educational attainment and economic growth, which has been shown to positively influence organizational innovativeness (Acs et al., 1994). In sum, interactions in a regional cluster may strengthen professional and social linkages among firms and members leading to the creation of new ideas and products. Thus, we suggest the following moderator relationship:

Proposition 2a: The higher the population density within a region, the more positive the relationship between middle manager innovative behavior and organizational innovativeness.

Regional influence of normative institutions. According to Scott (2003), the normative pillar refers to sets of expectations within organizational context of what constitutes appropriate and therefore legitimate behavior. Within the context of business, one can argue that the extent of corruption operating has profound normative influences on organizational behavior and outcomes in general, and organizational innovativeness in particular. Therefore, the second institutional variable which we consider in this study is the extent of corruption operating within the region in which the organization operates.

Corruption can be defined as the misuse of public power for private benefit. It occurs when public officials secretly favor certain organizations over others so that the officials gain money and/or perquisites that are unofficial and unauthorized. In this study, we reason that when corruption is rampant and free, fair competition between firms is lessened. This reduction in competition should translate into less desire and effort to be innovative. In contrast, when corruption is minimal or nonexistent, we would expect that the emphasis on being innovative would be higher. This suggests the following normative institutional argument:

Proposition 2b: The lower the level of perceived corruption within a region, the more positive the relationship between middle manager innovative behavior and organizational innovativeness.

Regional influence of regulative institutions. The third and final pillars are regulatory institutions. They constrain and punish unlawful organizational behavior. When the regulative institutions function properly, the "rules of the game" are clear and transparent. In these institutional environments, hard work and innovation are rewarded. However, not all institutional environments operate with effective regulative institutions. Sometimes, regulations favor certain organizations over others, or more commonly, the regulations are clear and fair, but the execution of those regulations is flawed. A phenomenon that is very common in emerging countries.

Since organizational innovativeness is an uncertain process that often requires sustained investment over a long period of time for uncertain outcomes, societies often reward organizational innovativeness with a temporary monopoly in the form of intellectual property rights. Intellectual property rights represent externally enforced rules and regulations that protect organizations which created the intellectual property and punish organizations which did not create it but try to use it.

Innovators have used property rights laws, in the form of patents, to protect their inventions and the economic rents generated. Corporations have also used patents as a form of protection from competitive threats (Cockburn & MacGarvie, 2006) and evidence of their innovativeness. In fact, Hall et al. (2005) found corporations were rewarded through change in market value for appropriation of innovation rents via patenting. Property rights protection provides the foundation for innovation rents appropriation which in turn motivates both individual and corporation to engage in often risk-laden and highly uncertain innovative activities. Thus, we suggest the following moderator relationship:

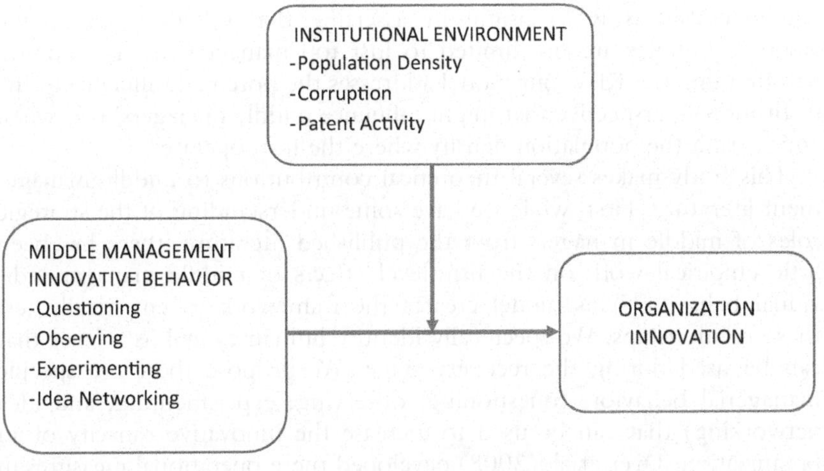

Fig. 3.2 Proposed moderator model (*Source* Authors)

Proposition 2c: The higher the level of patent activity within a region, the more positive the relationship of middle manager innovative behavior and organizational innovativeness.

In today's global economy, corporations large and small interact in a truly global marketplace in which goods, services, capital, people, and ideas move freely across geographic boundaries. Therefore, organizational innovativeness cannot be measured in a vacuum. Understanding the forces in the external environment allows managers to mitigate threats but possibly more importantly, leverage opportunities. As shown in Fig. 3.2, we propose a framework that captures the role of environmental context in the middle manager innovative behavior relationship with organizational innovation.

Research Implications

Utilizing an activity-based approach to explain the effect of individual behaviors on firm outputs, we are able to develop a multi-level model for the phenomena. As the resource-based view (RBV) predicts, middle management innovation behavior could operate as a valuable and unique resource that would lead to competitive advantages. This model refines and extends this RBV insight by asserting that valuable and unique resource bundles are not limited to just top management. In addition to extending the RBV, our model addresses the potential influence of the institutional perspective that might influence middle managers' role when considering the population density where the firm operates.

This study makes several theoretical contributions to middle management literature. First, while we have some understanding of the strategic roles of middle managers from the published literature, there has been little empirical work on the firm-level effects of middle manager individual behavior. This model creates the framework to empirically test these relationships. We specifically identify human capital as a lever that can be used during the recovery stage. We propose there are specific managerial behaviors (questioning, observing, experimenting, and idea networking) that can be used to increase the innovative capacity of an organization. Dyer et al. (2008) developed these operational measures in an inductive grounded theory study, which included 72 successful and unsuccessful innovative entrepreneurs and 310 executives. Though the literature is still fragmented and empirically underdeveloped, there have been several studies that have asserted operational measures for middle manager individual-level behavior, such as Sieger et al., 2013, Dyer et al, 2008, and Pearce et al, 1997. Our assertion does not diminish the role of managerial empowerment, managerial authority, decision-type, or the decision-making process in firm-level outcomes. We argue that scholars should unpack the decision-making process by bringing focus to behaviors that are integral to the decision-making process, such as questioning, observing, experimenting, and networking.

Second, we address several voids in the middle management literature. Our study explores the influence of boundary-spanning middle managers in the context of organizational innovativeness (Wooldridge et al., 2008). As an internal information conduit, middle managers contribute to organizational knowledge through their constant interaction with line managers and top managers. As an external information conduit, middle managers interaction with other managers external to the firm at professional meetings (i.e., trade associations, conferences, and customer events) contributes significantly to idea generation. For firms to survive in this new normal, top management should champion key middle managers to make decisions, encourage information sharing across managerial silos, trust managerial input at multiple levels, and leverage interconnections and interdependencies to promote organizational innovativeness.

Third, our novel research design also suggests that the location of organizational units matters. Culture, languages, legal systems, and macroeconomic conditions could have a significant impact on firm innovation, which is critically important for firms rebuilding in a post-COVID-19 environment. Humanity has faced a number of grand challenges, from poverty, food insecurity, deforestation, violent conflicts, climate change, infectious disease, but none have struck global and domestic business commerce with the acuteness, the severity, and completeness of the coronavirus (COVID-19) pandemic (Brammer et al., 2020). The early months of the global pandemic required business leaders to re-envision service and product delivery in a mostly virtual space, to overcome supply chain disruptions, and reimagine traditional business practices. This socially disruptive extreme event led to unprecedented levels of innovation throughout all aspects of economic and social life globally (Brammer et al., 2020). In the post-pandemic environment (recovery stage), businesses will need to think and operate creatively to survive in a high uncertainty environment.

Countries have implemented various fiscal supports and economic policies to counteract the economic and financial impact of the pandemic. Though necessary, these mitigation strategies are being employed at differing levels. For example, Mexico did not initiate large fiscal stimulus as part of their COVID-19 response. In fact, the Mexican government spent only 1.9% of gross domestic product for COVID-19 relief, which is the lowest amount of any G20 country (Segal, 2020). And is significantly lower than its North American neighbors, Canada at 19.7% and the United States at 26.46% (Cattan & Silver, 2021). Our model illustrates how this macro-level activity may support (or discourage) organizational innovation, a needed outcome for business survival in high-uncertain environments.

Conclusion

Competing in this "new normal" will require executives to question the processes and procedures that were successful in the past. We provide a framework to test a firm's ability to create a competitive advantage using resource-based view assertions in context. Our model unearths the importance of managerial activity, by focusing on the internal process of organizational innovation. It is not the mere resources, but the development and application of resources by the firm's managers that serve as basis for superior performance (Jiménez-Jiménez & Sanz-Valle, 2011). Specifically, we identify four sets of behaviors (questioning, observing, experimenting, and idea networking) that contribute to firm-level innovative outcomes. Managers who exhibit these behaviors become change agents within the firm. As firms navigate the rebuilding stage, managers, who challenge the status quo and seek to acquire knowledge and experiences from outside the firm, will be critical drivers of innovation. Improving the innovative capability of an organization, improves its ability to adapt to, explore, and exploit the opportunities and challenges in an environment characterized by high uncertainty.

Our proposed relationships also include external environmental moderators at both the micro- and macro-level, in an effort to explore the impact of exogenous factors on firm resource bundles. In fact, we argue that in today's globally integrated society the institutional environment in which a firm operates matters. Firms operating in urban centers will likely be more innovative, due to more intense and a higher rate of interactions of firms and their employees leading to a higher rate of idea creation and new product development, than firms in more rural, less populated areas. Likewise, firms located in communities with high patent activity will experience agglomeration effects that will help them be more innovative than their counterparts. However, firms situated in environments, where managerial trust is low and fairness is not the norm, will have managers with little desire to engage in firm-related innovative activity. Consequently, organizations facing a rebuilding stage of indeterminate duration can increase innovation by leveraging the human capital represented by their middle managers through a specific set of behaviors, while controlling for the exogenous factors likely to derail innovation and promoting the factors likely to enhance innovation.

Acknowledgements This work was partially supported by Asociacion Mexicana de Cultura AC.

References

Acs, Z. J., Audretsch, D. B., & Feldman, M. P. (1994). R&D spillovers and innovative activity. *Managerial & Decision Economics, 15*(2), 131–138.

Ahuja, G. (2000). Collaboration networks, structural holes, and innovation: A longitudinal study. *Administrative Science Quarterly, 45*(3), 425–455.

Ahuja, G., & Lampert, C. M. (2001). Entrepreneurship in the large corporation: A longitudinal study of how established firms create breakthrough inventions. *Strategic Management Journal, 22*(6–7), 521–543.
Ahuja, G., & Katila, R. (2001). Technological performance and the innovation performance of acquiring firms: A longitudinal study. *Strategic Management Journal, 22*(3), 197–220.
Amit, R., & Schoemaker, P. J. H. (1993). Strategic assets and organizational rent. *Strategic Management Journal, 14*(1), 33–46.
Balogun, J., & Johnson, G. (2004). Organizational restructuring and middle manager sensemaking. *Academy of Management Journal, 47*(4), 523–549.
Barney, J. (1991). Firm resources and sustained competitive advantage. *Journal of Management, 17*(1), 99–119.
Bartlett, C. A., & Ghoshal, S. (1993). Beyond the M-form: Toward a managerial theory of the firm. *Strategic Management Journal, 14*(S2), 23–46.
Birkinshaw, J., Hamel, G., & Moi, M. J. (2008). Management innovation. *Academy of Management Review, 33*(4), 825–845.
Bonesso, S., Gerli, F., Pizzi, C., & Boyatzis, R. E. (2020). The role of intangible human capital innovation diversification: Linking behavioral competencies with different types of innovation. *Industrial and Corporate Change, 29*(3), 661–681.
Brammer, S., Branicki, L., & Linnenluecke, M. K. (2020). COVID-19, societalization, and the future of business in society. *Academy of Management Perspectives*, *34*(4), 493–507.
Brandstätter, H. (2011). Personality aspects of entrepreneurship: A look at five meta-analyses. *Personality and Individual Differences, 51*(3), 222–230.
Broekel, T., & Brenner, T. (2011). Regional factors and innovativeness: An empirical analysis of four German industries. *Annals of Regional Science, 47*(1), 169–194.
Burgelman, R. A. (1983). A model of the interaction of strategic behavior, corporate context, and the concept of strategy. *The Academy of Management Review, 8*(1), 61–70.
Camison-Zornoza, C., Lapiedra-alcamí, R., Segarra-cipres, M., & Boronat-navarro, M. (2004). A meta-analysis of innovation and organizational Size. *Organization Studies, 25*(3), 331–361.
Cattan, N., & Silver, V. (2021, July 15). How Mexico forgot its Covid crisis. *Bloomberg*. https://www.bloomberg.com/news/features/2021-07-15/mexico-covid-crisis-amlo-government-s-response-ahead-of-delta-variant
Chabowski, B. R., Hult, G. T., Kiyak, T., & Mena, J. A. (2010). The structure of JIBS's social network and the relevance of intra-country variation: A typology for future research. *Journal of International Business Studies, 41*(5), 925–934.

Chan, C. M., Makino, S., & Isobe, T. (2010). Does subnational region matter? Foreign affiliate performance in the United States and China. *Strategic Management Journal, 31*(10), 1226–1243.

Cowen, A. P., Rink, F., Cuypers, I. R. P., Gregoire, D. A., & Weller, I. (2022). Applying Coleman's boat in management research: Opportunities and challenges in bridging macro and micro theory. *Academy of Management Journal, 65*(1), 1–10.

Cockburn, I. M., & MacGarvie, M. (2006). Entry, exit and patenting in the software industry. *SSRN*.

Damanpour, F. (1987). The adoption of technological, administrative, and ancillary innovations: Impact of organizational factors. *Journal of Management, 13*(4), 675–688.

Damanpour, F. (1991). Organizational innovation: A meta-analysis of effects of determinants and moderators. *Academy of Management Journal, 34*(3), 555–590.

De Clercq, D., Dimov, D., & Thongpapanl, N. (2010). The moderating impact of internal social exchange processes on the entrepreneurial orientation–performance relationship. *Journal of Business Venturing, 25*(1), 87–103.

Deng, G., Shi, J., Li, Y., & Liao, Y. (2021). The COVID-19 pandemic: Shocks to human capital and policy responses. *Accounting & Finance, 61*(4), 5613–5630.

Denrell, J., Fang, C., & Winter, S. G. (2003). The economics of strategic opportunity. *Strategic Management Journal, 24*(10), 977–990.

Dew, N., Velamuri, S., & Venkataraman, S. (2004). Dispersed knowledge and an entrepreneurial theory of the firm. *Journal of Business Venturing, 19*(5), 659–679.

DiMaggio, P. J., & Powell, W. W. (1983). The iron cage revisited: Institutional isomorphism and collective rationality in organizational fields. *American Sociological Review, 48*(2), 147–160.

Drucker, P. (1969, November). Management's new role. *Harvard Business Review*, 49–54.

Dutton, J. E., & Ashford, S. J. (1993). Selling issues to top management. *Academy of Management Review, 18*(3), 397–428.

Dutton, J. E., Ashford, S. J., O'Neill, R. M., & Lawrence, K. A. (2001). Moves that matter: Issue selling and organizational change. *Academy of Management Journal, 44*(4), 716–736.

Dyer, J. H., Gregersen, H. B., & Christensen, C. M. (2008). Entrepreneur behaviors, opportunity recognition, and the origins of innovative ventures. *Strategic Entrepreneurship Journal, 2*, 317–338.

Fischer, C. S. (1995). The subcultural theory of urbanism: A twentieth-year assessment. *American Journal of Sociology, 101*(3), 543–577.

Floyd, S. W., & Lane, P. J. (2000). Strategizing throughout the organization: Managing role conflict in strategic renewal. *Academy of Management Review, 25*(1), 154–177.

Floyd, S. W., & Wooldridge, B. (1996). *The strategic middle manager: How to create and sustain competitive advantage*. Jossey-Bass.

Floyd, S. W. & Wooldridge, B. (1999). Knowledge creation and social networks in corporate entrepreneurship: The renewal of organizational capability. *Entrepreneurship: Theory & Practice, 23*(3), 123–143.

Freeman, M. A., Stuadenmaier, P. J., Zisser, M. R., & Andresen, L. A. (2019). The prevalence and co-occurrence of psychiatric conditions among entrepreneurs and their families. *Small Business Economics, 53*, 323–342.

Goodale, J., Kuratko, D., Hornsby, J., & Covin, J. (2011). Operations management and corporate entrepreneurship: The moderating effect of operations control on the antecedents of corporate entrepreneurial activity in relation to innovation performance. *Journal of Operations Management, 29*(1/2), 116.

Grimpe, C., Murmann, M., & Sofka, W. (2019). Organizational design choices of high-tech startups: How middle management drives innovation performance. *Strategic Entrepreneurship Journal, 13*, 359–378.

Guillen, M., & Garcia-Canal, E. (2009). The American model of the multinational firm and the "new" multinationals from emerging economies. *Academy of Management Perspectives, 23*(2), 23–35.

Guth, W. D., & MacMillan, I. C. (1986). Strategy implementation versus middle management self-interest. *Strategic Management Journal, 7*(4), 313–327.

Hall, B. H., Jaffe, A., & Trajtenberg, M. (2005). Market value and patent citations. *RAND Journal of Economics, 36*, 16–38.

Hauschildt, K., & Konradt, U. (2012). The effect of self-leadership on work role performance in teams. *Leadership, 8*(2), 145–168.

Hitt, M. A., Ireland, D. R., Camp, M. S., & Sexton, D. L. (2001). Guest editors' introduction to the special issue: Strategic entrepreneurship: Entrepreneurial strategies for wealth creation. *Strategic Management Journal, 22*(6/7), 479–491.

Hornsby, J. S., Kuratko, D. F., & Zahra, S. A. (2002). Middle managers' perception of the internal environment for corporate entrepreneurship: Assessing a measurement scale. *Journal of Business Venturing, 17*(3), 253–273.

Hornsby, J. S., Kuratko, D. F., & Zahra, S. A. (2005). A model of middle-level managers entrepreneurial behaviour. *Entrepreneurship, Theory and Practice, 29*(6), 699–716.

Huallachain, B. O., & Lee, D. S. (2011). Technological specialization and variety in urban invention. *Regional Studies, 45*(1), 67–88.

Huy, Q. (2002). Emotional balancing of organizational continuity and radical change: The contribution of middle managers. *Administrative Science Quarterly, 47*(1), 31–69.

Ireland, R., Hitt, M. A., & Sirmon, D. G. (2003). A model of strategic entrepreneurship: The construct and its dimensions. *Journal of Management, 29*(6), 963.

Jiménez-Jiménez, D., & Sanz-Valle, R. (2011). Innovation, organizational learning, and performance. *Journal of Business Research, 64*(4), 408–417.

Johnson, G., Melin, L., & Whittington, R. (2003). Guest editors' introduction: Micro strategy and strategizing: Towards an activity-based view. *Journal of Management Studies, 40*(1), 3–22.

Johnson, S. L., Madole, J. W., & Freeman, M. A. (2018). Mania risk and entrepreneurship: Overlapping personality traits. *Academy of Management Perspectives, 32*(2), 207–227.

Judge, W. Q., Douglas, T., & Kutan, A. (2008). Institutional antecedents of corporate governance legitimacy. *Journal of Management, 34*, 765–785.

King, A. W., Fowler, S. W., & Zeithaml, C. P. (2001). Managing organizational competencies for competitive advantage: The middle-management edge. *Academy of Management Executive, 15*(2), 95–106.

Kodama, M. (2005). Technological innovation through networked strategic communities: A case study on a high-tech company in Japan. *SAM Advanced Management Journal, 70*(1), 22–35.

Kuratko, D. F., Ireland, R. D., Covin, J. G., & Hornsby, J. S. (2005). A model of middle-level manager's entrepreneurial behavior. *Entrepreneurship: Theory & Practice, 29*(6), 699–716.

Kwaku, A. G., & Ko, A. (2001). An empirical investigation of the effect of market orientation and entrepreneurship orientation alignment on product innovation. *Organization Science, 12*(1), 54–74.

Leonard, D., & Rayport, J. F. (1997). Spark innovation through empathic design. *Harvard Business Review, 75*, 102–115.

Lumpkin, G. T., & Dess, G. G. (1996). Clarifying the entrepreneurial orientation construct and linking it to performance. *Academy of Management Review, 21*(1), 135–172.

Machado-Vieira, R., Luckenbaugh, D. A., Ballard, E. D., Henter, I. D., Tohen, M., Suppes, T., & Zarate, C. A., Jr. (2017). Increased activity or energy as a primary criterion for the diagnosis of bipolar mania in DSM-5: Findings from the STEP-BD study. *The American Journal of Psychiatry, 174*(1), 70–76.

March, J. G. (1991, February). Exploration and exploitation in organizational learning. *Organization Science*, 71–87.

McGuirk, H., Lenihan, H., & Hart, M. (2015). Measuring the impact of innovative human capital on small firms' propensity to innovate. *Research Policy, 44*(4), 965–976.

Meyer, C. B. (2006). Destructive dynamics of middle management intervention in post-merger processes. *Journal of Applied Behavioral Science, 42*(4), 397–419.

Meyer, J. W., & Rowan, B. (1977). Institutionalized organizations: Formal structure as myth and ceremony. *American Journal of Sociology, 83*(2), 340–363.

Miller, D., & Shamsie, J. (2001). Learning across the life cycle: Experimentation and performance among the Hollywood studio heads. *Strategic Management Journal, 22*(2), 725–745.

Mollick, E. (2012). People and process, suits and innovators: The role of individuals in firm performance. *Strategic Management Journal, 33*(9), 1001–1015.

Montobbio, F., & Sterzi, V. (2011). Inventing together: Exploring the nature of international knowledge spillovers in Latin America. *Journal of Evolutionary Economics, 21*(1), 53–89.

Nonaka, I. (1994). A dynamic theory of organizational knowledge creation. *Organization Science, 5*(1), 14–37.

Organization for Economic Cooperation and Development. (2005, 2011). *Oslo manual-guidelines for collecting and interpreting innovation data*. Eurostat.

Pearce, J. A., Kramer, T. R., & Robbins, D. K. (1997). Effects of managers' entrepreneurial behaviour on subordinates. *Journal of Business Venturing, 12*, 147–160.

Penrose, E. T. (1959). *The theory of the growth of the firm*. John Wiley.

Porter, M. E. (1990). *The competitive advantage of nations*. The Free Press.

Ramoglou, S., & Tsang, E. W. K. (2016). A realist perspective of entrepreneurship: Opportunities as propensities. *Academy of Management Review, 41*(3), 410–434.

Scott, W. R. (2003). *Organizations: Rational, natural, and open systems* (5th ed). Prentice Hall.

Segal. (2020, April 30). *Breaking down the G20 Covid-19 fiscal response*. Center for Strategic and International Studies. https://www.csis.org/analysis/breaking-down-g20-covid-19-fiscal-response

Sieger, P., Zellweger, T., & Aquino, K. (2013). Turning agents into psychological principals: Aligning interests of non-owners through psychological ownership. *Journal of Management Studies*, 50, 361–388.

Smith, W. K., & Tushman, M. (2005). Senior teams and managing contradictions: On the team dynamics of managing exploitation and exploration. *Organization Science, 16*, 522–536.

Sleptsov, A., & Anand, J. (2008). Exercising entrepreneurial opportunities: The role of information-gathering and information-processing capabilities of the firm. *Strategic Entrepreneurship Journal, 2*, 357–375.

Sparrow, P., & Cooper, C. (2014). Organizational effectiveness, people and performance: New challenges, new research agendas. *Journal of Organizational Effectiveness, 1*(1), 2–13.

Takács, E., Abcouwer, T., & de Boer, R. (2021). Management and leadership skills and attitude in uncertainty. *Proceedings of the European Conference on Management, Leadership & Governance*, 401–410.
Wernerfelt, B. (1984). Consumers with differing reaction speeds, scale advantages and industry structure. *European Economic Review, 24*, 254–270.
Wooldridge, B., & Floyd, S. W. (1990). The strategy process, middle management involvement, and organizational performance. *Strategic Management Journal, 11*(3), 231–241.
Wooldridge, B., Schmid, T., & Floyd, S. W. (2008). The middle management perspective on strategy process: Contributions, synthesis, and future research. *Journal of Management, 34*(6), 1190–1221.
Zahra, S. A. (1993). Corporate entrepreneurship and financial performance: The case of management leveraged buyouts. *Journal of Business Venturing, 10*(3), 225–247.
Zahra, S. A., & Covin, J. G. (1995). Contextual influences on the corporate entrepreneurship-performance relationship: A longitudinal analysis. *Journal of Business Venturing, 10*(1), 43–58.

CHAPTER 4

Co-Creating Value Through People-Centered Leadership: Lessons Learned from the COVID-19 Crisis

Santiago García-Álvarez
and Andrée Marie López-Fernández

Introduction

The World Health Organization declared COVID 19 a pandemic within the first quarter of 2020 (CDC, 2022). The severity of the virus drove governmental and organizational leaders to impose lockdown policies that led to remote work which, in turn, triggered a significant change in organizations worldwide (Mehta, 2021). According to Linton et al., (2016) well-being may be classified into six dimensions: "mental, social, spiritual,

S. García-Álvarez (✉) · A. M. López-Fernández
Facultad de Ciencias Económicas y Empresariales, Universidad Panamericana, Mexico City, Mexico
e-mail: sgarciaa@up.edu.mx

A. M. López-Fernández
e-mail: alopezf@up.edu.mx

E. Murillo et al. (eds.), *Creating Economic Stability Amid Global Uncertainty*, https://doi.org/10.1007/978-3-031-41386-5_4

physical, activities and functioning, and personal circumstances." Furthermore, the COVID-19 pandemic highlighted the importance of mental and emotional health (Gorgenyi-Hegyes et al., 2021). Collaborators and organizational leaders worldwide have determined that a work-model change may aid in achieving and maintaining physical, emotional, and mental health which, consequently, positively impact individual and organizational performance.

Telework, also known as home office and remote work, is not a modern practice; in fact, it began in the '70s and was known as telecommuting (Nilles, 1975). Today, entire work environments have completely changed with access to mobile devices and Internet; multiple jobs can be performed anywhere and at any time as long as collaborators have a computer, or a suitable device, and an Internet connection (Messenger, 2019). However, there were many preconceived notions related, in general, to flexible work models; the most common being that workers would not be productive, and even that they would go as far as to take advantage of the situation and simply not complete their tasks and functions.

Adhocracy is a way of organizing that can offer benefits in today's challenges through more decentralized and people-oriented leaderships. It is a mode of operation with a main coordinating mechanism based on mutual adaptation and one of its key design parameters is selective decentralization (Mintzberg, 1983). High-tech or innovative companies, among other similar firms, often require more flexible and interdisciplinary teams, where greater power is given to experts, and managers focus more on ensuring that collaborators have adequate resources to carry out their work. At the same time, the pandemic drove firms in various industries and sectors to redesign their organizations toward more flexible and interdisciplinary teams. Historically, NASA has been an example of adhocracy, bringing together scores of experts to develop specific projects, that is, an ad hoc organization that begins and finishes tasks with defined dates (Chandler & Sayles, 1971). More recently, several companies have adopted adhocratic styles in order to react quickly to market demands (Gachet & Brézillon, 2005) and even the public sector has considered adhocracies as a way to foster innovation (Lindquist & Buttazzoni, 2021).

In this framework, the COVID-19 pandemic has represented a new defining moment for organizations across industries and sectors worldwide. Lockdown policies forced people to work from home, in a more flexible and technology-based way. There are numerous challenges for organizations in the wake of a post-COVID-19 lockdown phase, including: an increasing need for greater organizational flexibility, optimal use of technology, a person-centered leadership that enables collaborators to perform their jobs and contribute with their competencies and qualifications without compromising efficiency. Based on this, adhocracy is presented as a model that can be useful for building work communities that respond to the needs of the post-COVID-19 pandemic world.

The general objective of this conceptual study was to analyze the effects of lockdown policies on business dynamics. Specific objectives included: (i) to assess the changes in work models and the implications for collaborator well-being and organizational performance, and (ii) to propose an adhocracy-based model for the co-creation of value in organizations post-lockdown. This chapter is sectioned as follows, section two includes a revision of previous literature on the study's constructs, section three includes an analysis and discussion of the proposed conceptual model, and section four includes concluding remarks and future research directions.

Literature Review

Adhocracy in the Context of Organizational Design and Leadership

Organizational design is a relevant discipline in the world of management; it encompasses three approaches: restructuring, reengineering, and rethinking (Keidel, 1994), all of which require activity coordination between members of an organization to achieve objectives, an essential task for any company, government, nongovernmental organization (NGO), or institution. The COVID-19 pandemic not only posed a need for organizations to address their design, but also revealed that traditional approaches to change management are insufficient in the face of a global crisis (Choflet et al., 2021).

Numerous studies have been developed in this regard. One of the classic authors in organizational structure is Simon, whose research was fundamentally based on rational thought; along with March, he established guidelines to generate stability in organizations through rational behavior (March & Simon, 1958). Other authors have defended less rigid and more dynamic organizational models such as the famous work by Ansoff (1974) and research later developed by Bolman and Deal (1995).

Henry Mintzberg produced a synthesis of the literature on organizational structure existing at the time, developing what became a classic on Organizational Design (Mintzberg, 1983). Mintzberg highlighted in a special way the concept of adhocracy, with notable advantages but also with some disadvantages, representing an attractive organizational model but sometimes difficult to apply. A few decades before, Bennis and Slater (1968) and Toffler (1975) had already discussed the concept of adhocracy; however, Mintzberg took on the concept and developed it extensively, defining it as an organic structure with a selectively decentralized essence, which makes great use of linked devices (Mintzberg, 1983).

Many authors expanded concepts of the adhocracies. For example, Bailey and Neilsen (1992) posited that Mintzberg had privileged adhocracies as an effective way of working in small organizations and providing standardized and innovative services, but that he had not worked out how to maintain the system over time; they propose a learning process and the existence of stages of development. Subsequently, numerous authors have studied adhocracies from different perspectives. Campbell (1992) used it to analyze an employee wellness program structured on the basis of innovation and mutual adaptation. Alvesson (1992) analyzed a computer consultancy company with adhocratic features where leadership is conceived as social integrative action. Conrad et al. (1997) conducted a study on customer satisfaction where adhocracy is one of their four important cultural elements.

Years later, Gachet and Brézillon (2005) discussed the changes in traditional companies from hierarchical styles toward adhocratic structures, where paths in decision-making need to be shortened and lighter structures established to react quickly to changes in the market. More recently, Wei et al. (2014) studied organizational culture as a strategic resource where adhocracy is one of its prototypes to exemplify organic systems. Martela (2019) took up Mintzberg directly in his study to solve six fundamental organizational problems. Kim and Chang (2019), for their part, analyzed organizational culture and performance by comparing adhocratic cultures with others. Lindquist and Buttazzoni (2021) analyzed adhocracies as a way to foster a more innovative and open culture for government and public service institutions. And, Cabri and Fioretti (2022) took up adhocracies to provide a theoretical unifying framework for flexible organizational forms.

According to Mintzberg, there are three main types of coordination in organizations: mutual adaptation, direct supervision, and standardization (Mintzberg, 1983). Furthermore, organizations have five fundamental parts: core operations, strategic apex, middle line, technostructure, and the staff (Mintzberg, 2012). Subsequently, Mintzberg studied how the organization's parts relate to the types of coordination. He analyzed different scenarios, contingencies, and forces that move in organizational structures. Finally, he concluded that there are five main structural configurations that are summarized in Table 4.1 (Mintzberg, 2012, p. 341):

Some configurations are more centralized and rely on formal structures, as are the cases of machine and professional bureaucracies. Others prefer to clearly set objectives but leave greater flexibility in mediums, as is the case of the divisional form. Adhocracy, however, differs from bureaucracy (Irwansyah, 2021) as it refers to work focused on projects, where hierarchies matter less, guidelines are less vertical, a leading role is given to experts who support from their disciplines, interdisciplinary work is required, as well as an important degree of adaptation among the different team members (Mintzberg, 1983). Adhocracy, therefore, favors

Table 4.1 Mintzberg's five main structural configurations

Structural configuration	Main coordination mechanism	Organization's fundamental part	Decentralization type
Simple structure	Direct supervision	Strategic apex	Vertical and horizontal centralization
Machine bureaucracy	Work process normalization	Technostructure	Limited horizontal decentralization
Professional bureaucracy	Ability normalization	Core operations	Vertical and horizontal decentralization
Divisional form	Result normalization	Middle line	Limited vertical decentralization
Adhocracy	Mutual adaptation	Support *staff*	Selective decentralization

innovation, leadership focuses on coordinating and facilitating, success depends on people's qualities in the team, there are few normalization rules, and people are focused on the common good of the proposed project (Mintzberg, 1983). Moreover, because innovativeness is associated with resilience (Do et al., 2022) and the latter is central to a firm's organization (Raetze et al., 2022), it has been central for organizations' survival during the COVID-19 pandemic.

NASA is an example of adhocracy, as it organizes teams to carry out specific innovative projects. In this case, much of the work is temporary and people adapt to projects regardless of their position (Chandler & Sayles, 1971). Due to the technological revolution witnessed in recent decades, many technological innovation companies have emerged as well as various digital platforms with applications. In this framework, adhocracy has played a leading role.

Adhocracy Characteristics

Schein defines an organization as "the planned coordination of the activities of a group of people to seek the achievement of an explicit or common goal or purpose, through the division of labor and functions, and through a hierarchy of authority and responsibility" (Schein, 1997, p. 14). Historically, organizational leaders have looked for solutions to divide work and coordinate effectively, thus, Mintzberg's research on organizational structure, alternatives, and configurations is applicable. According to Mintzberg, in 1979, the simple structure and machine bureaucracy were structures of the past, the professional bureaucracy and divisional form of the present, and adhocracy of the future (Mintzberg, 1983). Adhocracy is actually typical of the second half of the twentieth century and the beginning of the twenty-first century. Although it is true that its pure application is not simple, its organizational design concept is valuable for the challenges that organizations face in a world as complex as the current one in the midst of health, social, and economic crises.

In regard to the design and definition of how an organization works, key concerns are usually related to departmentalization, collaborators by area, job functions, coordination, and, fundamentally, decision makers. Adhocracies achieve work coordination through simple informal communication (Mintzberg, 2012), and, therefore, mutual adaptation is constituted as their main coordination mechanism; it is the easiest way to organize and typical of start-ups, for example. Although there may certainly be leaders' direct supervision, adhocratic work seeks that team members adapt to each other, each contributing with their expertise and knowledge capital—i.e., know-how, know-what, know-who, and know-why (Jurczak, 2008). There may be previously established patterns and procedures; however, this normalization does not constitute the basis for coordination among collaborators but simply a complementary mechanism; further, given that innovation is one of the main pillars in adhocracies, spaces for creativity and flexibility are required, minimizing the rigidities typical of conventional structures (Mintzberg, 2012).

The organization's fundamental part is the so-called "Support Staff," that is, people who are not usually in the flow of operations but have and contribute with high specialization, expertise, and carry out tasks that are not easy to learn (Mintzberg, 2012). Managers try to facilitate the work of qualified people involved in processes and decisions, but their work is more oriented toward articulating insights and key findings than giving direct instructions. In this way, power is distributed among the entire work team and not just managers; in fact, those who contribute more often end up acquiring greater influence possibilities, not based on their status but on their experience or knowledge. In other words, adhocracy tends toward organic decentralization because of its work environment and nature.

The work environment is dynamic and complex; dynamic, due to the nature of the innovative work typical of these configurations, which are also surrounded by a rather uncertain and unpredictable environment. Complex, because they are usually sophisticated markets, such as technology, which require specialized knowledge (Mintzberg, 2012). In a dynamic environment, the structure needs to be more organic; future conditions are not predictable and, therefore, operations and procedures are less susceptible to standardization. Organizations must move fast and act less prompted by rules and more driven by innovation. Being a complex environment, the required work is not simple, it needs specialization and truly prepared people, which is why decentralization toward experts is important (Mintzberg, 2012). Dynamic and complex environments are particularly observed when in the midst of a crisis, be it social, economic, and/or health related such as that of the COVID-19 pandemic and, consequently, organizations are directly affected.

Decision-Making in an Adhocracy

One of the most important organizational aspects is defining decision makers. According to Carlos Llano, participation in decision-making is the leitmotif of current management literature (Llano, 2000). Hence, the need to choose between centralization and decentralization, a typical situation of organizational theory, arises. Centralization favors precision in decision-making and is a tool that achieves greater control, and decentralization helps react quicker to local conditions (Mintzberg, 2012). In the case of adhocracies, the tendency is to decentralize as much as possible and leave decisions in experts' hands. Specifically, adhocracies favor horizontal decentralization, where decision processes are controlled by analysts, specialists, or operators (Mintzberg, 2012). Adhocracies can grant greater power to the following members of the organization (Mintzberg, 2012):

1) Analysts: design organizational systems or processes and, therefore, know operation details;
2) Experts: possess specialized knowledge, called Staff, and are required in more technical than political decisions; and
3) Operatives or members: all organizational members, for example a Kibbutz, where a distribution of tasks is favored.

Some examples may serve to illustrate the adhocratic behavior of certain organizations which are closer to a democratic or meritocratic function. In hospitals, most decisions are made by the doctors themselves, who are the experts and have the competencies to solve and tend to each patient's needs. In research centers, researchers themselves usually make decisions regarding research areas, and individual and collective guidelines, standards, timelines, etc. And, as an example of a for-profit corporation, Toyota realized that some decisions had to be made closer to the action—operation—rather than within top management (Tabuchi & Vlasic, 2013).

Adhocracy as an Alternative Leadership Style

Adhocracy's main advantages are: flexibility, dynamism, adaptability, democratization, de-bureaucratization, and knowledge appreciation, among others; disadvantages include: a risk of politicized environments due to the involved leadership, economies of scale are lost, and important differences in workloads may arise, etc. There are some alternatives in order to solve difficulties presented by adhocracies' poor structure (Galbraith, 1971):

1) Liaisons: facilitate mutual adaptation without resorting to hierarchy;
2) Groups and committees: ad hoc groups to perform specific tasks with well-defined start and end dates;
3) Integrating managers: coordinate people without exercising formal authority; and
4) Matrix structure: facilitates the coordination of multiple interdependencies.

Organizations should be conceived as open systems, with multiple purposes and dynamically interacting subsystems, as well as multiple links (Schein, 1997); adhocracy's effectiveness largely depends on the harmony of such statement. Then, another concern emerges: whether the person who carries out certain functions, will also decide which functions to perform and how to do so. According to Carlos Llano, it is essential that collaborators' work involve inventive and creative skills, rather than be limited to repeating activities (Llano, 2006); in fact, in this way, work is more humane, since it involves human functions beyond task repetition. Llano also insists that those who achieve objectives must participate in their definition at the same time (Llano, 2006). Thus, it is possible not only to design good jobs, but also to develop collaborators with and through them. These are precisely some of adhocracy's strengths, which represent an alternative model for people-centered leadership capable of responding to the challenges of the post-lockdown world.

COVID-19 Lockdown Effects on Work Dynamics

On March 11, 2020, about three months after the first case of COVID-19 was detected, the World Health Organization (WHO) declared COVID-19 a pandemic (CDC, 2022). It rapidly became clear that no one was exempt from infection; further, without a vaccine and given its high rate and velocity of contagion, the only way to restrict the scale of infection and deaths was by enforcing lockdown policies. Although various governmental leaders around the world instituted and enforced lockdown policies, many organizations did not comply with these policies because: (i) their operations partially or entirely could not be performed at home, and (ii) their work was classified as essential, including healthcare, law enforcement, food, agriculture, education, transportation and logistics, wholesalers, etc. (CDC, 2021) and, therefore, could not be absent from their workplaces.

In addition to the virus' biological and physiological effects, the lockdown, although necessary to ensure the population's health and safety, also created turmoil. The health crisis notwithstanding, the COVID-19 pandemic quickly exacerbated economic and social crises (Pak et al., 2020; Pitterle & Niermann, 2021). It created an unparalleled complex and dynamic environment for businesses worldwide as they were negatively impacted by the disruption of entire local and global supply chains (Lopes de Sousa Jabbour et al., 2020); moreover, organizational structures and overall business dynamics were significantly altered.

Lockdown guidelines were enforced to ensure social distancing at different moments with varying durations in each country. This meant that those collaborators that could, would work from home. There was no time for organizations to design and execute strategies to adapt to the new work model because the change was sudden and in most cases immediate (George et al., 2022). And, even though the practice has been around for over forty years (Nilles, 1975), it still posed significant challenges such as: a major change in leaders' and collaborators' mindsets, real-time learning and training, and the aggregated psychological and physical effects. As organizations were not set up for the shift, many collaborators did not have the necessary equipment, such as a computer, Internet connection (existing, stable, high velocity), a desk or proper chair to work from home.

Previous research conducted before the COVID-19 pandemic showed that remote work benefits included: reduced costs (Kitou & Horvath, 2008; Robèrt & Börjesson, 2006) related to infrastructure, and environmental impact from transportation traffic (Harpaz, 2002), as well as turnover rate and absenteeism (Gibson et al., 2002), a more inclusive workforce (Mello, 2007), and increased productivity (Kitou & Horvath, 2008; Mello, 2007), morale and motivation (Kurkland & Bailey, 1999), among others. However, disadvantages included physical and psychological health issues such as stress, depression, and overwork (Tavare, 2017) causing burnout, among others; and, impediments for an effective transition to remote work included the lack of an organizational culture to guide collaborators in the operation, as well as contractual frameworks (Pyöriä, 2011) that would govern the work model. Therefore, even with years of previous research on remote work, the abrupt work-model shift in the midst of a serious and frightening pandemic exposed lack of organizational preparedness.

During the lockdown, some of the collaborators working from home experienced varying degrees of negative psychological effects (Le & Nguyen, 2021) such as, increased stress, anxiety, and depression, as well as fatigue (Patanjali & Bhatta, 2022). These consequences could have been due to the effects of change (George et al., 2022), the existence of a pandemic, the confinement itself, the drastic shift that required adopting digital technologies, and/or the increased pressure to deliver high levels of productivity under the circumstances. That being said, studies also found that working from home during COVID-19 was associated with increased productivity and reduced commute time (Cramer & Zaveri, 2020; Patanjali & Bhatta, 2022), as well as significant savings, and improved job satisfaction, health, and well-being (Cramer & Zaveri, 2020), among others.

Many collaborators and organizational leaders found that the advantages of remote work outweighed the disadvantages. For instance, the University of Kent and University of Birmingham developed a study regarding remote work during the COVID-19 lockdown and found that the experience had informed collaborators' perceptions and preferences for flexible work models (Heejung et al., 2020); further, the McKinsey Global Institute found that changes such as remote work and online meetings were expected to continue being enforced in organizations after the lockdown (McKinsey Global Institute, 2021), and Ferrari et al., (2021) stated that not only would the new work models stay, but also that hybrid models were the most likely option.

Work Dynamics Post-COVID-19 Lockdown

In the first year of COVID-19, almost every decision was made with a great degree of uncertainty. While vaccine development and release was a major turning point, vaccination speed and reach has been insufficient; in May 2022, "only 57 countries had vaccinated 70% of their population" and, unfortunately, most of them did not include developing countries or emerging markets (WHO, 2022a). And, as of July 2022, COVID-19 continues to take a toll. Despite the fact that over 12 billion doses of vaccines have been administered, there are still over 560 million confirmed cases and over 6.3 million deaths globally (WHO, 2022b). Therefore, the pandemic continues which means that health concerns should remain a priority. That being said, every other sector and industry is operating regularly because, globally, the priority shifted to economic stability and growth.

Once the lockdown was lifted, many organizational leaders compelled their collaborators to return to in-person activities in a pre-pandemic mode or in an attempt to return to ***normal***. A year into the vaccination process, most countries were no longer on lockdown, but many collaborators wanted to continue working remotely. Some of their reasons included: (i) realizing they were more productive working from home, (ii) being less likely to get sick, being able to spend quality time with their families, and prioritize physical and emotional well-being, and, (iii) significant savings as they were spending less on transportation and food. That being said, other organizational leaders took a different approach, that is, the Great Confinement (Esparza-Rodriguez et al., 2021) drove them to lean into the notion of remote work and hybrid models.

Mello (2007) previously posited that the time collaborators spent commuting would most likely be used to work, which is precisely what occurred during lockdown periods. This led to an increase in productivity, but also anxiety, overwork, and burnout. The latter negatively affect collaborator satisfaction, colleague relationships, and performance (Alexander et al., 2021). Because collaborators began to value and prioritize their physical and mental health, millions quit their jobs which led to the great resignation (Fuller & Kerr, 2022). Therefore, one of the major lessons learned by collaborators and leaders around the world is that a work-personal life balance is required (Gorgenyi-Hegyes et al., 2021) to ensure mental health. And, fostering a work-personal life balance would, in turn, positively impact collaborators' well-being, satisfaction, productivity, and individual and organizational performance.

As a result, different work models have been adopted, including: home office, remote work, and flexible work hours (Gorgenyi-Hegyes et al., 2021), among others. While home office is self-explanatory, remote work means that collaborators can perform their functions and activities from anyplace as long as they have a device (computer, laptop) and Internet connection. Flexible work hours or schedules entail that collaborators define the times they start and end their work days (Golden, 2001); they positively impact productivity, decrease absenteeism, turnover rate, stress

(Shepard III et al., 1996) and increase engagement, as well as commitment and satisfaction (Scandura & Lankau, 1997). There are also hybrid models, *i.e.*, those combining office work and remote work (Ferrari et al., 2021), which can enhance performance through a decrease in costs and by making the most of collaborators' efforts (Alexander et al., 2021).

These work models affect and are affected by an organization's structure, culture, systems, and teams (Mello, 2007); this means that the firm's corporate philosophy, governance, and culture need to be aligned with the dynamics of each work model. Leaders should foster a climate that prioritizes the use of technology and autonomy rather than them monitoring (Messenger, 2019) collaborators' every move. And, in order to prevent mental health issues, or at least reduce the risk, policies to protect collaborators' mental health should be developed and executed (Le & Nguyen, 2021). These are not only important for collaborator well-being, but also for firms' growth; for instance, a detriment of collaborators' mental health negatively impacts productivity and, according to Alexander et al., (2021), may cost the global economy about $1 trillion per year.

Collaborators also need support to guarantee productivity and should be empowered with a sense of autonomy (Patanjali & Bhatta, 2022) for effective decision-making. Therefore, remote work's degree of success depends on leadership's effectivity in collaborator management and, the level of effectivity, will impact individual and organizational performance (Messenger, 2019).

Person-Centered Leadership

The taxonomy of leadership is vast and each proposed style has its particularities and degrees of involvement with followers. Transactional leaders, for instance, are result-oriented, more prone to a centralized structure and decision-making, and less innovative; transformational leaders are more democratic, participatory, people-oriented, innovative, and aligned with a decentralized structure and decision-making. Furthermore, in a culture informed by adhocracy, meaning an "externally orientated, intensely creative, and high adaptable" (Toh, 2022) culture, leaders are more likely to embrace risk, innovation, are visionaries (Masood et al., 2006), and creative, flexible (Kargas & Varoutas, 2015; Mozaffari, 2008) and inclusive.

It seems ineffectual to discuss any style of leadership not centered on the individual; in other words, a style of leadership not focusing on the collaborator is counterproductive. Person-centered style of leadership has been defined as a "complex, dynamic, relational and contextualised practice that aims to enable associates and leaders achieve self-actualisation, empowerment and well-being" (Cardiff et al., 2018). People's needs, including their feelings, are at the center of this leadership style (Plas, 1996), they are not ignored and when mentioned, they are not dismissed. Therefore, it views individuals integrally (Chou et al., 2015).

This style of leadership, given the abovementioned characteristics, is also associated with ethical leadership. The latter has a positive impact on collaborator and sustainable performance (Dey et al., 2022) as well as collaborator trust in the organization and decreases absenteeism (Eluwole et al., 2022). Further, trust in organizations has a significant impact on the manner in which crises are managed, such as that of COVID-19, and both collaborator well-being and their experience at work (Jiang et al., 2022). This occurs because person-centered leadership is concerned with the efficiency and effectivity of collaborator performance obtained by means of their well-being. According to Plas (1996), it is precisely the lack of attention to and consideration of collaborators as individuals that has led to the failure of participatory leadership styles. Therefore, person-centered leadership is deemed effective and necessary in order to direct desired levels of productivity and performance, particularly, in the midst of managing a crisis.

In terms of work models, according to Neirotti et al. (2013), remote work may be profitable for organizations when their business models are tailor-made to each organization's needs in relation to location, structure, and technology. Doing so is possible when the organizations' leaders' approach to management is democratic and flexible enough to adapt to changes in the environment, be them swift or gradual. Moving forward with different types of work models requires a people-centered style of leadership. Therefore, in order to co-create value through different work models, organizations should foster a more flexible approach with a person-centered leadership that advocates for collaborators' well-being, creativity, innovativeness, and autonomy, for an efficient operation and effective performance.

Adhocracy in a Post-COVID-19 Lockdown World

As previously stated, the confinement caused by COVID-19 drove many organizations to adapt to the pandemic and, at the same time, change the way they function and operate. This required different coordination strategies. Successful organizations in confinement stood out for their flexibility and adaptability, similar to that presumed by adhocracy configurations. After the general confinement, many organizations have returned to face-to-face activities, however, others have maintained more flexible work arrangements learned during COVID-19.

In many organizations, the environment is dynamic—marked by uncertainty—and complex—demanding sophisticated solutions. This context requires work to be as organic as possible, so that the solutions can be fast as well as effective. This context results in an adhocracy model that can be successful today. Mutual adaptation becomes a fundamental principle of operation and a coordinating mechanism. The *staff* takes a leading role, and decision-making necessarily goes through experts, analysts, or collaborators working directly in the operation. And, selective decentralization is required, which is based precisely on collaborators' expertise.

In this framework, there is a need for clarity of purpose and flexibility of means, giving rise to a leadership that requires facilitation, coordination, and development as fundamental characteristics, often in an interdisciplinary manner. For this style of leadership, collaborator development becomes a fundamental pillar through active participation in decision-making and innovation. Given the high dependence on the *staff*, the organization's common good depends on their function and being able to add value.

At the same time, with the reality of digital transformation, today's organizations have contact with numerous stakeholders around the world, accentuating the advantages and disadvantages of adhocracies. Some of its strengths include: contact with global experts, interdisciplinarity, decrease of barriers and response times, and the possibility of reducing overhead when outsourcing non-essentials. However, confusion in decision-making, ambiguity of certain dependencies, lack of control, blurred limits, and/or lower loyalty toward organizations represent important challenges (Daft, 2016).

Therefore, the greater the organizational flexibility, the greater leadership's ability to foster a participatory and autonomous environment in which collaborators can be creative, innovative, and productive. In other words, adhocracies in a post-COVID-19 lockdown world can have a disruptive effect on traditional work models that may, in turn, lead to positive results for collaborators' well-being, as well as individual and organizational performance. Based on the above discussion of constructs, the following propositions have been framed:

P1: Complex and dynamic environments, derived from a crisis, impact business environments and organizational design.
P2: Adhocracy, through decentralized and people-oriented leadership, influences organizational culture.
P3: Organizational culture influenced by adhocracy positively impacts the development of new work dynamics in a complex and dynamic environment.
P4: Culture informed by adhocracy fosters the development of work communities whereby value may be co-created, thus, positively impacting the business environment.

Model Analysis and Discussion

The proposed conceptual model to co-create value through adhocracy organizational design is included in Fig. 4.1. The model illustrates how a complex and dynamic environment (Mintzberg, 2012), such as that caused by the COVID-19 pandemic and the subsequent lockdown, directly impact business environments and, therefore, firms' organizational design (P1). In other words, the multiple changes in the environment, particularly abrupt ones, shaped the way business operations and collaborators were managed during lockdown and once related policies were lifted. It quickly became apparent that a traditional approach to change management falls short of organizations' and collaborators' needs in a crisis of COVID-19's magnitude. While the Great Confinement (Esparza-Rodriguez et al., 2021) drove a significant number of collaborators worldwide to change from a tradition work model to home office, it was a shift in organizational design and culture focused on a balance of well-being and productivity that led to more flexible work models post-COVID-19 lockdown.

Adhocracy's characteristics, then, provide an ideal foundation for organizations' redesign. As adhocracy is a way of organizing that can offer benefits for such challenges through a more decentralized and people-centered leadership, it has the ability to ensure greater stability for environment changes which have directly impacted organizations' design. That is because its adaptability quality, as well as flexibility, dynamism, and

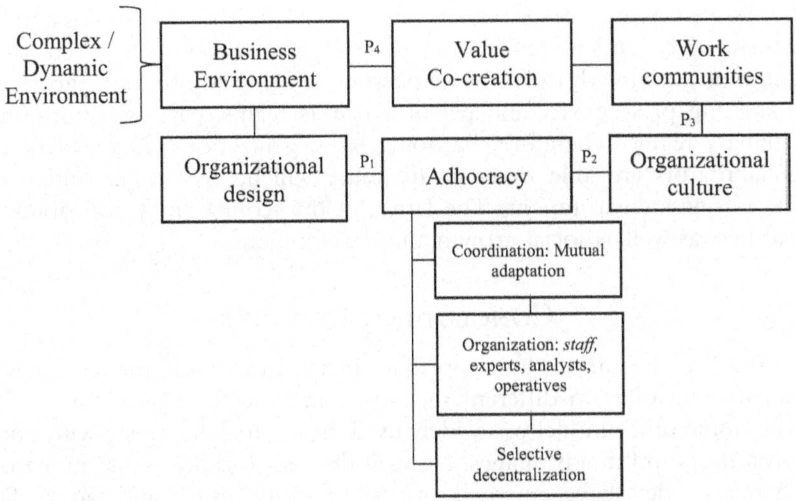

Fig. 4.1 Conceptual model to co-create value through adhocracy culture (*Source* Authors)

democracy, enable organizational leaders to rise to environmental challenges while focusing on collaborators' physical, emotional, and mental well-being in parallel with their levels of efficiency, productivity, and overall performance.

In that sense, mutual adaptation coordination, organization including *staff*, experts, analysts, and operatives, and selective decentralization (Mintzberg, 1983), are key aspects that influence people-centered leaderships and an organization's culture to effectively adapt to change by adopting new work dynamics (P2-3). These new work models may be operational and effective as adhocracy provides a more organic organization and fosters the minimization of rigidities associated with traditional organizational design. As such, a firm's culture influenced by adhocracy is, for all intents and purposes, equipped with the expertise, knowledge, competencies as well as resilience to face the challenges of an uncertain and ever-changing environment.

Adhocracy, by influencing organizational culture, gives rise to a type of adhocracy culture; in other words, the culture is informed by adhocracy, as per Mintzberg's contribution. The latter's characteristics have the potential to enable organizational leaders to not only be people-centric, but also to create work communities (P4). That is, a sense of community generated by and for collaborators to explore the bounds of creativity and innovation with the ultimate purpose of achieving strategic goals and increasing productivity and performance as teams, particularly interdisciplinary teams. Therefore, by doing so, organizations, *i.e.*, leaders and collaborators are able to co-create value which, as a result, influences the business environment. The latter, in due course, may contribute to business as well as social growth and development.

Concluding Remarks

COVID-19 has meant an important change in the way many organizations work today in different industries and sectors around the world. The home office model was widely used during lockdown, showing some advantages and disadvantages. Now, in the post-lockdown era, numerous flexible models have emerged—a mix of home office and face-to-face work—and are having positive results. Technology has been a catalyst for these forms of organization, in a more flexible and dynamic way. Adhocracy is an organizational style that has historically responded to complex and dynamic environments, such as COVID-19 and current post-lockdown phase. One of its main strengths is that it favors person-centered leadership styles, allowing greater development of each individual who is also more involved in decision-making and setting goals, growing personally while carrying out their duties.

With adhocracy, organizational culture works on mutual adaptation and the use of informal means of coordination. Leadership is more oriented toward coordinating activities and allowing experts to act in a committed manner; thus, the work community strengthens thanks to collaborative work. Leadership must foster this collaboration without allowing effectiveness to diminish, keeping the organization's goals clear and objectives explicit. As expected, adhocracy does not work on all situations. It is important to use this structure at the right time and with the right projects. It is not always convenient as it can be expensive to operate due to the few economies of scale it offers. It is particularly important to monitor the coordination mechanisms used by leadership and the organization given an ad hoc work that requires matrices and various articulation mechanisms. At the same time, a pure application of adhocracy is not easy, and its implementation naturally requires flexibility to adapt its principles to specific situations. However, in that sense, it represents a way of organizing that has benefits in this complex world that COVID-19 has generated.

Rebuilding in the post-lockdown phase entails maneuvering in a persistent state of uncertainty and, in many cases, turbulent environment despite advances in health protocols and vaccination processes. In other words, management is faced with the challenge of rebuilding within an ongoing pandemic. The lessons learned during lockdown show that: alternative work models can have positive effects on collaborators' well-being and productivity and, therefore, performance, as long as it is fostered by a person-centered leadership. And, that rebuilding after the Great Confinement requires rethinking leadership, organization, and structures to be more flexible, dynamic, democratic, and decentralized. A successful recovery, then, requires embracing risk and diligently listening to and aligning collaborators' and organizational needs. For that reason, adhocracy is proposed as a model to leverage value co-creation based on an organizational design, culture, and leadership that ultimately build work communities that are not only productive but may also effectively impact business and social growth and development.

Future Research Directions

Future research could develop a longitudinal study of the effects of flexible work models across industries and sectors in order to evaluate varying degrees of performance. Also, it is suggested that future research could study the correlation of different leadership styles with flexible work models in a post-COVID-19 lockdown world to determine whether there is a substantial difference in performance. Finally, it would be interesting to assess the effects of various flexible work models on collaborators' development and growth.

References

Alexander, A., De Smet, A., Langstaff, M., & Ravid, D. (2021, April 1). *What employees are saying about the future of remote work*. Retrieved July 21st, 2022 from McKinsey & Company: https://www.mckinsey.com/business-functions/people-and-organizational-performance/our-insights/what-employees-are-saying-about-the-future-of-remote-work

Alvesson, M. (1992). Leadership as social integrative action. A study of a computer consultancy company. *Organization Studies, 13*(2), 185–209. https://doi.org/10.1177/017084069201300202

Ansoff, I. (1974). Corporate structure present and future. *Vanderbilt University Working Paper*, *74*(4), 31–55.

Bailey, D., & Neilsen, E. H. (1992). Creating a bureau-adhocracy: Integrating standardized and innovative services in a professional work group. *Human Relations, 45*(7), 687–710. https://doi.org/10.1177/001872679204500703

Bennis, W. G., & Slater, P. E. (1968). *The temporary society*. Harper and Row.

Birkinshaw, J., & Ridderstrale, J. (2015). Adhocracy for an agile age. *McKinsey Quarterly*, 44–57.

Bolman, L. G., & Deal, T. E. (1995). *Organización y liderazgo: el arte de la decisión*. Addison-Wesley Iberoamericana.

Cabri, G., & Fioretti, G. (2022). Flexibility out of standardization. *International Journal of Organization Theory and Behavior, 25*(1–2), 22–38. https://doi.org/10.1108/IJOTB-11-2020-0197

Campbell, D. P. (1992). Employee wellness program marketing: An organizational theory perspective. *Health Marketing Quarterly, 9*(3–4), 5–17. https://doi.org/10.1300/J026v09n03_02

Cardiff , S., McCormack , B., & McCance, T. (2018, August). Person-centred leadership: A relational approach to leadership derived through action research. *Journal of Clinical Nursing, 27*(15–16), 3056–3069. https://doi.org/10.1111/jocn.14492.

CDC. (2021, March). *Interim list of categories of essential workers mapped to standardized industry codes and titles*. Retrieved July 16th, 2022 from: https://www.cdc.gov/vaccines/covid-19/categories-essential-workers.html

CDC. (2022, January). *CDC Museum COVID-19 Timeline*. Retrieved July 15th, 2022 from Online Exhibitions: https://www.cdc.gov/museum/timeline/covid19.html

Chandler, M. K., & Sayles, L. R. (1971). *Managing large systems*. Harper & Row.

Choflet, A., Packard, T., & Stashower, K. (2021, June). Rethinking organizational change in the COVID-19 era. *Journal of Hospital Management and Health Policy*, 5, 1–13. http://dx.doi.org/https://doi.org/10.21037/jhmhp

Chou, W.-J., Sibley, C. G., Liu, J. H., Lin, T.-T., & Cheng, B.-S. (2015). Paternalistic leadership profiles: A person-centered approach. *Group & Organization Management., 40*(5), 1–26. https://doi.org/10.1177/1059601115573358

Conrad, C. A., Brown, G., & Harmon, H. A. (1997). Customer satisfaction and corporate culture: A profile deviation analysis of a relationship marketing

outcome. *Psychology and Marketing, 14*(7), 663–674. https://doi.org/10.1002/(SICI)1520-6793(199710)14:7%3c663::AID-MAR2%3e3.0.CO;2-E
Cramer, M., & Zaveri, M. (2020, May 31). *What if you don't want to go back to the office?* Retrieved July 17th, 2022 from Business: https://www.nytimes.com/2020/05/05/business/pandemic-work-from-home-coronavirus.html
Daft, R. L. (2016). *Management*. Cengage Learning.
de Sousa Jabbour, A. B. L, Chiappetta, C. J., Hingley, M., Vilalta-Perdomo, E. L., Ramsden, G., & Twigg, D. (2020). Sustainability of supply chains in the wake of the coronavirus (COVID-19/SARS-CoV-2) pandemic: Lessons and trends. *Modern Supply Chain Research and Applications, 2*(3), 117–122. https://doi.org/10.1108/MSCRA-05-2020-0011
Dey, M., Bhattacharjee, S., Mahmood, M., Uddin, M. A., & Biswas, S. R. (2022, February). Ethical leadership for better sustainable performance: Role of employee values, behavior and ethical climate. *Journal of Cleaner Production, 337*, 130527. https://doi.org/10.1016/j.jclepro.2022.130527
Do, H., Budhwar, P., Shipton, H., Nguyen, H.-D., & Nguyen, B. (2022, March). Building organizational resilience, innovation through resource-based management initiatives, organizational learning and environmental dynamism. *Journal of Business Research, 141*, 808–821. https://doi.org/10.1016/j.jbusres.2021.11.090
Eluwole, K. K., Karatepe, O. M., & Avci, T. (2022, April). Ethical leadership, trust in organization and their impacts on critical hotel employee outcomes. *International Journal of Hospitality Management, 102*, 103153. https://doi.org/10.1016/j.ijhm.2022.103153
Esparza-Rodriguez, S. A., Martinez-Arroyo, J., & Sanchez-Vargas, A. (2021, May). Socioeconomic and structural profiles of the informal sector in the COVID-19 pandemics. *Nova Scientia, 13*(spe). https://doi.org/10.21640/ns.v13ie.2593.
Ferrari, E., Paladino, F., Pesce, F., Frecassetti, P., Lodovici, M. S., Aram, E., & Hadjivassiliou, K. (2021, June). *The impact of teleworking and digital work on workers and society. Special focus on surveillance and monitoring, as well as on mental health of workers*. Retrieved July 19th, 2022 from: https://www.europarl.europa.eu/RegData/etudes/STUD/2021/662904/IPOL_STU(2021)662904_EN.pdf
Fuller, J., & Kerr, W. (2022, March 23). The great resignation didn't start with the pandemic. Retrieved July 20th, 2022 from Harvard Business Review: https://hbr.org/2022/03/the-great-resignation-didnt-start-with-the-pandemic
Gachet, A., & Brézillon, P. (2005). A multi-level model. *Journal of Decision Systems, 14*(1–2), 9–37. https://doi.org/10.3166/jds.14.9-37
Galbraith, J. R. (1971, February). Matrix organizations design. *Business Horizons, 14*(1), 29–40. https://doi.org/10.1016/0007-6813(71)90037-1

George, T. J., Atwater, L. E., Maneethai, D., & Madera, J. M. (2022). Supporting the productivity and wellbeing of remote workers. *Organizational Dynamics, 51*(2), 1–9. https://doi.org/10.1016/j.orgdyn.2021.100869

Gibson, J. W., Blackwell, C. H., Dominicis, P., & Demerath, N. (2002). Telecommuting in the 21st century: Benefits, issues, and a leadership model which will work. *Journal of Leadership and Organizational Studies, 8*(4), 75–86. https://doi.org/10.1177/107179190200800407

Golden, L. (2001, March). Flexible work schedules: Which workers get them? *American Behavioral Scientist*, *44*(7), 1157–1178. https://doi.org/10.1177/00027640121956700

Gorgenyi-Hegyes, E., Nathan, R. J., & Fekete-Farkas, M. (2021). Workplace health promotion, employee wellbeing and loyalty during Covid-19 Pandemic-large scale empirical evidence from Hungary. *Economies, 9*(2), 55. https://doi.org/10.3390/economies9020055

Harpaz, I. (2002). Advantages and disadvantages of telecommuting for the individual, organization and society. *Work Study, 51*(2), 74–80. https://doi.org/10.1108/00438020210418791

Heejung, C., Hyojin, S., Forbes, S., & Birkett, H. (2020) *Working from home during the COVID-19 lockdown: Changing preferences and the future of work.* Retrieved July 17th, 2022 from the University of Kent: https://kar.kent.ac.uk/83896/1/Working_from_home_COVID-19_lockdown.pdf

Irwansyah, I. (2021, August). Adhocracy as a model for organizing government institution in simplifying Indonesian bureaucracy. *Jurnal Borneo Administrator*, *17*(2), 241–258. https://doi.org/10.24258/jba.v17i2.832

Jiang, L., Bettac, E. L., Lee, H. J., & Prob, T. M. (2022). In whom do we trust? A Multifoci Person-centered perspective on institutional trust during COVID-19. *International Journal of Environmental Research and Public Health.*, *19*(3), 1815. https://doi.org/10.3390/ijerph19031815

Jurczak, J. (2008). Intellectual capital measurement methods. *Economics and Organization of Enterprise.*, *1*(1), 37–45. https://doi.org/10.2478/v10061-008-0005-y

Kargas, A. D., & Varoutas, D. (2015). On the relation between organizational culture and leadership: An empirical analysis. *Cogent Business & Management.*, *2*(1), 1055953. https://doi.org/10.1080/23311975.2015.1055953

Keidel, R. W. (1994). Rethinking organizational design. *Academy of Management Perspectives.*, *8*(4), 12–28. https://doi.org/10.5465/ame.1994.9412071698

Kim, T., & Chang, J. (2019). Organizational culture and performance: A macro-level longitudinal study. *Leadership and Organization Development Journal*, *40*(1), 65–84. https://doi.org/10.1108/LODJ-08-2018-0291

Kitou, E., & Horvath, A. (2008, June). External air pollution costs of telework. *The International Journal of Life Cycle Assessment*, *13*(155), 155–165. https://doi.org/10.1065/lca2007.06.338

Kurkland, N. B., & Bailey, D. E. (1999). Telework: The advantages and challenges of working here, there, anywhere and anytime. *Organizational Dynamics, 28*(2), 53–68. https://doi.org/10.1016/S0090-2616(00)80016-9

Le, K., & Nguyen, M. (2021). The psychological consequences of COVID-19 lockdowns. *International Review of Applied Economics., 35*(2), 47–163. https://doi.org/10.1080/02692171.2020.1853077

Lindquist, E. A., & Buttazzoni, M. (2021). The ecology of open innovation units: Adhocracy and competing values in public service systems. *Policy Design and Practice, 4*(2), 212–227.

Linton, M.-J., Dieppe, P., & Medina-Lara, A. (2016). Review of 99 self-report measures for assessing well-being in adults: Exploring dimensions of well-being and developments over time. *BMJ Open, 6*(e010641). https://doi.org/10.1136/bmjopen-2015-010641

Llano, C. (2000). *La amistad en la empresa*. Instituto Panamericano de Alta de Alta Dirección de Empresas y Fondo de Cultura Económica.

Llano, C. (2006). *Análisis de la acción directiva*. Limusa.

March, J. G., & Simon, H. A. (1958). *Organizations*. Wiley-Blackwell.

Martela, F. (2019). What makes self-managing organizations novel? Comparing how weberian bureaucracy, Mintzberg's adhocracy, and self-organizing solve six fundamental problems of organizing. *Journal of Organization Design, 8*(1). https://doi.org/10.1186/s41469-019-0062-9

Masood, S. A., Dani, S. S., Burns, N. D., & Backhouse, C. J. (2006). Transformational leadership and organizational culture: The situational strength perspective. *Proceedings of the Institution of Mechanical Engineers, Part B: Journal of Engineering Manufacture, 220*(6), 941–949. https://doi.org/10.1243/09544054JEM499

McKinsey Global Institute. (2021, February 18). *The future of work after COVID-19 Report*. Retrieved July 17th, 2022 from: https://www.mckinsey.com/featured-insights/future-of-work/the-future-of-work-after-covid-19

Mehta, P. (2021, November). Work from home—Work engagement amid COVID-19 lockdown and employee happiness. *Journal of Public Affairs, 21*(4), e2709. https://doi.org/10.1002/pa.2709

Mello, J. A. (2007). Managing telework programs effectively. *Employee Responsibilities and Rights Journal., 19*, 247–261. https://doi.org/10.1007/s10672-007-9051-1

Messenger, J. C. (2019, November). Introduction: Telework in the 21st century – an evolutionary perspective. In J.C. Messenger (Ed.), *Telework in the 21st Century. An evolutionary perspective* (pp. 1–34). The ILO Future of Work series. https://doi.org/10.4337/9781789903751

Mintzberg, H. (1983). *Diseño de organizaciones eficientes*. El Ateneo.

Mintzberg, H. (2012). *La estructuración de las organizaciones*. Ariel.

Mozaffari, F. A. (2008). A study of relationship between organizational culture and leadership. In *International Conference on Applied Economics—ICOAE 2008*. pp. 679–688.

Neirotti, P., Paolucci, E., & Raguseo, E. (2013). Mapping the antecedents of telework diffusion: Firm-level evidence from Italy. *New Technology, Work and Employment, 28*(1), 16–36. https://doi.org/10.1111/ntwe.12001

Nilles, J. M. (1975, October). Telecommunications and organizational decentralization. *IEEE Transactions on Communications*, *23*(10), 1142–1147. https://jala.com/Telecomm%20and%20Org%20Decentralization.pdf

Pak, A., Adegboye, O. A., Adekunle, A. I., Rahman, K. M., McBryde, E. S., & Eisen, D. P. (2020, May). Economic consequences of the COVID-19 outbreak: The need for epidemic preparedness. *Frontiers in Public Health*, *8*(241), 1–4. https://doi.org/10.3389/fpubh.2020.00241

Patanjali, S., & Bhatta, N. M. K. (2022). Work from home during the pandemic: The impact of organizational factors on the productivity of employees in the IT industry. *Vision: The Journal of Business Perspective*, 1–13. https://doi.org/10.1177/09722629221074137

Pitterle, I., & Niermann, L. (2021, August). *The COVID-19 crisis: What explains cross-country differences in the pandemic's short-term economic impact?* DESA Working Paper No. 174. Retrieved July 16th 2022 from United Nations Department of Economic and Social Affairs: https://www.un.org/en/desa/covid-19-crisis-what-explains-cross-country-differences-pandemic%E2%80%99s-short-term-economic-impact

Plas, J. M. (1996). *Person-centered leadership. An American approach to participatory management*. Sage Publications.

Pyöriä, P. (2011). Managing telework: Risks, fears and rules. *Management Research Review., 34*(4), 386–399. https://doi.org/10.1108/01409171111117843

Raetze, S., Duchek, S., Maynard, M. T., & Wohlgemuth, M. (2022). Resilience in organization-related research: An integrative conceptual review across disciplines and levels of analysis. *Journal of Applied Psychology., 107*(6), 867–897. https://doi.org/10.1037/apl0000952

Robèrt, M., & Börjesson, M. (2006, July). Company incentives and tools for promoting telecommuting. *Environment and Behavior*, *38*(4), 521–549. https://doi.org/10.1177/0013916505283422

Scandura, T. A., & Lankau, M. J. (1997, July). Relationships of gender, family responsibility and flexible work hours to organizational commitment and job satisfaction. *Journal of Organizational Behavior, 18*(4), 377–391. https://doi.org/10.1002/(SICI)1099-1379(199707)18:4<377::AID-JOB807>3.0.CO;2-1

Schein, E. H. (1997). *Psicología de la organización*. Prentice Hall Hispanoamericana.

Shepard III, E. M., Clifton, T. J., & Kruse, D. (1996, January). Flexible work hours and productivity: Some evidence from the pharmaceutical industry. *Industrial Relations: A Journal of Economy and Society, 35*(1), 123–139. https://doi.org/10.1111/j.1468-232X.1996.tb00398.x

Tabuchi, H., & Vlasic, B. (2013, January 2). *Battered by expensive crises, Toyota declares a rebirth.* Retrieved July 28th, 2022 from The New York Times: https://www.nytimes.com/2013/01/03/business/battered-by-crises-toyota-declares-a-rebirth.html

Tavare, A. I. (2017). Telework and health effects review. *International Journal of Healthcare., 3*(2), 30–36. https://doi.org/10.5430/ijh.v3n2p30

Toffler, A. (1975). *El shock del futuro.* Plaza Janés.

Toh, S.-Y. (2022). (Re)constructing leadership: Complexity and flexibility. In S.N. Khan (Ed.), *Leadership and followership in an organizational change context* (pp. 22–56). IGI Global. https://doi.org/10.4018/978-1-7998-2807-5

Wei, Y., Samiee, S., & Lee, R. P. (2014). The influence of organic organizational cultures, market responsiveness, and product strategy on firm performance in an emerging market. *Journal of the Academy of Marketing Science, 42*(1), 49–70. https://doi.org/10.1007/s11747-013-0337-6

WHO. (2022a, May 22). *COVID-19 vaccines.* Retrieved July 22nd, 2022a from: https://www.who.int/emergencies/diseases/novel-coronavirus-2019/covid-19-vaccines

WHO. (2022b, July 22). *WHO coronavirus (COVID-19) dashboard.* Retrieved July 25th, 2022b from: https://covid19.who.int/

CHAPTER 5

COVID-19: An Opportunity to Explore Hybrid Work

Yvette Mucharraz y Cano, Diana Dávila-Ruiz, Ricardo Murcio Rodríguez, and Karla Cuilty-Esquivel

The COVID-19 pandemic accelerated the implementation of remote working arrangements. Before the lockdown, we observed positive and negative outcomes, the first ones linked to greater creativity and productivity levels, generating organizational commitment and job satisfaction (Scandura & Lankau, 1997), as well as the opportunity to improve work-life balance and quality of life (Sullivan, 2012). On the other end, some leaders may have lost control and experienced difficulties in maintaining communication across the organization. During the lockdown, working

Y. Mucharraz y Cano (✉) · K. Cuilty-Esquivel
Human Resources Management, IPADE Business School, Mexico City, Mexico
e-mail: ymucharraz@ipade.mx

K. Cuilty-Esquivel
e-mail: karlacuilty@ipade.mx

D. Dávila-Ruiz
Universidad Anahuac, Mexico City, Mexico
e-mail: diana.davilar@anahuac.mx

E. Murillo et al. (eds.), *Creating Economic Stability Amid Global Uncertainty*, https://doi.org/10.1007/978-3-031-41386-5_5

from home with school and domestic chores coexisted in a single space, the challenges of teleworking increased, and some negative effects were identified. In spite of this, different aspects should be analyzed to understand which could be the best work model for the future of work. While a high percentage of employees would like to continue working remotely, there are some activities that need to take place face to face, so the hybrid work scheme seems to be a viable option. The combination of on-site and remote work appears to facilitate business performance while reducing employees' work-life conflict, which is why different companies are shifting toward this type of scheme.

In this chapter, we will analyze how human, technological, and organizational levers were used and promoted because of the pandemic and enabled the emergence of a new hybrid work model, which is likely to change the future of work. Also, we will address the advantages and disadvantages of hybrid work, observing the phenomenon simultaneously from the talent and the organizational perspectives.

Previously, hybrid work has been identified by its characteristics, including "boundarylessness, multitasking, non-related work interruptions, and demand for constant learning" (Xie et al., 2019, p. 479), as well as flexibility in terms of time and space (Gratton, 2020). The pandemic has changed people's perception of hybrid work, so we make a distinction by defining hybrid work as the combination of work in and outside the office, where space, time, and home intersect as a novel combination of technological and human levers.

The hybrid model responds to the need to offer work schemes that are more malleable and allow for a better work-life balance. We have recently witnessed that one of the potential root causes for "the great resignation" in the United States in late 2021 was a strong desire to rethink the work model (Sull et al., 2022, para. 1), and employees are not just looking for higher remuneration but demanding a higher quality of life. Employees have a strong preference for hybrid work, especially executive women, who have encountered benefits in this work model, which also seems to promote and activate organizational resilience (Mucharraz

---

R. Murcio Rodríguez
Organizational Behavior Department, IPADE Business School, Mexico City, Mexico
e-mail: rmurcio@ipade.mx

y Cano, 2020). Moreover, employees are particularly interested in joining organizations with healthy and innovative cultures that offer vertical and horizontal growth opportunities, specifically companies that offer remote work opportunities (Sull et al., 2022), and these employees may act as levers to promote the development of hybrid work in companies. Thus, the post-COVID-19 era will call for more freedom at work, and the hybrid model will become more and more common and necessary, perhaps even the basic reality for organizations to attract and retain talent, especially female talent. This new reality requires a clearer and stronger definition of boundaries and expectations.

Besides the proposed definition of hybrid work, this chapter outlines the evolution of remote work, its potential benefits for the mitigation of work-life conflict. It also explores how hybrid work can build a mechanism integrating the employees' professional and personal lives, without underestimating its potential downsides, such as the so-called Zoom fatigue, isolation, and burnout, among other mental health issues (Sokolic, 2022). At the end of the chapter, we analyze the conditions that would make hybrid work feasible, including the necessary technology to work under this scheme.

Working from Home and Other Working Arrangements: The Evolution

The COVID-19 pandemic has hastened the business transformation process originated during the Fourth Industrial Revolution, and hybrid work has been introduced more quickly and widely than expected, combining teleworking and in-office work. Internet technologies have supported the reconstruction and changing nature of the workplace, working hours, and employment relationship (Burgess & Connell, 2020). During the lockdown, this became evident for a large percentage of companies and their employees.

This new reality brings with it the challenge of integrating business processes to hybrid work, as observed by some authors (Moglia et al., 2021). Organizations will face profound changes—not only with their employees, but also with their clients, providers, and suppliers—while implementing new ways of working (Mahmooda & Mubarik, 2020), which will pose several difficulties and opportunities in the years to come. Nevertheless, new technology levers such as online meetings, virtual private network connectivity, and different software tools that allow employees to share their work progress and information easily can enable us to overcome these challenges. Technological advances and new types of work organization have seemed to improve people's quality of life, productivity, and salaries, allowing for better time management between professional and personal activities. In this sense, the flexibilization of work could minimize work-life conflict, make employment relationships more dynamic, and build diverse and cross-functional work teams that can yield better results (Burgess & Connell, 2020), and it is clear now that organizations will face profound changes.

Although at the moment, working remotely is viewed as a somewhat innovative trend, especially in emerging markets, working from home can be considered as an ancient practice. In the Middle Ages, many trades such as shoemaking, carpentry, smithing, and farm work were performed from home. Even the greatest kings and pharaohs were all working from home. The big change happened during the First and Second Industrial Revolutions, when working at factories was implemented as the main source of economic resources for a large portion of the population (Groumpos, 2021). The mechanization process, which introduced large and heavy machinery, led to the need for a common space to perform different types of specialized work, where employees performed their tasks in a joint and coordinated fashion. In 1800, 6% of the American population was concentrated in cities, yet by 1900, this number had reached 40% (Groumpos, 2021, p. 466).

In 1973, due to the oil crisis, Jack Nilles and others wrote a report proposing the idea of working from home (Nilles et al., 1974). In 1976, their revolutionary ideas were enshrined in a book that presented teleworking as a viable option to face the United States' oil import problem (Nilles, 1976). Since that moment, the rise of households with computers has facilitated remote work. According to the United States Census Bureau's (2010) "Current Population" survey, only 8.2% of households had a computer at home in 1984 and 15% in 1989 (para. 1).

In the 1980s, flexible work meant choosing your own lunch schedule or having the freedom to organize your week before proposing a project (Dunham et al., 1987). In the late 1990s and early 2000s, remote work began to spread, leading to a lot of research on the topic (Kelliher & Anderson, 2010). This could be related to the European Economic Community's interest in promoting employees' flexibility and employability, as established by the 1998 Treaty of Amsterdam. As a result of the quick and rising increase in the unemployment rate, employment became a priority for the European Union (Goetschy, 1999). Besides, more and more households had computers as well as the possibility to connect to the Internet. In the United States, 36.6% of households had a computer by 1997. This was also the first year in which the percentage of households with Internet access (18%) was reported (United States Census Bureau, 2010, para. 1).

During this period, Jack Nilles' ideas became a real and attractive possibility, especially for employees and governments. Internet access and the use of electronic mail facilitated close remote communication in both the work and personal arenas. This enabled novel flexible work structures in terms of both the times and places in which work could be performed.

In sum, it may seem paradoxical that the Third and Fourth Industrial Revolutions appeared to be pushing work structures for people to return to their homes. However, this is what has been happening, especially in some professions (Pérez-Pineda, 2020), which include desk jobs that do not require close contact with clients and can be performed with the use of technology.

Since 2010, it became evident that work structures were undergoing a transformation that required new professional agreements. Most of the existing legal framework was insufficient for the novel specifications required by the job market. The term alternative agreements was intended to encompass all the contracts that lay outside of the traditional schemes that had prevailed in the workplace over the previous centuries. Cappelli and Keller (2012, pp. 583–584) identified 10 working arrangements:

1. Full-time employees (they follow the traditional structure);
2. Part-time employees (they follow the traditional structure, but work less than 35 hours per week);
3. On-call employees (they receive a salary and have traditional controls, but do not have to follow an established schedule; they are called upon and must be available when the organization needs them);
4. Direct-hire temporary employees (they follow the traditional structure for a limited period, like seasonal workers);
5. Professional employee organizations (they have an indirect work relationship with the company, as the company hires a third-party agency that is in charge of hiring the employees and is legally responsible for them);

6. Leased employees (a company hires an agency for a specific talent; the agency provides the staff and, when the job is done, they are reassigned to a different company);
7. Agency temporary workers (an agency provides workers for short-term assignments; the agency supervises the workers, but the final result is controlled by the client);
8. Independent contractors (the client-provider relationship takes place on a project basis);
9. Day laborers (these workers are hired on a one-job basis, typically lasting between one and three days; they do not have a formal contract and often receive their payment in cash); and
10. Vendors on-premises (a company hires a vendor to provide a service; the vendor then pays for the necessary workers, materials, etc.).

In consequence, thanks to the levers of technology and human organization progress, a wide variety of hiring options emerged in the labor market. When observing the characteristics of jobs, a constant space provided by the company could be found in only three of the schemes. Workers frequently used their personal spaces, such as their homes, to perform their professional activities. The time invested in work shifted from a schedule with fixed entry and exit times to a multiplicity of schedules that could be structured by the employer and the employee and that are now under the umbrella of remote work.

The Covid-19 Pandemic, the Fourth Industrial Revolution, and Hybrid Work

The COVID-19 pandemic and the human, technological, and organizational levers that it triggered have substantially reshaped the way we work and led us to ponder the possibility of developing new schemes, which include an additional variable: hybrid work. In other words, this emergent scenario was not isolated but rather stemmed from the evolution of work and the accelerated changes in innovation and technology.

Previous industrial revolutions brought challenges to employability while technological innovations tend to render certain jobs or products obsolete. In the case of the current revolution, the speed, the simultaneity of the changes, and the fact that the modifications include complete systems (Schwab, 2016) are leading to a complex scenario. Current evidence seems to indicate that the Fourth Industrial Revolution will differ from its predecessors in that it will create fewer jobs, and unemployment will increase due to the new technologies implemented on a large-scale basis (Schwab, 2016).

In the year 2000, the term Fourth Industrial Revolution was used to identify the progress toward "the networking of all systems [leading] to 'cyber-physical production systems' and, therefore, smart factories, in which production systems, components, and people communicate via a network and the production is nearly autonomous" (Groumpos, 2021, p. 466).

The number of people working from home before the pandemic represented 7.9% of the workforce, or approximately 260 million people. These estimates are based on data from 118 countries (Soares et al., 2021, p. 1). According to Germain and McGuire (2014), virtual work teams prevailed in companies with a wide geographical distribution and were a growing trend in the face of globalization. Remote work arrangements also continued to increase (Spreitzer et al., 2017). When contact restrictions were put in place due to the pandemic, this percentage increased, reaching an estimated 14.9% to 19.9%, which means that approximately 447 to 638 million people were working from home (Soares et al., 2021, p. 11). Technology seemed to provide communication options to deal with social distancing. As the pandemic progressed and the confinement measures started to be eased, it was necessary to implement hybrid work schemes, especially for parents, considering that in some countries, schools continued to be closed despite the opening of workspaces. Also, there was an intermittent opening of operations, especially during the COVID-19 waves that followed, in which contagions increased and there was the need to isolate active cases or those at risk. For some, hybrid work was an alternative by choice, and some individuals preferred to go back to the workplace some days despite having the possibility to work remotely on a daily basis.

The pandemic led companies and workers to consider digital virtuality as an unlimited and geographically expandable environment (Bennett & McWhorter, 2021) which can be combined with work in the employers' facilities. Based on the workers' expectations and needs, a hybrid work scheme may also address talent attraction and retention. The teleworking aspect of this scheme allows for flexibility to accommodate employees' personal and family needs, while the on-site work aspect may mitigate some of the negative effects experienced during the pandemic due to the constant exposure to online platforms, such as Zoom fatigue (Daigle, 2020). With this information, better strategies for new work schemes can be established.

The interaction between the Fourth Industrial Revolution and the pandemic marked a before and an after in the history of humankind. The work environment will surely never be the same because the opportunity to combine the possibility of being in the workplace and at home, at least partially, was a comfortable experience for many, and companies have gotten a taste of some of its benefits during the lockdown, including cost efficiencies, talent engagement, motivation, job satisfaction (Sokolic, 2022), and the possibility to enable business continuity alternatives to face contingencies.

From a theoretical viewpoint, some researchers have studied the concept of hybrid work in terms of work orientation styles, which include job, career, and calling. In this sense, a job implies setting an hourly rate for the work, a career involves a salary and benefits, and a calling refers to a more voluntary job or career altogether (Pitacho et al., 2021). Consequently, the concept of hybrid work can be defined more comprehensively based on the way this work is performed, considering a location that is not fixed and how the use of space, time, and technology interact.

Moreover, recently created work schemes need to keep on being analyzed from the human, business, and technological points of view. The future of employment will depend on the capacity of human adaptation to the creation and implementation of new technology. Within the new styles of work organization, hybrid work may become more and more frequent due to its benefits to individuals' well-being. Some studies have predicted that hybrid work will become "the most prevalent model of work organization in companies in the future" (Sokolic, 2022, p. 209).

Hybrid Work and the Pursuit of Balance

The aspiration to attain a balanced life while managing work and family responsibilities was already complicated, and the arrival of the COVID-19 pandemic uncovered the virtues and flaws of mixing one's work, family, and social lives. In a context where social distancing was not only desirable but also mandatory, in many cases, the desire to blend work with family became a reality for those who had this option, and they integrated their activities in a single space, which was their home (Dávila Ruiz et al.,

2020), allowing for the observation of its effects. Then, with the need to establish hybrid work schemes, the complexity increased, as in many cases, it was difficult to plan when it would be necessary to attend work in person and the time for teleworking. In this sense, instead of referring to work-life balance, especially in hybrid work, it may be more appropriate to use the concept of "work-life blend."

The term work-life blend seems to have emerged from practice (Joseph, 2019) as a response to the continuous search for the formula to balance one's personal and work life and was derived from the concept of "work-life balance." The two main characteristics of the work-life blend seem to be mixing work responsibilities and personal life and giving up on the possibility of reaching a balance.

Translating the difficulty to balance work and personal life responsibilities under the pandemic context, it is worth clarifying that the result was not the same for everyone. At the beginning of the confinement, work activities needed to be performed from home, and schools closed for more than 200 days (Organisation for Economic Cooperation & Development, 2021) in some places like Mexico, and this meant that people also needed to take care of their homes and family members. The differences were particularly noticeable for women (Bhumika, 2020; Yavorsky et al., 2021), and they were exacerbated by cultural factors in many countries, given that the responsibility for the family and children had long since lain primarily on women. In this scenario, hybrid work was a tool used by companies and employees to adapt to the circumstances by combining isolation and presence, reducing the possibility of contagion. After some months, with the introduction of hybrid work, the complexity increased, and a good proportion of female talent decided to resign in order to face the changing and unpredictable circumstances while opting for informal or part-time jobs.

Past literature has mentioned the conflict between personal and professional life (Frone et al., 1992; Martins et al., 2002), but even though the topic has been reviewed over and over, both from an empirical and a theoretical perspective, a unidimensional way to approach it has not been found. Unfortunately, the experience during the pandemic led to the first conclusion presented in this chapter, in which the conditions of the lockdown, particularly for women (Aguiar et al., 2021; Collins et al., 2021; Kerr et al., 2021; Mustajab et al., 2020; Queen & Harding, 2020), pushed the work-from-home model to the limit and led to the discovery of a possible undesirable effect: the lockdown's impact on mental health (Adams-Prassl et al., 2020).

Faced with the aforementioned scenario, it is necessary to propose an alternative work scheme that is fair not only to women but also to families and that facilitates productivity and social interaction. It would seem that hybrid work possesses some of these characteristics, so it is worth exploring its potential risks and benefits. However, hybrid work brings new challenges, especially in the way of leading when combining remote and face-to-face work (Antonacopoulou & Georgiadou, 2021).

Finally, there is also a paradigm worth questioning: whether work and personal life are independent. This includes questioning the notion of work itself, which refers exclusively to paid work as if it had a greater value, leaving out family and/or household work (Goodman & Kaplan, 2019). The social contribution coming from the family should have greater recognition, as it is geared toward the common good and even contributes to the development of future generations. In this sense, the idea of balancing our personal and professional lives should be viewed not just in light of the short-term economic priorities, but in an integral way, taking into account people's development and fulfillment.

Freedom or Slavery in Hybrid Work: The Flexibility Trap

Reconciling individual and organizational needs represents a challenge in the implementation of hybrid work schemes. Also, it is important to analyze the implications of attending work, home, and family responsibilities simultaneously. First, it is necessary to distinguish between working from home, remote work from any other place, and hybrid work in which schedules, on-site attendance, and days off are not fixed, as well as the work scheme taking place in the circular economy "most frequently depicted as a combination of reduce, reuse and recycle activities" (Kircherr et al., 2017, p. 221), where energy and renewable materials are favored.

As previously mentioned, the pandemic was particularly straining for women. In addition to balancing their workload in the home and taking care of others, the attention required by school-age children demanded an extraordinary effort. Unfortunately, during this scenario, employers were rarely considerate toward their workers, and workloads increased exponentially in the face of an economic crisis that affected most companies. Working with no schedule and no boundaries became the norm, in some cases even incurring what has been referred to since before the pandemic as "modern slavery," meaning the exploitation of workers to benefit companies (Crane, 2013, p. 49).

The aforementioned conditions in which work took place due to the COVID-19 pandemic reached a breaking point. Employees and executives worked nonstop and with complete willingness, both on their computers responding to emails or instant messages and participating in virtual meetings until reaching what was dubbed "Zoom fatigue" (Fosslien & West Duffy, 2020, para. 1). The new work habits became the norm, and even when it was possible to work on site, Zoom meetings continued to be a recurrent practice, and therefore, some of the apparent benefits of coming back to the workplace were diluted. In the future, it will be necessary to reconsider if this is the best way to work, i.e., if responding to more emails or messages or attending more virtual meetings leads to greater efficiency or if, on the contrary, it undermines people's ability to reflect, act, and genuinely connect in work teams. If what the world needs most nowadays is innovation, creativity could be hindered by this relentless way of working, which does not allow employees to interact with their ecosystems or with something greater than themselves and their immediate environment.

Thus, from this point forward, it is essential to redirect working conditions toward the dignification of work, which should never come before people and their families. The ideals that led to the struggle that has taken place throughout history to avoid labor exploitation should take on a new meaning, which is not to rise up in arms but to peacefully reconcile the interests of both companies and people in favor of human rights (Kolben, 2009) and to effectively achieve what has been dubbed decent work (International Labour Organization n.d.).

Hybrid Work: Intersecting Organizational and Family Expectations

As we have already mentioned, the pandemic did not lead to the invention of a new way of working; moving from traditional work arrangements has been on the rise since the 1980s as an alternative to reconcile work demands and employees' personal needs (De Menezes & Kelliher, 2017; Richardson & McKenna, 2014). Nowadays, hybrid work is related to a work arrangement without the traditional 8-hour office work schedules and combines on-site attendance with remote work. However, the trend was received with fear and concerns; only a few companies had allowed it and most maintained traditional work relationships. COVID-19 accelerated the implementation of hybrid work and put it to the test in ways that had never been seen or even imagined. It forced companies and employees to question established employment agreements, thus creating the need to rethink the existing relationships, regulations, and expectations in professional and personal lives, leading different authors and cases to express the need to re-regulate these relationships (Ajzen & Taskin, 2021).

Over the last decade, important studies about the relevance of alternate work arrangements and their profound implications have been carried out (Huws, 2013). In general terms, there are two main concerns: (a) the compelling need to make work more flexible to meet personal and professional expectations and commitments; and (b) the considerable impact that this new way of working has had on our personal lives, affecting our mental, familial, and social health, with a considerable increase in stress, even leading to the already well-known burnout (Mucharraz y Cano et al., 2022). Both scenarios require that we take moment and study the expectations that the post-COVID-19 world will have regarding the new working conditions.

The study of the mentioned scenarios requires the consideration of one of the main levers that has accelerated the adoption of alternate work arrangements, technological development. In this sense, technology has changed how we carry out our work activities, generating a more globalized world that, since the beginning of this century, has been developing and evolving in an accelerated way. Virtual work, carried out online, persisted with the possibility of checking email from devices outside the office (Huws, 2013), evolving to this day, when a whole business model can rely on distance work, which can be carried out from anywhere in the world without any complication. The complexity emerged when, during the first stage of the pandemic under the Great Confinement, three elements that were normally separated intersected in the same place: (a) family, (b) work, and (c) school. The three environments were integrated into a highly complex and uncertain context and, in most cases, amid an economic crisis. With this background and as the pandemic progressed, many employers required talent to not only operate virtually but go back to working on site, at least partially, with some employees resisting to re-engage in face-to-face activities. Also, employees with a lot of distractors at home sought hybrid work to maintain their concentration (Appel-Meulenbroek et al., 2022). To keep core activities in the workplace while combining them with virtual ones, the activation of the organizational lever in hybrid work schemes will require the development of operational frameworks and policies.

All these elements, integrated abruptly and unexpectedly, require finding their respective spaces, involving a learning process and the definition of new work and family relationships. The new rules, functions, and responsibilities of the people in these environments need to be studied.

According to Sull et al. (2022), there are some fundamental elements that will help organizations retain talent in the future, and one of the most important ones will be reaching an agreement that will allow people to be satisfied with their work scheme. It is necessary to continue doing research on the response to hybrid work, the pros and cons, and the way it is implemented in different industries, geographies, and organizations. Companies will be required to reconcile the coexistence of teleworking, hybrid, and fully on-site work with the same workforce.

Some of the studies on emerging work arrangements have shown that people are looking for the possibility to work remotely but are also displaying great differences based on their industries, sectors, social levels, and quality of work. In terms of the benefits that have been identified, employees expect to maintain remote work in the future, at least some days of the week, in the form of a hybrid arrangement, as can be seen in Parker and Clark's study, where 73% of the interviewees wish to continue working remotely (Parker & Clark, 2022, p. 21). However, hybrid work is not for everyone, as home spaces and needs differ from person to person (Appel-Meulenbroek et al., 2022). There are still challenges regarding domestic chore arrangements to address the responsibilities and activities that historically have required more involvement from women (Parker & Clark, 2022). In this sense, hybrid work may open up the option of generating new arrangements in the household, where men could be more involved in family- and household-related activities.

Additionally, one basic question that needs to be investigated is how hybrid work impacts the productivity of companies. The pandemic generated the opportunity to study the phenomenon, but the results are still inconclusive (Sokolic, 2022). The variables to be explored for the future include employees' level in the organization—considering their income and job function—Internet access, digital agility, level of knowledge developed to achieve their objectives, time and place where they perform their work activities, reconciliation of family schedules and needs, and ways of increasing productivity under hybrid work. Another element to consider, especially in cities with a large urban concentration, is the commuting time for the days in which on-site attendance is required (Appel-Meulenbroek et al., 2022), as it may decrease productivity due to the time and energy dedicated to being physically present.

It seems that employees expect to be able to continue having access to work schemes with freedom, which will allow them to have a better quality of life. Employers will not only need to improve the working conditions they offer but also create open organizational cultures and be willing to offer their employees development opportunities and a better quality of life. Companies will have to take care of two fundamental aspects so as not to lose productivity: (a) awareness and (b) availability (Ocker et al., 2007), which means that employees will need to have the willingness to be technologically, physically, mentally, and emotionally available while also being aware of other team members' ability and availability to work. The organizations that better manage work arrangements, and even adapt them individually, when possible, will be more attractive employers in the future.

Technology, a Key Element of Hybrid Work

To help with the new challenges and create the possibility of productive work, it is necessary to rely on technology. Sixty-nine percent of executives work remotely from their mobile devices and laptops and remain connected to perform their work (Global Return to Workplace Study 2021, as cited in Steelcase Inc., 2021), even when working on site. The BYOD model (Bring Your Own Device) is helping employees' by supporting and integrating a variety of hardware and software solutions, so people can connect more easily and productively at home, the office, or another location (Barlette et al., 2021).

It's now possible to imagine companies leveraging their productivity with technology, and employees having the same experience from home, based on cheap prices and great support from software development (Ellis et al., 2022; Gratton, 2020). In the future, companies are going to be able to provide people in the office a better virtual presence by designing important elements such as cameras, acoustics, content, and lighting. The hybrid scheme will further promote physical and virtual spaces and enable people inside and outside the office to communicate and interact (Appel-Meulenbroek et al., 2022). Now, it is also becoming possible to provide an engaging experience for employees when working on site.

Movement technology will allow both remote and co-located participants to move around the room with the help of mobile furniture and displays. Audio and acoustics considerations for an optimal sound for both parties are now a priority for companies because communication is positively correlated with business success (Olson, 2002). Considering the size, boundaries, and materials of the space as well as the direction of microphones and speakers for the best audio on both ends will be a main concern.

Meetings carried out through virtual and augmented reality will continue to enable interaction through avatars among individuals representing different continents and time zones. Also, the tendency of recruitment for the metaverse will be at play in the future (Dwivedi et al., 2022). These technological trends will be perfected further to better serve organizations, but they are already a reality.

While considering technology as one of the levers for change in the post-pandemic period, in hybrid work schemes it is necessary to address the definition of boundaries. One of the main risks is falling in an atemporal category (i.e., where the time for each activity is not limited), putting mental health at risk due to the lack of rest and the potential isolation, even at a professional level (Golden et al., 2008). This new nature of work might make it impossible to allocate time for personal activities or use time interchangeably, lacking the proper focus to perform each task, especially when applying a hybrid work scheme.

Among the levers on the human side, organizations have adopted a variety of new ways to manage workers' time in hybrid schemes, as it is not only a new configuration regarding the days in which an employee needs to attend the facilities and work on site. Even on the same day, part of the work may be performed on site and the other remotely, not necessarily from home. In the past, such arrangements were common for the sales workforce (Harris, 2003), but especially during the pandemic, they became the norm in many companies.

Conclusion: The Need for Plasticity in Work Schemes

Work arrangements have been evolving throughout history. However, the COVID-19 pandemic and the lockdown forced us to experience alternate work schemes, including hybrid work. We analyzed how human, technological, and organizational levers were used and promoted because of the pandemic and enabled the emergence of a new hybrid work model, which is likely to change the future of work. This situation helped us to break paradigms and try new ways of working, combining remote and on-site work. In the post-pandemic period, it seems hybrid work will play a big role in the years to come, allowing people to find better quality of life and personal development, and organizations to achieve greater productivity and efficiency. This will be made possible thanks to the technology levers which are now in place to promote this new reality, a trend that did not start with COVID-19 but that has been promoted and tested during this time. Companies and employees have found advantages in the hybrid work scheme, using it as a tool that facilitates life balance, under certain parameters. It is possible to assert that the new ways of social, family, and work organization will develop and promote hybrid work. In this sense, the best scheme seems to be more like a tailor-made formula for each individual and organization rather than a universal one, as each human being has its own particular complexities and environment. The desire to strike the perfect balance between working from home and outside the home may seem illusory, but it becomes evident in the work-life blend concept that intends to integrate rather than separate the two domains.

To achieve this, organizations need to be prepared with the right technology to establish better ways of communicating with their employees, as well as facilities that will allow for greater connectivity with people in and outside the office. Likewise, it is the ideal time for companies to reconsider new ways of organizing themselves, and thanks to the paradigm shifts, reach new agreements that facilitate greater equity and the right to rest and have decent work, while also promoting productivity and efficiency.

Additionally, organizations can implement hybrid work schemes to strengthen their talent attraction and retention programs as well as to consolidate their reputation in the talent market. The factors that define hybrid work include the best use of space, time, and technology. The post-pandemic period seems to be the best moment to implement hybrid schemes. To succeed, it is essential to create the right conditions from both the infrastructure and the human sides and to make the necessary arrangements to achieve efficiency. The work environment will tend to merge office space with employees' personal spaces, making hybrid working schemes increasingly prevalent in the future, which may be beneficial for both employees and organizations to accomplish higher goals.

References

Adams-Prassl, A., Boneva, T., Golin, M., & Rauh, C. (2020). The impact of the coronavirus lockdown on mental health: Evidence from the US. *Economic Policy*. https://doi.org/10.1093/epolic/eiac002

Aguiar, J., Matias, M., Braz, A. C., César, F., Coimbra, S., Gaspar, M. F., & Fontaine, A. M. (2021). Parental burnout and the COVID-19 pandemic: How Portuguese parents experienced lockdown measures. *Family Relations, 70*(4), 927–938. https://doi.org/10.1111/fare.12558

Ajzen, M., & Taskin, L. (2021). The re-regulation of working communities and relationships in the context of flexwork: A spacing identity approach. *Information and Organization, 31*(4), Article 100364. https://doi.org/10.1016/j.infoandorg.2021.100364

Antonacopoulou, E. P., & Georgiadou, A. (2021). Leading through social distancing: The future of work, corporations, and leadership from home. *Gender, Work & Organization, 28*(2), 749–767. https://doi.org/10.1111/gwao.12533

Appel-Meulenbroek, R., Kemperman, A., Van de Water, A. Weijs-Perrée, M., & Jan Verhaegh (2022). How to attract employees back to the office? A stated choice study on hybrid working preferences. *Journal of Environmental Psychology, 81*, Article 101784. https://doi.org/10.1016/j.jenvp.2022.101784

Barlette, Y., Jaouen, A., & Baillette, P. (2021). Bring your own device (BYOD) as reversed IT adoption: Insights into managers' coping strategies. *International Journal of Information Management, 56*, 1–16. https://doi.org/10.1016/j.ijinfomgt.2020.102212

Bennett, E. E., & McWhorter, R. (2021). Virtual HRD's role in crisis and the post COVID-19 professional virtual HRD's role in crisis and the post COVID-19 professional. *Advances in Developing Human Resources, 23*(1), 5–25. https://doi.org/10.1177/1523422320973288

Bhumika, B. (2020). Challenges for work-life balance during COVID-19 induced nationwide lockdown: Exploring gender difference in emotional exhaustion in the Indian setting. *Gender in Management, 35*(7–8), 705–718. https://doi.org/10.1108/GM-06-2020-0163

Burgess, J., & Connell, J. (2020). New technology and work: Exploring the challenges. *The Economic and Labour Relations Review, 31*(3), 310–323. https://doi.org/10.1177/1035304620944296

Cappelli, P., & Keller, J. (2012, October). Classifying work in the new economy. *The Academy of Management Review, 38*(4), 575–596. https://doi.org/10.5465/amr.2011.0302

Collins, C., Landivar, L. C., Ruppanner, L., & Scarborough, W. J. (2021). COVID-19 and the gender gap in work hours. *Gender, Work & Organization, 28*(S1), 101–112. https://doi.org/10.1111/gwao.12506

Crane, A. (2013). Modern slavery as a management practice: Exploring the conditions and capabilities for human exploitation. *Academy of Management Review, 38*(1), 49–69. https://www.jstor.org/stable/23416302

Daigle, T. (2020, May 27). 'Zoom fatigue' is setting in: What it is and how to prevent it. *CBC*. https://www.cbc.ca/news/science/zoom-fatigue-is-setting-in-1.5585933

Dávila Ruiz, D., Mucharraz y Cano, Y., & Gómez Minakata, C. (2020). *Home-office: La nueva revolución industrial*. Bosch México.

De Menezes, L. M., & Kelliher, C. (2017). Flexible working, individual performance, and employee attitudes: Comparing formal and informal arrangements. *Human Resource Management, 56*(6), 1051–1070. https://doi.org/10.1002/hrm.21822

Dunham, R., Pierce, J., & Castañeda, M. (1987). Alternative work schedules: Two field quasi-experiments. *Personnel Psychology, 40*, 215–242. https://doi.org/10.1111/j.1744-6570.1987.tb00602.x

Dwivedi, Y. K., Hughes, L., Baabdullah, A. M., Ribeiro-Navarrete, S., Giannakis, M., Al-Debei, M. M., Dennehy, D., Metri, B., Buhalis, D., Cheung, C., Conboy, K., Doyle, R., Dubey, R., Dutot, V., Felix, R., Goyal, D. P., Gustafsson, A., Hinsch, C., Jebabli, I., Janssen, M., Kim, Y., Kim, J., Koss, S., Kreps, D. Kshetri, N., Kumar, V., Ooi, K. B., Papagiannidis, S., Pappas, I.O., Polyviou, A., Park, S., Pandey. M., Queiroz, M. M., Raman, R., Rauschnabel, P. A., Shirish, A., Sigala, M., Spanaki, K., Wei-Han, G., Tiwari, M. K., Viglia, G. & Fosso, S. (2022). Metaverse beyond the hype: Multidisciplinary perspectives on emerging challenges, opportunities, and agenda for research, practice, and policy. *International Journal of Information Management, 66*, Article 102542. https://doi.org/10.1016/j.ijinfomgt.2022.102542

Ellis, R., Goodacre, T., Mortensen, N., Oeppen, R. S., & Brennan, P. A. (2022). Application of human factors at hybrid meetings: Facilitating productivity and inclusivity. *British Journal of Oral and Maxillofacial Surgery., 60*(6), 740–745. https://doi.org/10.1016/j.bjoms.2021.12.055

Fosslien, L., & West Duffy, M. (2020, April 29). How to combat zoom fatigue. *Harvard Business Review*. https://hbr.org/2020/04/how-to-combat-zoom-fatigue

Frone, M. R., Russell, M., & Cooper, M. L. (1992). Antecedents and outcomes of work-family conflict: Testing a model of the work-family interface. *Journal of Applied Psychology, 77*(1), 65–78. https://doi.org/10.1037/0021-9010.77.1.65

Germain, M.-L., & McGuire, D. (2014, May 5). The role of swift trust in virtual teams and implications for human resource development. *Advances in Developing Human Resources, 16*(3), 356–370. https://doi.org/10.1177/1523422314532097

Goetschy, J. (1999). The European employment strategy: Genesis and development. *European Journal of Industrial Relations, 5*(2), 117–137. https://doi.org/10.1177/095968019952002

Golden, T. D., Veiga, J. F., & Dino, R. N. (2008). The impact of professional isolation on teleworker job performance and turnover intentions: Does time spent teleworking, interacting face-to-face, or having access to communication-enhancing technology matter? *Journal of Applied Psychology, 93*(6), 1412–1421. https://doi.org/10.1037/a0012722

Goodman, R., & Kaplan, S. (2019). Work–life balance as a household negotiation: A new perspective from rural India. *Academy of Management Discoveries, 5*(4), 465–486. https://doi.org/10.5465/amd.2018.0105

Gratton, L. (2020, November 9). *Four principles to ensure hybrid work is productive work*. MIT Sloan Management Review. https://sloanreview.mit.edu/article/four-principles-to-ensure-hybrid-work-is-productive-work/

Groumpos, P. P. (2021). A critical historical and scientific overview of all industrial revolutions. *IFAC-PapersOnLine, 54*(13), 464–471. https://doi.org/10.1016/j.ifacol.2021.10.492

Harris, L. (2003). Home-based teleworking and the employment relationship: Managerial challenges and dilemmas. *Personnel Review, 32*(4), 422–437. https://doi.org/10.1108/00483480310477515

Huws, U. (2013). Working online, living offline: Labour in the internet age. *Work Organisation, Labour and Globalisation, 7*(1), 1–11. https://www.jstor.org/stable/10.13169/workorgalaboglob.7.1.0001

International Labour Organization. (n.d.). Decent work. International Labour Organization. https://www.ilo.org/global/topics/decent-work/lang--en/index.htm

Joseph, S. V. (2019, October 17). Forget work-life balance. Try achieving work-life blend instead. *Forbes Magazine*. https://www.forbes.com/sites/shelcyvjoseph/2019/10/17/forget-work-life-balance-try-achieving-work-life-blend-instead/?sh=7e2d68873d94

Kelliher, C., & Anderson, D. (2010). Doing more with less? Flexible working practices and the intensification of work. *Human Relations, 63*(1), 83–106. https://doi.org/10.1177/0018726709349199

Kerr, M. L., Rasmussen, H. F., Fanning, K. A., & Braaten, S. M. (2021). Parenting during COVID-19: A study of parents' experiences across gender and income levels. *Family Relations, 70*(5), 1327–1342. https://doi.org/10.1111/fare.12571

Kirchherr, J., Reike, D., & Hekkert, M. (2017). Conceptualizing the circular economy: An analysis of 114 definitions. *Resources, Conservation and Recycling, 127*, 221–232.

Kolben, K. (2009). Labor rights as human rights? *Virginia Journal of International Law, 20*(2), 50–484.

Mahmooda, T., & Mubarik, M. (2020, November). Balancing innovation and exploitation in the fourth industrial revolution: Role of intellectual capital and technology absorptive capacity. *Technological Forecasting & Social Change, 160*, Article 120248. https://doi.org/10.1016/j.techfore.2020.120248

Martins, L. L., Eddleston, K. A., & Veiga, J. F. (2002). Moderators of the relationship between work-family conflict and career satisfaction. *Academy of Management Journal, 45*(2), 399–409. https://doi.org/10.2307/3069354

Moglia, M., Hopkins, J., & Bardoel, A. (2021). Telework, hybrid work and the United Nation's sustainable development goals: Towards policy coherence. *Sustainability, 13*(16), Article 9222. https://doi.org/10.3390/su13169222

Mucharraz y Cano, Y. (2020). Organizational resilience after an extreme environmental event: An empirical study. *Paper presented to the EURAM 2020 online conference: The business of now: The future starts here. December 4–6, 2020.*

Mucharraz y Cano, Y., Dávila Ruiz, D., & Cuilty, K. (2022). The female face of COVID-19: Burnout in working women and the quest for resilience [Abstract]. *Academy of Management Proceedings, 2022*(1). https://doi.org/10.5465/AMBPP.2022.14832abstract

Mustajab, D., Bauw, A., Rasyid, A., Irawan, A., Akbar, M. A., & Hamid, M. A. (2020). Working from home phenomenon as an effort to prevent COVID-19 attacks and its impacts on work productivity. *TIJAB: The International Journal of Applied Business, 4*(1), 13–21. https://doi.org/10.20473/tijab.V4.I1.2020.13-21

Nilles, J. (1976). *The telecommunications-transportation tradeoff: Options for tomorrow*. John Wiley & Sons, Inc.

Nilles, J., Carlson, F., Gray, P., & Hanneman, G. (1974). *Telecommunications-transportation tradeoffs*. National Technical Information Service.

Ocker, R., Huang, H., Trauth, E., & Purao, S. (2007). The tension between expectations of availability and the reality of availability in hybrid teams. In K. Crowston, S. Sieber, & E. Wynn (Eds.), *Virtuality and virtualization*: Proceedings of the International Federation of Information Processing

Working Groups 8.2 on Information Systems and Organizations and 9.5 on Virtuality and Society, July 29–31, 2007, Portland, Oregon, USA (pp. 119131). International Federation for Information Processing

Olson, J. (2002). Research about office workplace activities important to US business -and how to support them. *Journal of Facilities Management, 1*(1), 31–47. https://doi.org/10.1108/14725960310807827

Organisation for Economic Cooperation and Development. (2021). *The state of global education: 18 Months into the Pandemic.* https://doi.org/10.1787/1a23bb23-en

Parker, R., & Clark, B. Y. (2022). *Unraveling the great resignation: Impacts of the COVID-19 pandemic on Oregon workers.* University of Oregon: Institute for Policy Research and Engagement. https://papers.ssrn.com/sol3/papers.cfm?abstract_id=4019586

Pérez-Pineda, J. A. (2020). Los sectores económicos con mayores beneficios para el 'home-office' en México. In L. Coronado Contreras & L. F. Llanos Reynoso (Eds.), *Home-office: La Nueva Revolución Industrial* (pp. 313–329). Wolters Kluwer España.

Pitacho, L., Jardim da Palma, P., Correia, P., & Pereira Lopes, M. (2021). Why do people work? An empirical test of hybrid. *Social Sciences, 10*(8), Article 284. https://doi.org/10.3390/socsci10080284

Queen, D., & Harding, K. (2020). Societal pandemic burnout: A COVID legacy. *International Wound Journal, 17*(4), 873–874. https://doi.org/10.1111/iwj.13441

Richardson, J., & McKenna, S. (2014). Rcordering spatial and social relations: A case study of professional and managerial flexworkers. *British Journal of Management, 25*, 724–736. https://doi.org/10.1111/1467-8551.12017

Scandura, T. A., & Lankau, M. J. (1997). Relationships of gender, family responsibility and flexible work hours to organizational commitment and job satisfaction. *Journal of Organizational Behavior, 18*(4), 377–391.

Schwab, K. (2016). *The fourth industrial revolution* (1st ed.). World Economic Forum.

Soares, S., Bonnet, F., Berg, J., & Labouriau, R. (2021, March 31). *Policy brief: From potential to practice: Preliminary findings on the numbers of workers working from home during the COVID-19 pandemic.* International Labour Organization. https://www.ilo.org/wcmsp5/groups/public/---ed_protect/---protrav/---travail/documents/briefingnote/wcms_777896.pdf

Sokolic, D. (2022, February). Remote work and hybrid work organizations. *Paper presented to the 78th International Scientific Conference on Economic and Social Development-Aveiro.* https://www.esd-conference.com/upload/book_of_abstracts/Book_of_Abstracts_esdAveiro2022_Online.pdf

Spreitzer, G., Cameron, L., & Garrett, L. (2017). Alternative work arrangements: Two images of the new world of work. *Annual Review of Organizational*

Psychology and Organizational Behavior, 4, 473–499. https://doi.org/10.1146/annurev-orgpsych-032516-113332

Steelcase Inc. (2021, July 22). *Hybrid collaboration is hard*. https://www.steelcase.com/eu-en/research/articles/topics/work-better/hybrid-collaboration-hard/

Sull, D., Sull, C., & Zweig, B. (2022). Toxic culture is driving the great resignation. *MIT Sloan Management Review, 63*(2), 1–9. https://sloanreview.mit.edu/article/toxic-culture-is-driving-the-great-resignation/

Sullivan, C. (2012). Remote working and work-life balance. In Reilly, N., Sirgy, M., & Gorman, C. (Eds.), *International handbooks of quality-of-life* (pp. 275–290). Springer Publishers. https://doi.org/10.1007/978-94-007-4059-4_15

United States Census Bureau. (2010, Febraury). Current Population Survey [Data file]. https://www.census.gov/data/tables/time-series/demo/computer-internet/computer-use-1984-2009.html

Xie, J. L., Elangovan, A. R., Hu, J., & Hrabluik, C. (2019). Charting new terrain in work design: A study of hybrid work characteristics. *Applied Psychology, 68*(3), 479–512. https://doi.org/10.1111/apps.12169

Yavorsky, J. E., Qian, Y., & Sargent, A. C. (2021), The gendered pandemic: The implications of COVID-19 for work and family, *Sociology Compass, 15*(6), Article e12881. https://doi.org/10.1111/soc4.12881

PART II

Lever Deployment in an Emergent Economy

CHAPTER 6

VAT Elasticities on Imports as a Lever to Forecast Collection: Mexico 2010–2021

Javier Moreno Espinosa, Leovardo Mata Mata, and Jaime Humberto Beltrán-Godoy

Introduction

Public finances, specifically government revenues and spending budgets, have received considerable attention due to the need to know the future behavior of government revenues and the public spending budget. Therefore, the analysis of government revenues and expenditures should be

J. Moreno Espinosa (✉)
Facultad de Ciencias Económicas y Empresariales, Universidad Panamericana, Mexico City, Mexico
e-mail: jmorenoe@up.edu.mx

L. Mata Mata · J. H. Beltrán-Godoy
Faculty of Economics and Business, Universidad Anáhuac México, Naucalpan, Mexico
e-mail: leovardo.mata@anahuac.mx

J. H. Beltrán-Godoy
e-mail: jaime.beltrang@anahuac.mx

E. Murillo et al. (eds.), *Creating Economic Stability Amid Global Uncertainty*, https://doi.org/10.1007/978-3-031-41386-5_6

carried out continuously and under a systemic approach to identify the different factors that influence tax collection and public spending.

This chapter will review what concerns income and specifically the relationship between the collection of Value Added Tax (VAT) and imports of merchandise classified in the 99 chapters of the International Harmonized System (HS). Please refer to Annex A1 for a listing of the 99 chapters (all Annexes are available in PDF format in an open access repository at https://tinyurl.com/Annex1-9).

"*The HS contributes to the harmonization of customs and trade procedures, and the non-documentary trade data interchange in connection with such procedures, thus reducing the costs related to international trade. The HS is also extensively used by governments, international organizations and the private sector for many other purposes such as internal taxes, trade policies, monitoring of controlled goods, rules of origin, freight tariffs, transport statistics, price monitoring, quota controls, compilation of national accounts, and economic research and analysis. The HS is thus a universal economic language and code for goods, and an indispensable tool for international trade*" (World Customs Organization).

Analyzing this relationship will make it possible to estimate the impact of imports of goods on VAT collection, with a good breakdown to identify the main items that generate value-added tax collection. Estimating the VAT collection elasticity concerning imports of goods classified in the harmonized system contributes to the design of fiscal policy in terms of the possible improvement in the income of the Mexican Treasury.

The relevance of this analysis lies in the fact that the Mexican economy has registered a growing degree of commercial openness, going from 56.7% in 2010 to 74.5% in 2020, a percentage that reflects the importance of export and import foreign trade operations to the behavior economy of Mexico. The value of imports concerning the Gross Domestic Product (GDP) went from 28.5% in 2010 to 35.7% in 2020, which places imports as the primary source of VAT collection. Figure 6.1 shows the proportion that imports represent concerning GDP between 2010 and 2020.

Considering that VAT is the second source of income for the Mexican Treasury, it is relevant to estimate the elasticities of VAT collection concerning imported products and classified in the harmonized system to identify and suggest policy measures. Specific fiscal measures allow increasing VAT collection from imports of goods (Moreno, 2019).

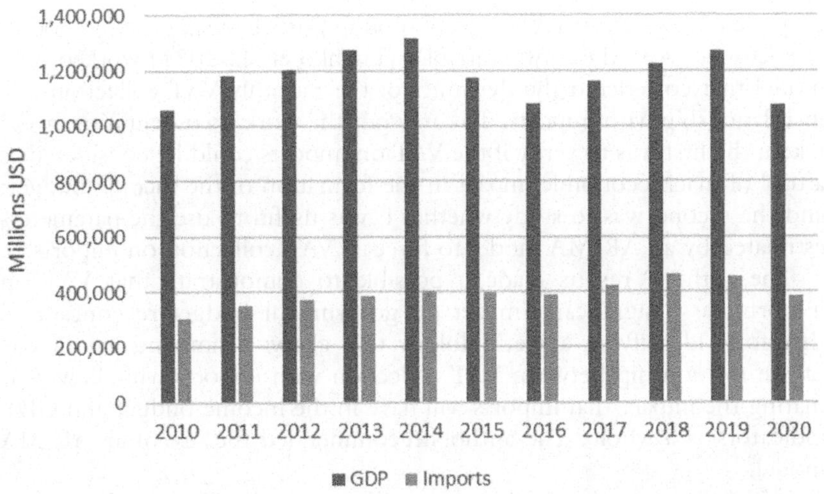

Fig. 6.1 Gross Domestic Product and Imports of Mexico 2010–2020 (millions of dollars) (*Source* Own elaboration with data from INEGI and the World Bank)

The International Monetary Fund (IMF, 2001) determined that there are four approaches to forecasting tax revenue. The first one is the effective rate approach. The second is known as the elasticity approach; this one establishes a stable empirical relationship between the growth of tax revenues and the corresponding increase in the tax base, which is known as an elasticity. The increase in tax revenue is obtained as a product of the projected increase in the tax base by the elasticity. The third method is known as a model-based approach; it is an econometric estimation using a general equilibrium model which takes into account the interdependence of the tax system and the economy. The fourth method is based on trends and autocorrelation that consider past trends with some specifications on the source of collection.

Elasticity is a measure of sensitivity that captures the reaction of VAT collection to the change in the behavior of imports of goods, in this case, goods classified in the international harmonized system (Pindyck & Rubinfeld, 2013).

Estimating the magnitude in which VAT collection is impacted by specific imports of goods classified in the harmonized system will help to make more accurate forecasts on value-added tax collection. As an example of calculating VAT collection on imports by using the method of elasticity between these two variables (Luchko et al., 2021) worked on a model that considered the dynamics of the monthly VAT collection and its relationship with imports. To carry out the work, two definitions were taken: the first was to verify if the VAT on imports could be considered as a tool of macroeconomic impact in the formation of the income budget; and the second was to study whether it was useful to use the parameters estimated by an ARIMA model to forecast VAT collection on imports.

The authors' results made it possible to demonstrate that VAT on imports has a significant impact on government budget revenues and, therefore, identifying a methodology that allows estimating parameters of the relationship between VAT collection with imports will allow estimating the impact that imports will have in the income budget and GDP indicators as a whole. The authors recommended the use of an ARIMA model.

In this research, the elasticity approach was used, following the recommendation of the IMF in its Manual of Fiscal Transparency, as a valid method for estimating tax revenues. The scope of this research was the calculation of the elasticities of the different items of imports, the forecast of VAT collection should be made by multiplying the elasticity with the tax base of imports, a simple operation to perform.

The elasticity defined as the change in VAT collection with respect to the change in imports of each of the 99 chapters of the harmonized international system will allow identifying the relationship and magnitude between both variables; that is, a positive elasticity means that in the face of positive movements in imports, VAT collection should also present a positive movement and vice versa. Therefore, if at any time, imports of any chapter show positive behavior and the elasticity is positive, collection should grow, but if VAT collection for merchandise imports decreases, there may be illegal trade practices, such as smuggling, tax evasion, and undervaluation of goods. The economic orientation derived from the elasticities makes it possible to monitor behaviors that do not correspond to the correlation established between imports and tax collection.

Literature Review

To achieve the objective of this article, it is necessary to prepare a literature review that covers the following areas: general aspects of VAT, advantages of analyzing and estimating the elasticity of the tax concerning imports, and estimation methods through the use of regression and ARIMA models.

VAT is an indirect tax on consumption; that is, it does not directly affect the income of a taxpayer but is based on the cost of some product or merchandise, therefore, the one who pays this tax is the final consumer. VAT is a tax that obliges taxpayers (individuals and legal entities) who, in national territory, carry out the following acts or activities: sale of goods, provision of independent services, grant the use or temporary enjoyment of goods and import goods or services.

According to Value Added Law, what is meant by importing goods into the national territory should be understood as:

- The introduction of goods to the country. It should be considered an import when the goods are destined to the temporary import customs regimes for elaboration, transformation, or repair in maquila or export programs; tax deposit to undergo the process of assembly and manufacturing of vehicles; of elaboration, transformation, or repair of fiscalized premises; and, of strategic fiscalized premises.
- The acquisition by persons residing in the country of intangible assets disposed of by non-resident persons.
- The temporary use or enjoyment, in national territory, of intangible assets provided by non-residents in the country.
- The temporary use or enjoyment, in national territory, of tangible goods whose material delivery had been made abroad.
- The exploitation in national territory of independent services for the provision of obligations to be performed by one person in favor of another; the transport of people; insurance, guarantee, and re-guarantee; mandate, commission, mediation, agency, representation, brokerage, consignment, and distribution; technical assistance and technology transfer; and any other obligation to give, not to do or to allow, assumed by one person in favor of another; when provided by non-residents in the country, except for international transportation.
- When a temporarily exported good returns to the country having added value abroad for repairs, additions, or any other concept that implies an additional value.

Typically, imports of goods that enter the country pay VAT through the import request document, which is the tax and customs declaration on foreign trade and serves as the basis for applying 16% as the general tax rate. There is a 0% rate and exemptions from the tax payment on some specific acts or activities. Regardless of the action, activity, or geographical area within the national territory.

(Luchko et al., 2021) mentioned that one of the most widely reviewed topics in the economic literature on VAT includes aspects of tax administration, payment problems, causes of tax evasion, tax reimbursement, refund, fraud and the tax behavior. However, he also stated that the estimation of VAT collection had been carried out in current times using simple methods under the belief that the tax is very stable, and that no greater sophistication is required to make forecasts of VAT collection. The authors recommended the use of an ARIMA model, but they also mention the usefulness of estimating the parameters of the relationship of VAT collection on imports of goods through the method of elasticities.

(Ebrill et al., 2002) considered that VAT can be a good option to obtain income and modernize an entire tax system. The findings suggest that VAT can efficiently boost government revenue. They proposed an index of efficiency in collecting the tax called "index C" and that instead of using the GDP, it considers consumption and is calculated as the relationship between VAT income and consumption, divided by the general tax rate. The tax is said to work very well when this index C is equal to one hundred percent. The increase in the efficiency of the system has to do with various factors, among which the following stand out: the relationship between trade and VAT (presumably, it is easier to collect VAT at the point of importation than domestically); the high literacy rates of taxpayers and the length of time the tax has been in force (the longer the tax has been in force, the better its return).

Bogetic and Hassan (1993) determined that VAT revenues usually depend on three groups of factors: the structural variables are the rate, the taxable base, and the tax thresholds; the amount of taxable activity and fiscal discipline. Ordinarily, VAT revenues can be estimated as a function of the rate, tax base, and thresholds established in the VAT Law and the economic variables that affect the tax base and compliance with tax obligations in accordance with the corresponding legal framework. The authors also suggest making the difference between taxed and non-taxed activities to identify the main contributors to tax collection.

Stock (1999) suggests that the historical trend can be useful in estimating VAT collection; however, it is necessary that the estimates have a theoretical economic basis that allows the generation of robust estimators for the collection of the tax. He established that making economic forecasts is a very common activity when it comes to defining the fiscal and budgetary policy of governments. The difficulty of making future estimates of collection revenue requires choosing the appropriate technique to make the estimate so that the estimators are robust, and the uncertainty generated by using statistical techniques to make the corresponding estimates is mitigated.

Gamboa and Sophia (2002) concluded that despite the fact that there are different methodologies for carrying out tax forecasts, they showed that calculating the elasticity of the tax by means of a regression using ordinary least squares is the most efficient procedure, and they considered it as the best forecasting methodology for calculating revenue for a tax. The authors used linear and logarithmic functions in their investigations for the purpose of working with an ordinary least squares regression. The review of the works of these authors made it possible to define that in this article, the elasticity of VAT collection will be calculated based on imports of goods classified in the 99 sections of the International Harmonized System.

Andrejovska and Pulikova (2018) studied the impact of some macroeconomic variables (gross domestic product, employment rate, public debt, foreign direct investment, effective tax rate, and statutory tax rate) on total tax collection in the 28 member countries of the European Union. They used the regression analysis: pooling model, the fixed effects model, and random effects model. The main hypothesis was that GDP is the indicator that has the greatest impact on tax collection. The results showed that there is a strong correlation between tax collection and the employment rate, followed by foreign direct investment and GDP.

Desai and Hines (2002), established that, in most countries that have adopted VAT as a consumption tax, imports have been taxed in the same way as a domestic consumption product while exports are not taxed under the belief that not paying VAT encourages the export of goods, at the expense of imports and domestic consumption. International trade theory makes a different prediction; countries that have adopted VAT as a source of revenue have no effect on imports and exports. The reason is that the exchange rate is adjusted to neutralize the effects of VAT on export and import incentives; for this reason, international trade theory estimates that VAT has no influence on international trade patterns.

Rudzkis and Maciulaityte (2007) studied the use of econometric methods to estimate tax revenues and concluded that the models to be used should be simple and short-term. However, the regression analysis was proposed in two stages: an econometric analysis as the first stage and the determination of the tax base forecast algorithms as the second stage. The cross estimation was used to evaluate the robustness of the algorithms used.

Soto-Ferrari et al. (2019), examined the capabilities and efficiency of the ARIMA models, the forecasting capabilities and developed procedures that allow the improvement of the forecasts made.

Büyüksahin and Ertekin (2019) concluded that there are several methods to make forecasts using linear and nonlinear models separately or with a combination of both. The combination of the models can be effective in improving the efficiency of the forecasts. They highlighted that a hybrid autoregressive integrated moving average (ARIMA) model and artificial neural networks (ANN) can also be useful in time series forecasting.

Tiao (2001) indicated that time series related to business, economics, and some other fields of science tend to show trend patterns, seasonal fluctuations, cycles, and periodic variability. Therefore, to carry out the analysis of this information, it is necessary to achieve an understanding of the known factors that affect the behavior of the phenomenon under study, in addition to the possible causes that are little known at the time of the analysis.

From the review of the literature, it can be concluded that an important source of tax revenue is the VAT, estimating the collection of this tax with respect to imports could be carried out using different methods. It can be done by using the effective rate of payment, by estimating an elasticity, by general equilibrium models and with trend and autocorrelation analysis; it is difficult to determine which is the best method to forecast tax revenues, all methods have advantages and disadvantages. The scope of this research, following the IMF recommendation on the elasticity method, is the estimation of the elasticity of VAT collection on imports for each of the 99 chapters defined in the international harmonized system.

Economic Analysis

The Data

Imports of goods as an independent variable of the analysis carried out have shown an average annual growth rate of 4.81% between 2010 and 2021, going from 301,481.2 to 505,715.6 million dollars. In terms of percentage participation, in this period, imports have behaved in a stable manner with positive and negative variations of less than one percentage point. The exceptions have been presented in the following chapters:

- Chapter (85) machines and electrical equipment with a drop of 3.5 percentage points, going from 23.5% to 20.0%; electronic circuits and microstructures and electrical telephony or telegraphy devices stand out for their participation, which have seen their imports into the national territory decrease.
- Chapters (98–99) unclassified products with an increase of 2.09 percentage points from 1.9% to 4.0%. The increase in these chapters indicates that an ambiguous tariff classification can be generated, which can produce repercussions in the collection of taxes due to the erroneous calculation of the taxable base.
- Chapter (72) iron and steel foundry with an increase of 1.05 percentage points from 2.40% to 3.46%, intermediate products of iron and unalloyed steel and rolled products of other steels with a width greater than 600 millimeters stand out for their participation.

The VAT collection series $X_t = \{X_{1t}, X_{2t}, \ldots, X_{nt}\}$ were obtained from the open data of the Tax Administration Service (SAT) of the Ministry of Finance and Public Credit and are presented monthly for the period 2010–2021. Likewise, the VAT collection data was converted to US dollars at the exchange rate to settle obligations in foreign currency published by the Bank of Mexico.

The collection of variables of the information set X_t are transformed under the natural logarithm and seasonally adjusted using the Census X12-ARIMA method. It is essential to point out that before proceeding to estimate the elasticities between the variables of the X_t set and VAT, it is necessary to verify the order of integration of each of the variables used, as developed in the following section.

The imports of the 99 chapters were obtained from the Bank of Economic Information of the National Institute of Statistics and Geography (INEGI) monthly from the period 2010–2021. These data are public and are presented in US dollars. Import values were also seasonally adjusted using Census X12-ARIMA.

Order of Integration and Control Variables

The order of integration is obtained through stationarity tests on the seasonally adjusted time series and in logarithms. Specifically, the Augmented Dickey-Fuller (DFA) and Phillips-Perron (PP) tests have the existence of a unit root in the data set as the null hypothesis (Tsay, 2015). Hence, the rejection of H_0 yields evidence of the stationarity of the random variable of interest. In contrast, the Kwiatkowski–Phillips–Schmidt–Shin (KPSS) test has the existence of stationarity as the null hypothesis, so it seeks not to reject H_0 (Enders, 2014).

In this document, the DFA, PP, and KPSS tests were carried out for each VAT collection time series. It can be seen in Annex A4 that the base hypothesis of DFA and PP is rejected for all cases and that the null hypothesis is not rejected for the KPSS test. This indicates that the time series in first difference are stationary.

Likewise, to consider the possible structural changes in the time series, the unit root tests of Andrews (2003), Andrews and Ploberger (1994), and Zivot and Andrews (1992) were also carried out. These authors have the null hypothesis that the time series has a unit root with a structural break at the intercept, trend, or both.

This set of tests was carried out to complement the results of the KPSS, DFA, and PP tests, which are not robust to breaks in the time series. Annex A9 reports the test statistics in absolute value, where the null hypothesis is rejected since the test statistics are higher than the corresponding critical values with 90% confidence.[1] There is no evidence for a unit root with structural change. In other words, the VAT collection data series are integrated time series of order one, $I(1)$.

The variables in Annex A1 allows us to investigate the existence of comovements and, therefore, the presence of cointegration relationships.

[1] The critical values for the Zivot-Andrews and Andrews-Ploberger tests at 90% confidence are 4.58, 4.11, and 4.82 in Intercept, Trend, and Both, respectively (R Core Team, 2022).

This set of long-term equilibrium relationships, captured in the different elasticities, are estimated under a VEC model.

In this regard, the analysis of multivariate systems with endogenous variables begins with a VAR model of p lags given by

$$y_t = A_0 + A_1 y_{t-1} + A_2 y_{t-2} + \cdots + A_p y_{t-p} + u_t$$

where A_i is an array of parameters of size $k \times k$, $i = 0, 1, 2, \ldots, T$; u_t is a vector of *i.i.d.* random perturbations with mean zero and covariance matrix Σ (Lütkepohl, 2013). If it is the case that the variables of the vector y_t present an equilibrium relationship in the long run (cointegration) and are not stationary time series, then the error correction model is defined as

$$\Delta y_t = A_0 + \Pi y_{t-1} + \sum_{i=1}^{T} \Gamma_i \Delta y_{t-i} + u_t$$

where Γ_i is a parameter matrix of size $k \times k$ and $\Pi = \alpha\beta'$ is a matrix of rank $0 < r < k$ such that $\Gamma_i = -\sum_{j=i+1}^{j-p} A_j$ and $\Pi = \sum_{j=1}^{p} A_j$. The interior coefficients of β correspond to the cointegration vector between the variables and α contains the adjustment parameters.

To verify the existence of cointegration, the Johansen tests corresponding to the specification

$$\Delta y_t = \alpha(\beta' y_{t-1} + \mu + \rho t) + \sum_{i=1}^{p-1} \Gamma_i \Delta y_{t-i} + \gamma + \tau t + \varepsilon_t$$

where the parameters ρ, γ, τ, and μ allow considering elements of restricted or unrestricted trend (Hamilton, 2000).

In this paper, the vector y_t comprises the time series for VAT collection, and merchandise imports are classified in the 99 sections of the International Harmonized System, see Annex A3. The objective is to estimate the long-term elasticities between the variables through a VEC specification, where the following binary variables have been incorporated as control variables, similarly to Moreno and Mata (2022):

$$d24 = \begin{cases} 1 & \text{if the observation is in the period } 2014 - 2020 \\ 0 & \text{another case} \end{cases}$$

$$d27 = \begin{cases} 1 \text{ if the observation is in the period } 2016 - 2020 \\ 0 \quad \text{another case} \end{cases}$$

$$c19 = \begin{cases} 1 \text{ if the observation is in the period de } 2020 - 2021 \\ 0 \quad \text{another case} \end{cases}$$

The dummy variable d24 captures the legal change to article 24 of the VAT Law, which establishes that when goods are introduced into the country, and these are destined for temporary importation customs regimes, they will be considered imports of goods. While the dummy variable d27 considers the legal change to article 27 of the VAT Law, which stipulates the value or tax base that will be taken into account for the importation of goods, making an analogy with the one that would correspond to the alienation of goods, use or enjoyment of goods, or provision of services, in national territory, as the case may be. Similarly, a dichotomous variable, c19, is added to consider the recent impact of the pandemic due to COVID-19.

The following section discusses the results of the VEC model and the elasticities corresponding to merchandise imports, see Annex A3 (available at https://tinyurl.com/Annex1-9).

Estimates and Results

According to the tables in Annex A4, it can be stated that the variables are integrated of order one, $I(1)$, non-stationary in level since they have a unit root, and I(0), stationary in their first difference (Tsay, 2015).

Long-term elasticities are estimated using a Vector Error Correction (VEC). This specification considers the existing cointegration relations between the variables (Hamilton, 2000). For the estimation of the VEC model, the number of optimal lags was determined using the Akaike (AIC), Schwarz (BIC), and Hanna-Quinn (HQIC) information criteria that correspond to the implicit VAR specification. In this case, the number of lags is one, which fits the minimum values in Table 6.1.

Then, the Johansen test is performed to verify the existence of cointegration based on the optimal number of lags. So, the number of cointegration vectors is found. Table 6.2 shows the results of the maximum eigenvalue and the trace test; it can be seen that there is evidence of four or five cointegration relationships. The model with the minor Schwarz

Table 6.1 Optimal lags in the VEC model

Lags	*AIC*	*HQIC*	*BIC*
0	−10.523	−10.025	−10.281*
1	−11.208*	−10.425*	−8.296
2	−11.144	−8.877	−5.564
3	−11.127	−7.776	−2.878
4	−11.205	−6.768	−0.286

Source Own elaboration
Note * Indicates the optimal lag according to the minimum of AIC, BIC, or HQIC

information criterion was chosen, corresponding to the quadratic trend case with five cointegration relations.

Through the results of Table 6.2, it can be stated that the variables in Annex A1 are cointegrated, which implies a long-term equilibrium relationship under a common trend. If the cointegration vector is normalized concerning $\ln(IVA_t)$, the long-term elasticities are obtained, as shown in Table 6.3.

In this case, the elasticities are positive, and if there are movements in the value of imports, there is a direct effect on VAT collection; that is, if imports grow, there is also a growth in tax collection, but this effect can also occur in the opposite direction when there is a decrease in the value of imports with its respective reduction in tax collection.

Table 6.2 Johansen test

Specification		*None* *No intercept* *No trend*	*None* *Intercept* *No trend*	*Linear* *Intercept* *No trend*	*Linear* *Intercept* *Trend*	*Quadratic* *Intercept* *Trend*
Test type	*Rank*					
Trace/ Maximum eigenvalue	0	458.721	429.133	402.008	431.815	457.128
	1	321.964	297.167	272.960	299.752	320.498
	2	251.890	227.234	203.503	229.815	250.434
	3	191.841	172.751	155.089	175.168	190.471
	4	141.776*	125.193	113.052	**127.013***	140.490
	5	101.931	**85.813***	**76.712***	87.631	**100.652***

Source Own elaboration
Note * Indicates the number of cointegration relations

Table 6.3 VAT Elasticities on Imports, 2010–2021

Chapter	*Elasticity*	*Percentage structure (%)*	*Average annual growth rate (%)*
Cap85 Machinery and electrical material	1.483	21.23	4.81
Cap84 Mechanical devices, boilers and their parts	1.341	16.50	4.75
Cap87 Land vehicles and their parts	0.932	8.89	9.76
Cap27 Mineral fuels and their products	0.477	8.33	9.25
Cap39 Plastics and their manufactures	1.245	5.56	7.64
Cap90 Optical and medical instruments and apparatus	0.977	3.55	10.28
Cap98 and 99 Unclassified products	0.561	3.11	6.50
Cap72 Iron and steel foundry	0.723	2.51	0.89
Cap29 USD Organic Chemicals	0.132	2.24	7.85
Cap73 Manufactures of cast iron or steel	1.274	2.23	7.86
Cap40 Rubber and its manufactures	1.123	1.58	5.00
Cap76 Aluminum and its manufactures	0.907	1.47	3.48
Cap48 Paper, cardboard and their manufactures	1.862	1.35	−0.10
Cap38 Chemical industry products	0.812	1.22	−8.93
Cap10 USD Cereals	0.408	1.20	7.56
Cap30 Pharmaceutical products	0.348	1.19	2.63
Cap02 Meat and edible offal	0.811	0.97	4.91
Cap12 Oil seeds and oleaginous fruits; various fruits	0.272	0.88	7.17
Cap94 Furniture, medical-surgical, not elsewhere specified	0.973	0.87	−7.26

(continued)

Table 6.3 (continued)

Chapter	*Elasticity*	*Percentage structure (%)*	*Average annual growth rate (%)*
Cap74 Copper and its manufactures	0.447	0.77	4.67
Cap33 Essential oils and resinoids	0.813	0.66	4.76
Cap83 Miscellaneous manufactures of common metals	1.291	0.61	5.29
Cap28 Inorganic Chemicals	0.815	0.56	5.08
Cap32 Tanning or dyeing extracts	1.409	0.54	5.34
Cap82 Common metal tools and fixtures	1.027	0.53	3.41
Cap95 Toys, articles for recreation and sports	0.317	0.53	5.24
Cap04 Milk, dairy products, eggs and honey	0.775	0.45	6.67
Cap61 Knitwear and clothing accessories	0.642	0.44	−1.22
Cap23 USD Waste from food industries	0.805	0.40	2.28
Cap44 Wood, charcoal and its manufactures	1.034	0.39	−8.01
Cap62 Garments and clothing accessories, except knitwear	0.747	0.36	7.76
Cap31 USD Credits	0.104	0.36	3.07
Cap15 USD Animal or vegetable fats	0.019	0.36	14.14
Cap70 Glass and its manufactures	1.276	0.34	4.59
Cap21 Miscellaneous food preparations	1.205	0.33	5.72
Cap71 Pearls, stones and precious metals	0.028	0.28	4.92
Cap52 Cotton	0.188	0.27	−7.24
Cap26 Metalliferous ores, slag	0.131	0.26	4.53
Cap86 Vehicles and material for railways	0.269	0.26	3.28

(continued)

Table 6.3 (continued)

Chapter	*Elasticity*	*Percentage structure (%)*	*Average annual growth rate (%)*
Cap08 Commercial fruit and nuts	0.870	0.26	4.51
Cap54 Synthetic or artificial filaments	1.065	0.26	4.55
Cap59 Coated fabrics, technical textile articles	0.712	0.26	−0.85
Cap47 Pulp of wood or fibrous materials	0.058	0.26	−1.33
Cap22 Beverages and vinegar	0.467	0.25	4.71
Cap64 Footwear, leggings and the like	0.700	0.25	8.29
Cap34 Soap, waxes, lubricants and candles	1.225	0.23	6.81
Cap17 Sugars and confectionery	0.389	0.23	6.35
Cap41 Skins and hides	0.284	0.22	4.97
Cap35 Albuminoidal substances	1.260	0.22	5.84
Cap96 Miscellaneous manufactures	1.230	0.22	2.55
Cap42 Manufactures of leather and gut	0.828	0.20	2.79
Cap69 Ceramic products	1.054	0.20	5.39
Cap56 Wadding, felt and cordage	1.455	0.20	0.66
Cap55 Synthetic or artificial discontinuous fibers	0.388	0.18	2.64
Cap60 Knitted fabrics	0.016	0.18	2.24
Cap68 Manufactures of piedar or similar	1.194	0.18	7.93
Cap49 Graphic industry products	0.008	0.18	2.49
Cap20 Preparations of vegetables, fruits, plants	1.107	0.17	4.97
Cap63 Other made-up textile articles	0.500	0.17	4.57
Cap19 Preparations of cereals or milk	0.840	0.16	2.34

(continued)

Table 6.3 (continued)

Chapter	*Elasticity*	*Percentage structure (%)*	*Average annual growth rate (%)*
Cap25 Salt, sulphur, soils and stones	0.595	0.15	−6.16
Cap03 Fish, crustaceans and molluscs	0.519	0.15	4.33
Cap11 Milling products	0.836	0.14	7.73
Cap18 Cocoa and its preparations	0.325	0.13	−1.92
Cap07 Vegetables, plants, roots and tubers	0.302	0.12	6.44
Cap16 Preparations of meat and aquatic animals	0.858	0.11	3.75
Cap58 Special fabrics with patches inserted	0.078	0.09	1.29
Cap91 Clockwork devices and their parts	0.287	0.09	6.23
Cap37 Photographic or cinematographic products	0.355	0.09	−4.81
Cap81 Other common metals and articles thereof	0.810	0.09	4.63
Cap09 Coffee, tea, yerba mate and spices	0.615	0.07	5.98
Cap88 Aircraft and their parts	0.092	0.07	4.27
Cap75 Nickel and its manufactures	0.751	0.07	3.55
Cap05 Other products of animal origin	0.813	0.06	5.08
Cap36 Gunpowder, explosives and matches	0.270	0.06	4.79
Cap57 Carpets and textile floor coverings	0.683	0.05	3.48
Cap01 Live animals	0.450	0.04	6.58
Cap79 Zinc and its manufactures	0.619	0.04	1.47
Cap13 Gums, resins, juices and vegetable extracts	0.319	0.04	5.18
Cap80 Tin and its manufactures	0.278	0.03	9.38

(continued)

Table 6.3 (continued)

Chapter	*Elasticity*	*Percentage structure (%)*	*Average annual growth rate (%)*
Cap65 Hats, headdresses and their parts	0.726	0.03	5.90
Cap89 Ships and floating artifacts	0.023	0.03	−5.67
Cap24 Tobacco and manufactured substitutes	0.093	0.03	6.57
Cap06 Plants and floriculture products	0.201	0.03	3.88
Cap51 Wool and animal hair, horsehair yarns and fabrics	0.148	0.02	−17.98
Cap92 Musical instruments	0.188	0.02	2.10
Cap93 Weapons and ammunition, their parts and accessories	0.115	0.02	0.63
Cap78 Lead and its manufactures	0.077	0.02	6.85
Cap67 Manufactures of hair and feather articles	0.497	0.01	1.09
Cap97 Objects of art or collectibles and antiques	0.113	0.01	3.70
Cap66 Umbrellas, parasols and canes	0.037	0.01	8.96
Cap53 Other vegetable textile fibers	0.347	0.01	−2.83
Cap45 Cork and its manufactures	0.412	0.01	6.30
Cap14 Braidable materials and other vegetable products	0.145	0.00	4.85
Cap46 Basketry manufactures	0.158	0.00	10.14
Cap43 Fur	0.010	0.00	3.06
Cap50 Silk	0.130	0.00	−0.92

Source Own elaboration with data of SAT, INEGI, and BANXICO

The maximum elasticity is 1.862 for paper, cardboard, and their manufacturers, while the smallest value is 0.008 for graphic industry products.

Sixteen chapters explain 82% of the value of imports; although the elasticities were estimated for all the components, 16 mainly explain the behavior of total imports, for which monitoring the behavior of these chapters is critical. Relevant due to its effects on VAT collection.

The imports made in chapter 85, related to machinery and electrical material, represent 21.3% of total imports during the period before the COVID-19 phenomenon (2010–2019), being the chapter with the most significant economic relevance in terms of customs value of imported goods. This concept becomes the VAT taxable base. The impact generated by the importation of electrical equipment and materials in that period was 1.510 percentage points when the value of what was imported increased by one percentage point, which means that these goods, being taxed with VAT, are significant contributors to the collection of the tax. However, in the 2020–2021 period, the COVID-19 phenomenon period, the elasticity of VAT collection concerning the value of imports was more significant. The value for that 2020–2021 biennium was 1.535, higher than the estimate obtained for the period 2010–2019 and for the entire study period that covers from 2010 to 2021 and whose elasticity was 1.483. Then, imports of equipment and electrical material were more sensitive during the pandemic period than in the rest of the study period; their relative contribution to VAT collection increased during the COVID-19 period.

The second chapter with the highest participation in the value of imports is 84, which refers to mechanical devices, boilers, and their parts, whose percentage participation in total imports in the years from 2010 to 2019 was 16.5%, and the elasticity of this chapter for the same period was 1.324. During the 2020–2021 period, the sensitivity of VAT collection to the customs value of imports was 1.262, slightly lower than the longer-term sensitivity. It is important to note that its elasticity did not undergo relevant changes, which allows us to infer that this chapter is a stable contributor to VAT collection.

The third chapter with the highest percentage participation with 9.0% in imports is 87, which refers to goods related to land transport and its parts and whose elasticity for the period 2010–2019 was 1.110; the elasticity for the 2020–2021 biennium was 0.970. This chapter presents values around one, which can be considered a more proportional effect on VAT collection concerning percentage movements in the value of imports.

The fourth chapter with the highest percentage share in total imports is 27, including mineral fuels and their products. This chapter represented

8.5% of total imports, and its elasticity in the period from 2010 to 2019 was 0.473, and in the period 2020–2021, it was 0.510. These elasticities of less than one mean that VAT collection derived from foreign trade operations is not highly sensitive to imports of mineral fuels and their derivatives in the short and long term.

These four chapters represented more than 55% of total imports from 2010 to 2019. However, Table 6.3 presents the elasticities by chapter ordered from highest to lowest in terms of their percentage share in total imports for the 2010–2021 period. Annexes A5 and A6 show the elasticities for the period 2010–2019 and the biennium 2020–2021.

Graphically, the behavior of the elasticities can be visualized by the color in Fig. 6.2, and the percentage participation in the imports of the main chapters by the size of the box can be observed (see Annex A7 and A8).

It is important to point out that the dummies d24 and d27 are not significant, although they reflect important changes in the regulatory

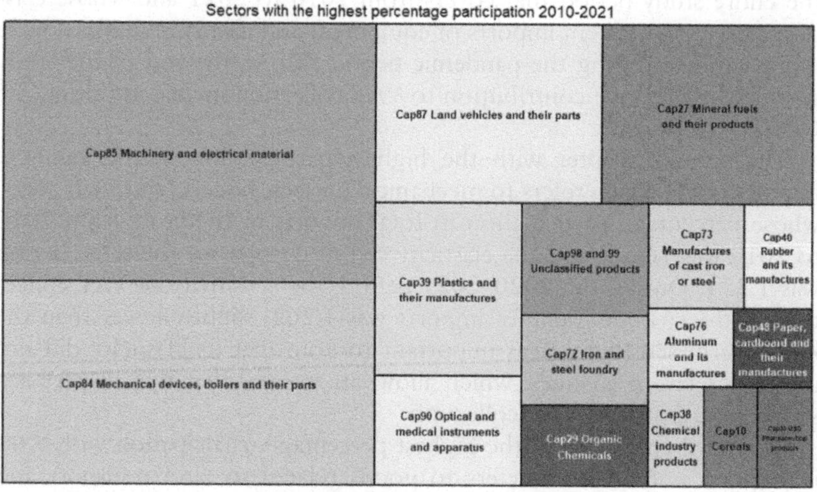

Fig. 6.2 Heat map 2010–2021 (*Source* Authors)

framework on imports and VAT collection. In contrast, the variable associated with the COVID-19 pandemic has a significant coefficient of less than zero, see Annex A3.

Conclusions

In international trade, a tariff increases the price of a good in the importing country and lowers the price in the exporting country. As a result of this price change, consumers face a loss in the importing country and a gain in the exporting country. Producers profit in the importing country and lose in the exporting country. Additionally, and due to the effects of the tariff, the government obtains income. In a small economy that cannot affect foreign prices, the net effect is that the cost of an unambiguous tariff outweighs the benefits. The results of an import tax are similar to those of a tariff; however, from the government's point of view, it obtains income from the taxation, or the taxes levied on imported goods (Krugman & Obstfeld, 1988).

From the government's point of view, collecting via the importation of goods is plausible; however, as observed in the estimation of the elasticities of the VAT collection concerning imports, sixteen chapters mainly explain the percentage structure of the total value of imports, which concentrates in a few chapters on the possibility of increasing VAT collection.

The goods imported in these 16 chapters have shown average growth rates for 2010–2019, ranging from 17% in chapters 98 and 99 that contain unclassified products, followed by chapter 87 related to land vehicles and their parts with a rate of 14.7%. In third place is chapter 27, referring to mineral fuels and their products with 8.2%, and in fourth place in Chapter 10, related to the importation of cereals with a rate of 7.7%.

With these significant growth rates, it could be inferred that as the import of goods from these taxed chapters grows, VAT collection should also grow; however, the chapter on unclassified goods has a percentage share of 2.9% and an elasticity of 0.590. It allows concluding that despite being a chapter with a two-digit growth rate, its importance in the structure of imports is minor. The elasticity is also less than one, which implies that the importation of goods from the chapters with a low percentage share will be below even though their contribution to VAT collection is growing significantly.

The import of goods from the chapters with the highest percentage share (chapters 85 and 84) during the 2010–2019 period registered an average annual growth rate slightly above 5%; both chapters also showed an elasticity greater than unity. Therefore, 37.8% of imports contributed to VAT collection from imports.

Relying on the importation of goods for tax collection generates revenue for the government; however, a country that taxes imports with VAT in the same sense as goods that are consumed domestically and does not tax exports to promote exports will very likely face inconveniences in the consumption of domestic and imported goods; for example, it may not affect imports and exports because the exchange rate can be adjusted and neutralize the effect on imports and exports (Desai and Hines, 2002).

The calculation of the elasticities was conceptualized as a lever that can contribute to the forecast of government tax revenues and better administration, surveillance, and auditing of the second source of the Government's tax revenues. It will allow identifying the sensitivity of the collection compared to the most crucial source in the generation of income by VAT are imports, which contribute approximately 70% of the collection of this tax.

Knowing the sensitivity of the collection against imports of goods by chapter allows locating the government's scarce resources in business intelligence and supervision activities on the importation of goods from the chapters of greater economic relevance and with greater sensitivity to movements in the entry of goods. That is, the supervision of the operations of the 16 main chapters that contribute more than 80 percent of imports should be prioritized, in order to ensure that the VAT payment is executed in accordance with the provisions of the legal framework.

If the customs authority allocates scarce resources in the surveillance of the most frequent illicit practices, such as, smuggling (technical and rough), money laundering, piracy, alteration of value (taxable base), declared false data, false or altered documents, use of simulated companies, triangulation of merchandise; the estimation of the elasticities by chapter and even by each tariff item will allow establishing behavior standards by an each specific item, in such a way that any pattern that deviates from the standard will allow quantifying the damage that will be generated to the collection of the tax and at the same time have a traffic light behavior of imports to monitor the deviations from the standard as a result of possible illicit practices that reinforce tax evasion.

As mentioned in the introduction, the tax authority could monitor the behavior of collection at the chapter level based on the behavior of imports; that is, if a chapter shows growth in imports and has a positive elasticity, it would be expected that VAT collection should also grow, but if the data shows a drop in collection, then that chapter should be reviewed more carefully because it contravenes the criterion of the positive relationship of the estimation of elasticity.

As an example of this conclusion, the month of December 2019 registered a positive percentage variation of 1.84% in the value of imports compared to the same month of the previous year, which, with a positive elasticity of 1.48, would be expected to have a positive behavior; however, the tax collection fell 2.18% in the same period.

In this same sense, the month of December 2021 registered a growth of 21.7% in the value of imports and collection in the same period (December 2021 vs December 2020) grew 25.4%. These percentages show the positive relationship that derives from the calculated elasticity of 1.48 between VAT collection and the value of imports. In this month the logic is fulfilled, not so in the month of December 2019.

With these examples, a traffic light can be established at the chapter level or by specific fraction of the tariff nomenclature to define the criteria or patterns that do not meet the expected relationship and thereby locate the audit resources available to the tax authority.

Future lines of research are to estimate the elasticities of imports by tariff item, by country, by cross analysis of HS chapter and means of transport, and by customs and means of transport. Estimating the elasticities from different perspectives will allow for a more intelligent monitoring of the different illicit practices that occur when goods are imported into the national territory.

References

Andrews, D. (2003). Tests for parameter instability and structural change with unknown change point: A Corrigendum. *Econometrica, 71*(1), 395–397.

Andrews, D., & Ploberger, W. (1994). Optimal tests when a nuisance parameter is present only under the alternative. *Econometrica, 62*(6), 1383–1414.

Andrejovska, A., & Pulikova, V. (2018). Tax revenues in the context of economic determinants. *Montenegrin Journal of Economics, 14*(1), 133–141. Retrieved February 16, 2022 from http://repec.mnje.com/mje/2018/v14-n01/mje_2018_v14-n01-a20.pdf

Bogetic, Z., & Hassan, F. (1993). *Determinants of value-added tax revenue a cross-section analysis (October 1, 1993)* (World Bank Policy Research Working Paper No. 1203). Retrieved February 15, 2022 from https://papers.ssrn.com/sol3/papers.cfm?abstract_id=1809969

Büyükşahin, Ü. Ç., & Ertekin, Ş. (2019). Improving forecasting accuracy of time series data using a new ARIMA-ANN hybrid method and empirical mode decomposition. *Neurocomputing, 361*, 151–163. https://doi.org/10.1016/j.neucom.2019.05.099

Desai, M., & Hines, J. (2002). *Value added taxes and international trade: The evidence*. International Tax Policy Forum. Retrieved February 15, 2022, from https://citeseerx.ist.psu.edu/viewdoc/download?doi=10.1.1.198.4287&rep=rep1&type=pdf

Ebrill, L., Keen, M., Bodin, J. P., & Summers, V. (2002, June) The allure of the value added tax. *Finance and Development, 39*(2), 58. Retrieved March 15, 2022 from https://www.elibrary.imf.org/view/journals/022/0039/002/article-A014-en.xml

Enders, W. (2014). *Applied econometric time series* (2nd ed.). Wiley.

Gamboa, A. M., & Sophia, J. (2002). *Development of tax forecasting models: Corporate and individual income taxes* (PIDS Discussion Papers Series, No. 2002-06). Retrieved march 3, 2022 from https://www.pids.gov.ph/publication/discussion-papers/development-of-tax-forecasting-models-corporate-and-individual-income-taxes

Hamilton, J. (2000). *Time series analysis*. Princeton University Press.

International Monetary Fund (IMF). (2001). *Manual on fiscal transparency*. Retrieved march 17, 2022 from https://www.imf.org/external/np/fad/trans/manual/manual.pdf

Krugman, P., & Obstfeld, M. (1988). *International economics: Theory and policy*. Scott, Foresman/Little, Brown College Division, Scott Foresman and Company.

Luchko, M., Drozd, I., Plutytska, K., Ruska, R., & Vovk, I. (2021). Analysis and modelling of value added tax revenues on imports: Some issues of application in Ukraine. *International Journal of Production Management and Engineering, 9*(1) section papers. Retrieved March 15, 2022 from https://polipapers.upv.es/index.php/IJPME/article/view/13984

Lütkepohl, H. (2013). *Introduction to multiple time series analysis*. Springer Science & Business Media.

Moreno, J. (2019). *Impuesto al Valor Agregado: Variables que condicionan su recaudación* (U. A. Norte, Ed.). Ciudad de México. Retrieved March 30, 2022 from https://anahuac.primo.exlibrisgroup.com/discovery/fulldisplay?docid=alma993734079005016&context=L&vid=52ANAHUAC_INST:UAMX&lang=es&adaptor=Local%20Search%20Engine

Moreno, J., & Mata, L. M. (2022). Perspectives for recovery of VAT collection derived from imports of goods. In A. M. López-Fernández & A. Terán-Bustamante (Eds.), *Business recovery in emerging markets* (pp. 23–40). Palgrave Studies in Democracy, Innovation, and Entrepreneurship for Growth. Palgrave Macmillan. https://doi.org/10.1007/978-3-030-91532-2_3

Pindyck, R., & Rubinfeld D. (2013). *Microeconomics* (8th ed.). Pearson Education.

R Core Team. (2022). *R: A language and environment for statistical computing*. R Foundation for Statistical Computing, Vienna, Austria. https://www.R-project.org/

Rudzkis, R., & Maciulaityte, E. (2007). Econometrical modelling of profit tax revenue. *Nonlinear Analysis: Modelling and Control, 12*(1), 95–112. Retrieved March 28, 2022, from https://doi.org/10.15388/NA.2007.12.1.14724

Soto-Ferrari, M., Chams-Anturi, O., Escorcia-Caballero, J. P., Hussain, N., & Khan, M. (2019, September). Evaluation of bottom-up and top-down strategies for aggregated forecasts: State space models and ARIMA applications. In *International Conference on Computational Logistics* (pp. 413–427). Springer. https://doi.org/10.1007/978-3-030-31140-7_26

Stock, J. H. (1999). *Forecasting Economic Time Series, Kennedy School of Government, Harvard University and the NBER*. Prepared for Companion in Theoretical Econometrics, Badi Baltagi (ed.), Basil Blackwell. Retrieved February 15, 2022 from https://www.eco.uc3m.es/~jgonzalo/teaching/timeseriesMA/forecastingsurvey.pdf

Tiao, G. C. (2001). Time series: ARIMA methods. *International Encyclopedia of the Social & Behavioural Sciences*, 15704–15709. https://doi.org/10.1016/B0-08-043076-7/00520-9

Tsay, R. (2015). *Analysis of financial time series* (2nd ed.). John Wiley & Sons.

World Customs Organization (w. d.). *What is the Harmonized System (HS)?* Retrieve July 13, 2022 from http://www.wcoomd.org/en/topics/nomenclature/overview/what-is-the-harmonized-system.aspx

Zivot, E., & Andrews, D. (1992). Further evidence on the Great Crash, the oil-price shock, and the unit root hypothesis. *Journal of Business and Economic Statistics, 10*(3).

CHAPTER 7

Employment, Gender Gap, and the Mexican Industry: The Effect of COVID-19 on the Dynamic Structure and Recovery in the Labor Market

Jorge O. Moreno, Cecilia Y. Cuellar, and Maria E. Ramos

J. O. Moreno (✉)
Facultad de Economía, Universidad Autónoma de Nuevo León (UANL), Monterrey, N.L., México
e-mail: jorge.morenotr@uanl.edu.mx

C. Y. Cuellar
Hibbs Institute of Business and Economic Research and Soules College of Business, The University of Texas at Tyler, Tyler, TX, USA
e-mail: ccuellartapia@uttyler.edu

M. E. Ramos
Facultad de Contaduría Pública y Administración, Universidad Autónoma de Nuevo León (UANL), San Nicolás de los Garza, N.L., México
e-mail: maria.ramosr@uanl.edu.mx

E. Murillo et al. (eds.), *Creating Economic Stability Amid Global Uncertainty*, https://doi.org/10.1007/978-3-031-41386-5_7

Introduction

The COVID-19 crisis represents, at the moment this chapter is written, the most critical challenge our society has faced in economics, financial, political, and public health over the twenty-first century.

In March 2020, the World Health Organization (WTO) declared the SARS-CoV-2 virus and the derived COVID-19 disease crisis a pandemic. As a result, almost two-thirds of the countries around the world paralyzed their economic activity, affecting all industrial sectors and employment worldwide. The effects of this period, known as the "Big Confinement," introduced sudden stops in most economic activities and changed dynamics with both temporal and permanent effects on the organization of the world economy (IMF, 2020). As an expected result, these effects permeated the labor market and potentially accentuated differences in job opportunities for women and men according to their skills, education, and experience across different industrial sectors (Siddiqui, 2020).

This complex scenario was particularly unfavorable for Mexico as the services sector, one of the country's primary sources of income, including entertainment and tourism, was the first to respond to the negative shock (Esquivel, 2020). Furthermore, the evidence from the different economic sectors of the country shows a sizeable structural impact on production and employment levels (Coparmex Nuevo Leon, 2020; ENOE, 2020). As a result, this economic impact translated into around half a million employment losses in the country's formal sector during the first half of the pandemic (INEGI, 2020).

Henceforth, identifying the relationships between the industrial structure and the different labor market segments is critical for understanding the employment dynamics, recovery, and connection with contingencies due to the COVID-19 economic crisis. These long-term relationships and their short-term components are valuable tools for evaluating the potential effectiveness of public policy to alleviate the impact on the labor market in the short and long run.

This chapter analyzes the dynamics, persistence, and changes in the Mexican labor market resulting from the COVID-19 economic shock, focusing on the impact on the gender gap. The labor market is divided into six segments according to two main dimensions: aggregate economy sectors (primary, secondary, and tertiary) and gender (men and women). This approach allows us to identify differentiating effects and heterogeneous changes across the labor market structure. The differentiated analysis between groups, mainly gender, will enable us to recover the heterogeneous structures in the market and thus compare long-term trends and dynamics in the Mexican labor market segments (Cuellar, 2019; Moreno & Cuellar, 2021; Cuellar & Moreno, 2022b).

With this objective, this research builds micro-founded employment time series, which recovers consistent and homologous Mexican labor market data over time. The aggregate data is organized quarterly from 1993:Q1 to 2021:Q4, focusing on urban areas and three industrial sectors: primary, secondary, and tertiary.[1] Following a theoretical neoclassical approach of production, factor demand, and economic growth (Akkemik, 2007; Moreno & Cuellar, 2021; Cuellar & Moreno, 2022b), the time series of employment in Mexico are segmented by industrial sectors and gender. Afterward, the empirical research strategy defines and estimates a VAR model that links each employment segment with the sectorial economic activity defined by the GDP to identify the depth and persistence of the first COVID-19 pandemic shock (*I-shock* COVID-19). Then, to perform the impact analysis, impulse-response functions are estimated by introducing the first shock observed in the economic activity of the Mexican GDP in the first quarter of 2020, sizable to the actual first impact of COVID-19, and forecast the trends of employment by segments. As a result of these estimates, we forecast the counterfactual trends to compare what would have happened if the *I-shock* COVID-19 shock had not existed. Finally, this methodology allows a comparative analysis with observed employment dynamics to identify structural changes and potential recovery in each employment segment with these forecasted trends.

This study contributes to the business and economic literature in four dimensions. First, the methodology uses *consistent* time series constructed from micro-data in all employment surveys for Mexico during the analyzed period. Second, this chapter analyzes the particular dynamics of the *industrial sector employment* in Mexico, identifying potential long-run structural changes in the labor market. Third, it estimates dynamic employment models by gender and industry segments and identifies heterogeneous impacts on the employment gender gap resulting from the *I-shock* COVID-19. Finally, this study estimates the long-run trends for recovery periods for each sectorial labor market segment. The research

[1] The urban areas historically represent more than 70% of the total employment in Mexico.

concludes by comparing the actual recovery to the long-trend estimates, which will measure the potential structural change in industrial employment and the employment gender gap.

Identifying changes in the long-run trends and the short-run observed components of employment is a valuable tool for analyzing public policies' potential impact on alleviating economic shocks during the pandemic. For instance, the evidence provided in this research suggests that the implementation of public policies by the Mexican federal government, such as "on-the-job training" scholarships (before to the COVID-19 crisis) or the prohibition of outsourcing jobs force them to become formal employment (during the COVID-19 crisis), might indeed have a limited or null effect on the long-run employment. These limited impacts could be related to the solid structural trends and traduced in limited effect in the short run over the labor structure due to the pandemic incidence.

The chapter is divided into six sections, including this introduction. The second section presents the theoretical framework and literature review, emphasizing previous findings related to the methodology, the regional labor market, and the COVID-19 crisis. The third section shows the data and methodology proposed to study regional employment dynamics divided by industrial sectors and gender. The fourth and fifth sections present the results and the discussion of the study. Finally, the sixth section presents the conclusions and implications of the analysis.

Theoretical Framework

The Labor Market, Productivity, and the Economy: The Model

This study uses a neoclassical theoretical framework (Arrow et al., 1961) applied to the labor market (Akkemik, 2007; Moreno & Cuellar, 2021; Cuellar & Moreno, 2022b). This framework assumes perfectly competitive markets, where the production function is of CES-type, and there are factors of production, which are capital (K) and labor (L); this function has returns to scale defined by the parameters s and ρ. In Eq. 7.1, "rho" is a positive parameter that measures the elasticity of substitution of capital and labor. From the optimality conditions, it can be observed that the marginal productivity of both factors equals their market price, r, and w (Eqs. 7.2, 7.3, and 7.4). Equation 7.5 takes logarithms from the labor's first-order condition and rearranges terms.

$$Q = f(K, L) = \theta\left[\beta L^{-\rho} + (1-\beta)K^{-\rho}\right]^{\frac{s}{\rho}} \tag{7.1}$$

$$f'(K, L) = f_k = r \tag{7.2}$$

$$f'(K, L) = f_L = w \tag{7.3}$$

$$\frac{\partial Q}{\partial L} = s\theta^{-\rho s}(1-\beta)Q^{1+\rho/s}L^{-1-\rho} = w \tag{7.4}$$

$$\ln L = \alpha_0 + \alpha_1 \ln Q + \alpha_2 \ln w \tag{7.5}$$

$$\alpha_0 = -\frac{1}{1+\rho}\ln(s(1-\beta)) - \frac{\rho s}{1+\rho}\ln\theta,\ \alpha_1 = -\frac{1+(\rho/s)}{1+\rho},\ \alpha_2 = -\frac{1}{1+\rho}$$

The α_0, α_1, and α_2 parameters of Eq. (7.3) are combinations of the structural parameters of production and show the equilibrium effect on the labor market derived from economic activity (expected positive) and wages (expected negative).

This neoclassical theoretical framework permits the recovery of the causal structural effects caused by the exogenous shocks derived from the COVID-19 pandemic on the different segments of the labor market in Mexico. The following subsection presents the data and methodology used to analyze the expected effects on the labor market structure.

Industrial Employment, Gender Gap, and the COVID-19 Crisis: The Evidence

The International Labour Organization (ILO) states that the COVID-19 pandemic affected labor markets in all regions, but the recovery patterns are very different. Europe and North America presented a faster recovery, with the most pessimistic outlook for Southeast Asia, Latin America, and the Caribbean. The differences between countries with the most robust labor market recovery are observed in high-income countries, while low-middle-income economies show a slow recovery (ILO, 2020).

In terms of the heterogeneous industrial effects, according to Gasca (2021), the pandemic in Mexico caused government institutions to decree a production stoppage in March 2020. Consequently, the policy caused a slowdown in GDP, presenting differences in the decline according to the productive sectors or regional patterns. In particular, the results in Gasca (2021) show a more significant decrease in states with high concentration and entities dedicated to the automotive and electronics industry (the central-western region and the north of the country). Jimenez-Bandala et al. (2020) review the panorama of the Mexican labor market and conclude that the regional recovery is asymmetric and uneven, reproducing the inequalities that existed before to the pandemic. The northern and western states presented a rapid readjustment in employment, but the center and south fell to a greater extent and presented a slow recovery.

Regarding the gender employment gap, the evidence in Latin America and Mexico is strong. Garcia et al. (2018) report a gender wage gap due to men, on average, dedicating more hours to work per week. The gender wage gaps by occupation are represented as follows: 60% in industrial and 61% in services.

Mancini (2016) concludes that women were not inserted in a large proportion in the manufacturing sector and "enter practically directly into the service sector or commerce." He also points out that women's entry into the labor market occurs later and with more qualifications than men. In a longitudinal analysis carried out for three generations of women, he observes that occupational mobility by the branch of activity is not very significant. He also points out the delay at the beginning of the labor trajectory and the increase in educational levels.

On the other hand, Fernandez and Lugo (2017) found that in 32 Mexican urban areas between 2005 and 2016, female employment increased compared to male. In particular, the female population was mainly in part-time shifts. They also identified that the weighted average of the participation rate of qualified women was equivalent in 2005 to 82% of that of men and rose to 85% in 2016. At the same time, the weighted average of the participation rate of unskilled women went from 80% of men in 2005 to 55% in 2016, and the labor gender gap has reduced for people with higher education. Despite this, there are still significant differences in income for women with low levels of education.

Cerquera-Losada et al. (2020) analyzed the gender wage gap in Colombia in 2017. When analyzing the productive characteristics, they conclude that women with even better characteristics (education, experience, among other variables) obtain lower remuneration than men. Furthermore, they indicate that, even though women have increased their participation with higher levels of education, the remuneration obtained still does not correspond.

In the Argentine labor market, Paz (2019) reveals that the context variable with the most significant weight in the salary gap is the participation of women in the non-formal segment, mainly among married women. Thus, married men outperform women precisely because they spend more time on paid work.

Felix-Verduzco and Inzunza-Mejia (2019) confirm the importance of professional education to increase labor participation but also verify the persistence of gender roles. Their analysis focused on women between 25 and 54 years old, and their crucial result is that the probability of labor participation is always higher in single women than in married women. For example, for the technical and professional levels of study, the probabilities of labor participation between married and single tend to converge when the potential labor income is high enough.

Pelaez and Rodriguez (2020) point out that men start their first job younger than women, particularly those with higher education. The fact that younger people remain in the educational system until reaching a higher educational level not only delays the start of working life but also tends to reduce the gender gap in the calendar of entry to the first job. This fact increases the probability of accessing the occupational stratum of higher status and hierarchy: directors, managers, and professionals (44.1% for men and 47.8% for women).

Bracamontes et al. (2020) analyzed the characteristics of the employed population in 2005 and 2017, identified the 11 different branches of the economy, and classified Mexico into regions of high, medium, and low exposure to trade openness. Between 2005 and 2017, the wage gap was reduced in the country, and each of the three regions favored women. However, higher wages are observed in the area most exposed to commercial opening, and higher wage differences favor men. The sectoral analysis shows that the labor participation of both genders in commerce, the manufacturing industry, and services has increased. Within the regions, gender differences persist in the regions of high exposure. It was found that most women continued to be located in commerce and most men in manufacturing; in those with low and medium exposure, most women and men were placed in commerce.

Ripani and Azuara (2021) point out that the pandemic labor crisis in Latin America affected the most vulnerable population to a greater extent, including the least educated young people and those in the informal sector. Workers with low education have lost jobs between 3 and 4 times more than those with high education, particularly women, accentuating regional inequality. However, female employment remained at lower pre-pandemic levels.

Gomez (2021) points out that in the Mexican labor market, the impact of the pandemic has been more significant on women. By 2020, the probability of a woman's employment decreased by four percentage points compared to the reduction experienced by men. The sectors with the most significant loss of employment were the services sector, specifically in the retail and wholesale business, food and beverage preparation, domestic work, leisure and cultural services, and light manufacturing.

Salce (2021) investigates the evolution of salary discrimination in Chile by gender by analyzing the information provided by the CASEN survey, from 1990 to 2017, with intervals of two or three years between each survey. The results reveal that when comparing a woman with a man with the same characteristics and equal qualifications, the woman will receive, on average, a lower salary than the man. In Chile, the wage gap has always favored men, standing at 9.8% in 2017. In addition, it has been observed that the labor market demands more educated women than men, yet the salary is lower than men. For example, in 2017, employed men had 8.9% fewer years of schooling than employed women.

On the other hand, in the case of the unemployed, it is observed that unemployed men had 4.3% more years of education than women in a similar situation for the same year. Another of the results indicates that potential discrimination is present mainly in the poorest and wealthiest extremes when separated by income quantiles into 10% of the population with minors and 10% with higher incomes. In addition, it shows that the most relevant variable that makes up wage discrimination is work experience, while years of education help reduce it.

So far, the literature analyzes the employment dynamics by industry and gender segments, mainly along and after the pandemic crisis. Hence, one of the main contributions of this work is to present a dynamic analysis of industry heterogeneity in the labor market, differentiating employment by gender. This approach permits the analysis of COVID-19 impact on employment in Mexico and estimates the potential recovery of employment in the defined market segments.

Empirical Strategy

Data

This research makes use of three historical employment surveys in Mexico: the National Urban Employment Survey (ENEU), the National Employment Survey (ENE), and the National Occupation and Employment Survey (ENOE). This quarterly micro-data is public and published by Instituto Nacional de Estadistica Geografia e Informatica (INEGI). The available periods for the ENEU are 1988 to 2004, for ENE from 1998 to 2004, and ENOE from 2005 to date.

The study constructs quarterly aggregate time series for each labor market segment in Mexico from 1993:Q1 to 2021:Q4. Therefore, the following time series are constructed for each market segment: *primary sector—male, primary sector—female, secondary sector—male, secondary sector—female, tertiary sector—male, and tertiary sector—female.*[2]

Thus, the main objective is to obtain the structural changes due to the COVID-19 pandemic and recover the new labor market structure defined by these segments. In addition, this approach allows us to construct a counterfactual trend (i.e., what would happen if the COVID-19 pandemic never existed) to identify structural changes in each employment segment. Finally, the pre-COVID-19 trend in employment is forecasted as implied by the parameter estimation of long-run trends and compared with the actual values of the employment post-COVID-19 to the analysis to estimate the COVID-19 impact on labor market segments.

We link employment to the Mexican economy's performance to accomplish the main objective. For this purpose, we use each industrial sector's GDP to measure economic activity extracted directly from INEGI's information bank. The real average hourly wages are estimated directly from the Mexican employment surveys.

To conclude, the construction of the time series of employment and wages is limited to the employment growth rates for this research. Therefore, the final micro-founded time series sample consists of individuals

[2] For further details on the methodological construction of the micro-founded time series, see Moreno and Cuellar (2021) and Cuellar and Moreno (2022a, b).

between 16 and 65 working and receiving a monetary payment greater than zero in homologated Mexican areas[3] for the defined period.

Econometric Specification

This chapter follows the labor market's dynamic neoclassical equilibrium approach, considering the relationship between economic activity and employment segments. This model implies long-run equilibrium causality relationships between production, productivity, employment, and wages (Arrow et al., 1961; Akkemik, 2007; and recently for Mexico Moreno & Cuellar, 2021; Cuellar & Moreno, 2022b).

The econometric strategy to analyze such long-run relationships is based on a Vectors Auto-Regressive (VAR) model in reduced and unrestricted form. This method permits studying the linear simultaneity between all the relevant variables and finding persistence between the same series in the long run, with the correct specification of the lags. Likewise, since the technique does not impose restrictions on the model, it avoids specification errors (Sims, 1980). This model also allows us to estimate the causal impact of the economy on employment, so this theory will enable us to propose an empirical model with simultaneous interactions between these variables.

The time series vector of interest $y_t = [y_{it} y_{jt} y_{kt}]'$ is presented in growth rates, where y_{it} is *i-employment segment* employment, y_{jt} is the GDP sector for the *j-industry sector* and y_{kt} is the real hourly wage *for gender k*. Each vector has its respective autoregressive component $(t-p)$ and a component associated with the white noise process, ε_t. The reduced VAR model can be represented in terms of its characteristic polynomials defined over the number of "L" lags, $A(L, \phi) and B(L, \theta)$ as follows:

$$y_t = A(L, \phi)y_{t-p} + B(L, \theta)\varepsilon_t \tag{7.6}$$

$$A'(L, \phi)y_t = B(L, \theta)\varepsilon_t \tag{7.7}$$

A unit root test will have to be performed on each vector to test the stationarity of each vector; details will be shown in the results section.

[3] Metropolitan areas included: Mexico City, Guadalajara, Monterrey, Puebla, Leon, Torreon, San Luis Potosi, Merida, Chihuahua, Tampico, Orizaba, Veracruz, Ciudad Juarez, Tijuana, Matamoros, and Nuevo Laredo.

Given the time stationarity of the series joint distribution, the system can be represented in terms of the Gaussian white noise process as in Eq. 7.6 using the Yule-Walker characteristic polynomials. The new characteristic polynomial described by $C(L, \phi, \theta)$ is unique for each VAR process defined over the number of lags (L). With this, a maximum likelihood method through the properties of the Gaussian process is used to recover the parameters associated with the original model, $\{\phi, \theta\}$.

$$y_t = \frac{B(L, \theta)}{A'(L, \phi)} \varepsilon_t = C(L, \phi, \theta)\varepsilon_t \tag{7.8}$$

Given that our primary objective is to analyze the impact of the I-shock of the COVID-19 pandemic on employment segments, each segment model's Impulse-Response Function (IRF) is used to capture the response of the model variables to an unanticipated "shock" in the idiosyncratic component of the model (ε_t). The variance decomposition of the orthogonal error term on the random innovations of each endogenous variable belonging to each model permits getting information on the correlations and variances for each exogenous shock.

Once the IRFs are obtained, where the impulse is in economic activity (GDP) and the response is in employment, employment levels are retrieved to compare pre-COVID-19 trends, I-shock COVID-19 trends, and the observed structure of employment.

Estimation and Results

Time Series Identification and Decomposition

The study analyzes and compares employment recovery trends segmented by sector and gender in Mexico. Once the model is estimated, the result is compared with the observed employment structure (the most recent data is 2021:Q4).

The methodology proposes to estimate two series with the actual employment to capture the impact of the first COVID-19 shock to analyze the structure and compare the recovery of jobs by the segment of the industrial sector and gender: (i) the *Pre-COVID-19 trend*: forecast the level of employment and are calculated based on the VAR model used in the methodology describing the expected level of employment if the COVID-19 crisis did not happen, (ii) *I-shock COVID-19 + Pre-COVID-19* trend time series forecast employment levels given the first shock due to the crises (GDP) and the respective trend from this impact, and (iii) *Actual employment*: theses series show the jobs levels observed for Mexico in each industrial sector segmented by gender.

These analyses allow us to recover the employment sectors' counterfactual gaps segmented by gender: (1) Pre-COVID-19 vs. Post-COVID-19 employment long-run trend; (2) Pre-COVID-19 vs. current employment trend; and (3) Post-COVID-19 vs. current employment trend.

Trends and gap impact on employment are estimated by introducing a negative shock equivalent to the observed effect of COVID-19 crises on GDP through the IRFs of the VAR model. Moreover, the VAR model will estimate the pre-COVID-19 trend, differentiating what would have been without the pandemic. Finally, the observed employment captures the magnitude of the structural effects, and with this, potential recovery scenarios are projected in the different employment sectors segmented by gender.

Unit Root Test and Selection Criterion Optimal Lags

Before estimating the model, the VAR's validity and stability are tested by performing unit root tests on each series of interest and optimal lags criterion tests. The time series are presented in growth rates, so two-unit root tests were performed: Augmented Dickey-Fuller (ADF) and Phillips-Perron unit root test to test the series' stability in the long term.

Table 7.1 presents the stationarity tests for the GDP, the employment sectors, and the real hourly wage. These time series are segmented by gender. It is observed that all series are stationary in both tests, so these series are consistent with order-one I(1) data.

This study uses an unrestricted VAR model, so a critical point is the order of the variables and the optimal number of lags to be used in the models. For the analysis, the theoretical framework model is used to sort variables in the following order: employment-GDP-real wages.

The reduced VAR model requires a lag criterion of estimation. According to the literature, it will be presented that the model should have one lag, given the size and periodicity of the series (Ivanov & Kilian, 2005).[4] Table 7.1 shows that three groups (SBIC) suggest zero lag (FPE, AIC, HQIC), propose one lag, and LR proposes five lags.

[4] This study does not recommend making inferences of individual coefficients due to the high multicollinearity among the variables (Akkemik, 2007). However, the model's statistical properties are reported in the annexes for information (Annex).

Table 7.1 VAR model: Tests and selection criteria

	Z-statistics for hypothesis testing unit roots				
Growth rates	**Augmented Dickey-Fuller (ADF)**			**Phillips-Perron Test (PP)**	
GDP	−7.53***			−79.46***	
Men					
Employment sector-Primary	−11.15***			−111.09***	
Employment sector-Secondary	−10.04***			−105.20***	
Employment sector-Tertiary	−15.11***			−130.93***	
Wage per hour	−13.64***			−148.32***	
Women					
Employment sector-Primary	−13.91***			−128.04***	
Employment sector-Secondary	−10.88***			−118.00***	
Employment sector-Tertiary	−16.79***			−128.97***	
Wage per hour	−12.78***			−134.85***	
p-value: 0.01***, 0.05**, 0.10*					
The selection criterion for optimal lags in VAR models					
Model: Employment sectors					
Lag	**LL**	**LR**	**FPE**	**AIC**	**HQICHQIC**	**SBIC**
0	1501.07		1.6e-24	−29.2562	−29.1624	**−29.0246***
1	1631.52	260.91	**6.1e-25***	**−30.2259***	**−29.2881***	−27.9098
2	1711.94	160.83	6.4e-25	−30.2145	−28.4325	−25.8138
3	1770.33	116.79	1.1e-24	−29.7712	−27.1451	−23.286
4	1833.94	127.22	1.8e-24	−29.4302	−25.96	−20.8605
5	1905.61	**143.33***	3.0e-24	−29.2472	−24.9329	−18.5929

*Selection criterion

Note Sample 102 observations. LL: log-likelihood, LR: likelihood ratio, FPE: final prediction error, AIC: Akaike's information criterion, HQIC: Hannan and Quinn information criterion, SBIC: Schwarz's Bayesian information criterion

Source Own estimations with time series constructed and homologized of employment surveys [ENEU-ENE-ENOE]. Seasonally adjusted series presented by growth rates

Employment Segment IRF's Analysis

Focusing on employment by gender and the industrial sector, the model follows the market-implied behavior after introducing the I-shock COVID-19. This section presents the main contribution of our research, which is to recover and quantify the impact of the I-shock COVID-19 on employment by segment defined on the industrial sector and gender in Mexico.

Firstly, the time series are segmented by industrial sector structure (*primary, secondary*, and *tertiary* employment) and gender to understand the labor market dynamics. It allows us to rely on Impulse-Response Functions to estimate the impact, using economic activity (Mexico's GDP) as the impulse variable. The response variables are the different sectors by gender in the labor market. For the VAR model (see Annex), the response variables are Primary/Secondary/Tertiary men's employment and the same sectors for women; all segments belong to the homologized cities of the standardized sample (Figs. 7.1 and 7.2).

The model introduces as *I-shock COVID-19* the observed change in economic activity (Mexico's GDP) for the first quarter of 2020 (INEGI, 2020), which represented a −2.2 standard deviation (s.d). Although the magnitude of the impulses in the IRFs frequently is introduced in one standard deviation, in the model, we use the first shock to observe its dynamics in the labor market. Figure 7.3 (see Annex) presents the Impulse-Response Functions for the model differentiated by the employment sector and segmented by gender structure.

Figure 7.3 in the Annex shows how the *I-shock COVID-19* impacts labor employment divided by gender and sector (high-definition pdf versions of this chapter's Figures are available at https://tinyurl.com/ch7-Figures). The model allows us to aggregate the negative impact in period $t+1$. With this, it is possible to observe that the primary sector labor market is inelastic to shocks in the Mexican economy. One of the reasons may be that the primary sector is highly dependent on external supply and demand, so the labor market has its behavior. On the other hand, Fig. 7.3 displays the impact of the COVID-19 shock on both jobs in the secondary and tertiary sectors. For Mexico, the manufacturing industry fell by 10.9% in the first four months (INEGI, 2020); in our model, this fall of the first shock represents 1.6% for men and 1.5% for women.

The first COVID-19 shock also significantly impacted tertiary sector employment due to the high adjustment cost of the sectors. The crisis hits those sectors more intensely with greater technological dynamism, resulting in changes in the country's production structure (CEPAL, 2020).

Also, the COVID-19 *I-shock* relative to gender has different dynamics between sectors. While in the secondary sector, the impact is more profound for women (1.6% vs. 1%), the opposite is true for the tertiary sector, where male employees received a greater shock than women (1.5% vs. 1.3%). The tertiary sector had the most significant impact from the pandemic since the first shock to hit Mexico was tourism (Esquivel, 2020). This sector accounts for a large part of tertiary employment.

These impulse-response functions allow us to recover the trend with the *I-shock* COVID-19 in employment sectors by gender, and then, with the VAR model, the pre-COVID-19 trends are estimated. The following section includes the differences between the employment losses derived from the I-shock and the losses derived from the structural effects triggered by the COVID-19 shock.

Discussion

Impact on Employment Sectors and Gender

As in previous works, employment in Mexico presents a particular structure and dynamics depending on the context and issues in which the data are analyzed (Moreno & Cuellar, 2021; Cuellar & Moreno, 2022b). First, this study introduces the economic I-shock derived from the COVID-19 pandemic. Then, it explores the impact on long-term employment growth trends among six primary, secondary, and tertiary segments segmented by gender. Once the trends are calculated, a counterfactual trend analysis is performed, i.e., the observed employment is analyzed against the pre-COVID 19 and I-shock-COVID-19 trends, giving a generalized context of what would have happened to employment if the pandemic had not occurred.

Figures 7.1 and 7.2 show the cumulative employment loss segmented by sector for men and women, compared to employment trends (one without the COVID-19 shock and the other including it). Our results are divided into impacts on elasticities, cumulative observed employment loss, and long-run employment growth trends.

The first result highlights the elasticities of employment in each economic sector. It can be observed that tertiary employment is more reactive or elastic to shocks produced by the economy, while primary sector employment is inelastic to these same shocks; this is in aggregate for both genders (see Fig. 7.3 in the Annex). This finding is in line with

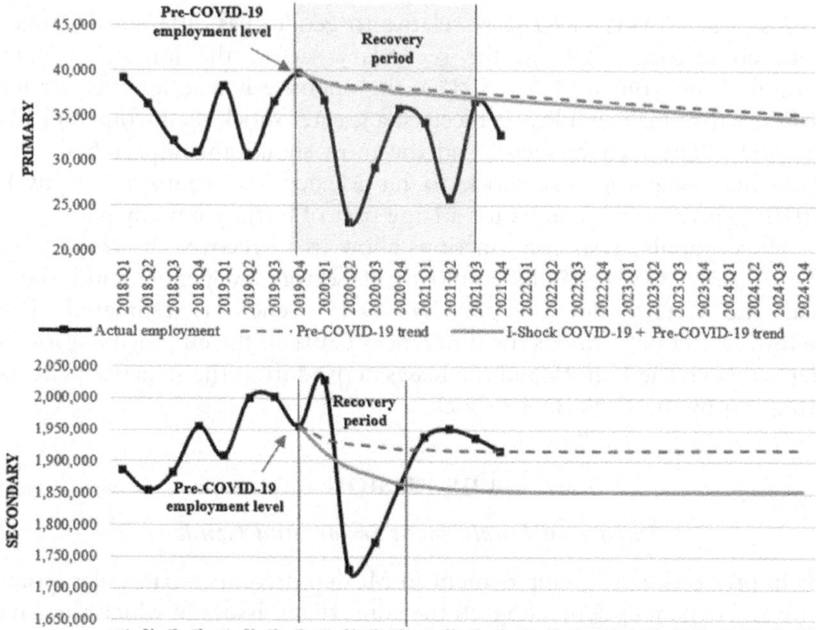

Fig. 7.1 COVID-19 shock and men's employment by sector (Primary/Secondary/Tertiary) (*Notes* Trend estimation uses a VAR model. The data on employment observed in the second 2020 quarterly was calculated by ETOE). *Source* Own estimations with time series constructed and homologized of employment surveys (ENEU-ENE-ENOE) by INEGI

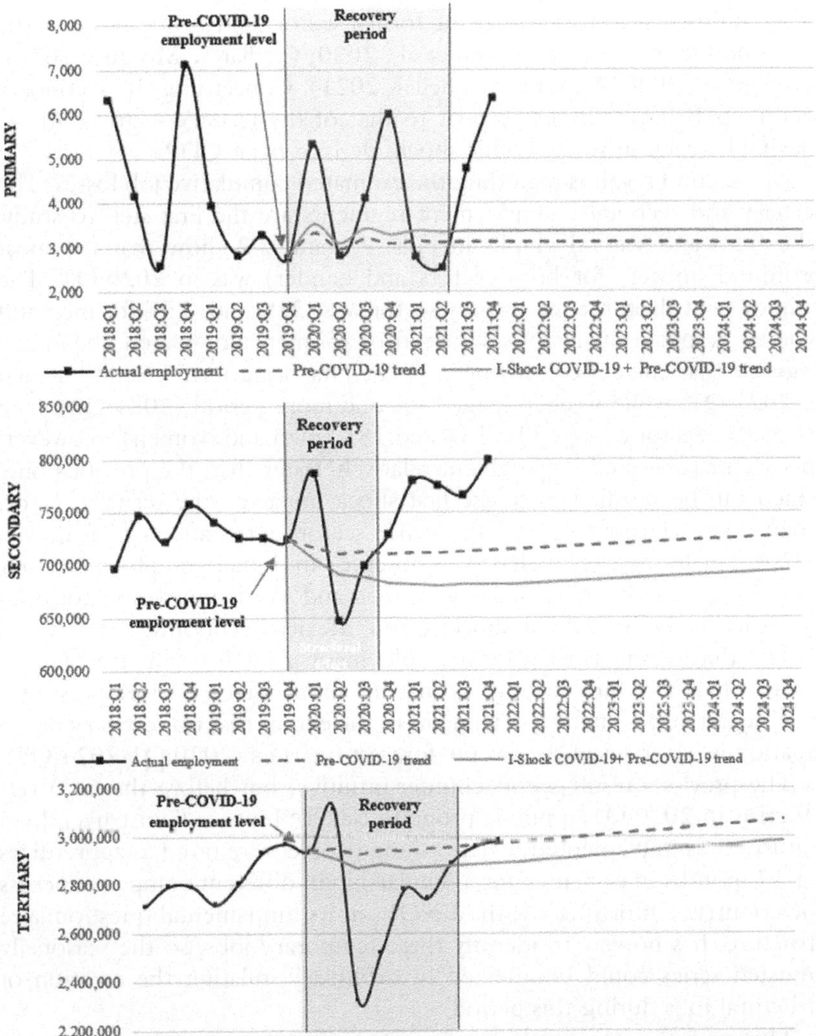

Fig. 7.2 COVID-19 shock and women's employment by sector (Primary/ Secondary/Tertiary) (*Notes* Trend estimation uses a VAR model. The data on employment observed in the second 2020 quarterly was calculated by ETOE). *Source* Own estimations with time series constructed and homologized of employment surveys (ENEU-ENE-ENOE) by INEGI

other authors, who found that the formal sector tends to be more elastic to economic shocks (Altamirano et al., 2020; Cuellar & Moreno, 2022a, b; Esquivel, 2020; Moreno & Cuellar, 2021). Concerning the secondary sector, its behavior is very similar to that of the tertiary sector, with an inevitable reaction to economic shocks derived from GDP.

The second result is regarding the estimated cumulative job losses. The tertiary and secondary employment segments are the first step to study. The third and second graphs in Figs. 7.1 and 7.2 show that the most profound impact (for both sectors and gender) was in 2020:Q2. The employment drop for the tertiary sector was -21% and -25% for men and women, respectively. Despite a sharp drop for men and women, the model suggests that current employment reached its "long-term" trend for men in 2021:Q1, while women lagged for one more period (2021:Q3). The secondary sector dropped by 15% and 18% (men and women). However, this sector recovered employment relatively faster than the previous one, which can be justified since the first shock impacted the tertiary sector. Then, like a chain reaction, the other sectors were affected (Esquivel, 2020). Finally, acyclical behavior is observed in primary employment, our model suggests that employment for men and women in this sector does not react to the impacts or shocks of the Mexican economy.

The third result is long-term employment growth trends (red line in the graphs). The model suggests that the initial shock is more persistent in all segments for men than women, to the extent that no recovery in job creation is observed in the twenty forecast quarters (2020:Q1-2024:Q4).

The previous result seems counter-intuitive, but before the COVID-19 crisis in 2019:Q1, a public program called "Jovenes Construyendo el Futuro" was implemented, where young people were hired as apprentices for 12 months in exchange for a scholarship in different companies across the country. Unfortunately, the ENOE, in its fundamental questionnaire structure, has no way to identify these temporary jobs, so the seasonally adjusted series could be affected by arbitrarily inflating the creation of structural jobs during this period.

This program may have temporarily inflated structural job creation during the 2019 crisis. So also, the recovery of structural jobs (current job series) could be overestimated during the crisis in the 2020–2021 period derived from this phenomenon.

Given the above two points, the long-term estimates suggest a slight downward trend, and stability would reflect the Mexican economy's underlying conditions. There has been no growth in GDP per capita, and the employment growth could only be due to the trend in employment. Therefore, the observed trend is the fall toward the data's natural growth equilibrium state.

Conclusions

This chapter analyzes the deepening and persistence of employment losses by gender and industrial sectors, showing the recovery trends in each market segment. To pursue this objective, the research builds a consistent micro-founded time series framework for the primary employment variables using quarterly data from 1993 to 2019 and following the same urban areas. As proposed by Cuellar (2019) and Moreno and Cuellar (2021), this methodology permits consistently defining and measuring all relevant dimensions directly from each micro data set in urban employment surveys in Mexico.

For pursuing the identification of employment structural trend components, the research estimates a VAR model linking each employment segment and aggregate production (defined by the real GDP) following the theoretical framework by Arrow et al. (1961) as proposed in Moreno and Cuellar (2021). This approach permits estimating long-run trends and short-run components in the segmented labor market. Then, the structural impact of the pandemic is estimated when considering the pre-COVID-19 forecasting of employment dynamics, given the initial observed shock on productivity, and compared with the actual employment levels observed over the year 2020. This approach allows for identifying the deepening and persistence of the initial shock of the recession.

The results suggest a structural and persistent effect on employment losses with lengthy recovery on employment levels, particularly in the male segment, and a more significant recovery rate relative to female employment. On the other hand, employment in the tertiary sector is more reactive to the first COVID-19 shock than in other sectors. Similarly, the secondary industrial sector shows a similar but less pronounced reaction, so all observed job losses are related to a structural change in the labor market. On the contrary, primary sector employment is inelastic to the initial shock.

The estimated outcomes of this research also suggest that public policies that artificially increase job opportunities, such as "Jovenes Construyendo Futuro" (an "on-the-job training" scholarship to promote employment among young workers with no experience) prior to the COVID-19 crisis or the prohibition of outsourcing to force switching those employment to formal during the COVID-19 crisis does not have long-run effects on employment. In the case of Mexico, the forecasted long-run employment levels for men and women, once the trend and seasonality of the series are considered, show a stable pattern in all sectors, contrary to the rapid recoveries of the observed series. Hence, these recovery rates might combine the policy effects and changes in the industrial employment structure.

This chapter proves that notwithstanding the adverse effects of the COVID-19 pandemic and the observed job recovery, long-run employment "binds the market." Hence, fundamental structural changes might include drift levels even by changes in the market structure but must be driven by policies that promote productivity and gender equality in the long run and not policies that artificially increase employment in the short run.

Annex

See Figure 7.3.

VAR Models and Impulse-Response Function to negative shock in GDP
Time set: quarters after I-shock COVID-19 related to the economic crisis

Model 1: Structure and dynamic of employment by economic sectors

	Men			Women		
Variable	*Primary*	*Secondary*	*Tertiary*	*Primary*	*Secondary*	*Tertiary*
L1.eter.m	−0.605	−0.0189	−0.203	−0.542	0.0719	0.131
L1.eter.w	−0.122	−0.131	0.0614	−0.418	−0.214	−0.475 **
L1.esec.m	0.647	0.0209	0.393 **	−0.619	0.388 *	0.226
L1.esec.w	−0.259****	0.119	−0.231 *	0.510	−0.235	−0.0972
L1.epri.m	−0.332	−0.0454	−0.0344	0.0000576	−0.0202	−0.00258
L1.epri.w	−0.00446	−0.00554	0.00183	−0.467 ***	−0.00736	−0.00332
L1.gdp	0.129	0.261	0.369 *	−1.100	0.409 *	0.316 *
L1.whr.m	0.839	0.0717	0.186	2.123	0.215	0.257 *
L1.whr.w	−0.217	0.135	−0.0946	−1.268	0.0270	−0.157
Constant	−0.0211	−0.0106	−0.0126	0.0123	−0.0125	−0.00578
N	106	106	106	106	106	106
RMSE	0.123956	0.038329	0.038496	0.425477	0.045331	0.036048
Chi2(prob)	0.0016	0.1524	0.0314	0.0003	0.0533	0.0048

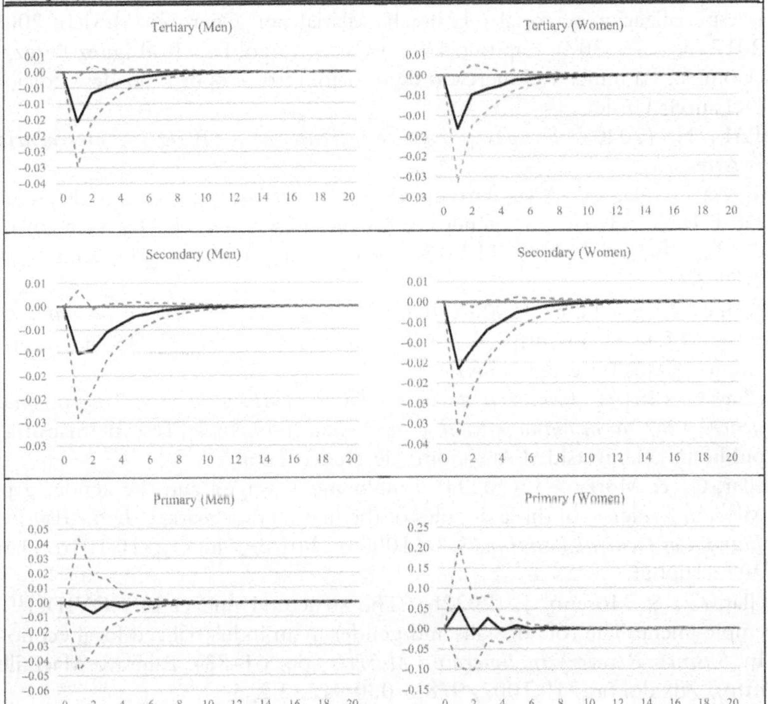

Fig. 7.3 VAR model: Estimation and Impulse-Response Functions (IRLs) (p-value 0.001***, 0.01**, 0.05* *Source* Own estimations with time series constructed and homologized of employment surveys (ENEU-ENE-ENOE). Seasonally adjusted series presented by growth rates)

References

Akkemik, K. (2007). The response of employment to GDP growth in Turkey: An econometric estimation. *Applied Econometrics and International Development, 7*(1), 65–74.

Altamirano, A., Azuara, O., & Gonzalez, S. (2020). ¿Cómo impactará la COVID-19 al empleo? *Posibles escenarios para America Latina y el Caribe. Banco Interamericano de Desarrollo.*

Arrow, K., Chenery, H., Minhas, B., & Solow, R. (1961). Capital-labor substitution and economic efficiency. *The Review of Economics and Statistics, 43*(3), 225. https://doi.org/10.2307/1927286

Bracamontes, J., Nuñez, J., & Rodriguez, R. (2020). Un análisis regional de la especialización sectorial y la brecha salarial por género en México, 2005 y 2017 (pp. 275–307). Capitulo 10, En Castro Lugo, D. y Rodríguez Pérez, R., (Comps). La mujer y el mercado de trabajo: retos y oportunidades; Ediciones DeLaurel; UAdeC.

CEPAL, N. (2020). *Sectores y empresas frente al COVID-19: emergencia y reactivación.*

Cerquera-Losada, O., Arias-Barrera, C. J., & Prada-Hernández, J. F. (2020). La Brecha Salarial por género en Colombia y en el Departamento de Caldas. *Ánfora, 27*(48), 113–136. https://doi.org/10.30854/anf.v27.n48.2020.671

Coparmex Nuevo Leon. (2020). *Lidera Nuevo Leon en empleos formales recuperados*. Taken from: https://coparmexnl.org.mx/2020/11/18/lidera-nl-en-empleo-formales-recuperados/

Cuellar, C. (2019). *Evolucion de la brecha salarial en Mexico: Un enfoque de genero y capital humano para el sector formal asalariado* [Tesis de maestría no publicada]. Universidad Autonoma de Nuevo Leon.

Cuellar, C., & Moreno, J. (2022a). Employment, wages, and the gender gap in Mexico: Evidence of three decades of the urban labor market. *Latin American Journal of Central Banking, 3*(2), 100055. https://doi.org/10.1016/j.latcb.2022.100055

Cuellar, C., & Moreno, J. (2022b). The structural impact of COVID-19 on employment: The role of skills and gender in an industrialized local economy. In *Business Recovery in Emerging Markets* (pp. 61–83). Palgrave Macmillan. http://dx.doi.org/10.1007/978-3-030-91532-2_5

Encuesta Nacional de Empleo Urbano (ENEU), anos de 1987 a 2000, INEGI. Taken from: www.inegi.gob.mx

Encuesta Nacional de Empleo (ENE), anos de 2001 a 2004, INEGI. Taken from: www.inegi.gob.mx

Encuesta Nacional de Ocupación y Empleo (ENOE), años de 2005 a 2020, INEGI. Taken from: www.inegi.gob.mx

Encuesta Nacional Telefonica de Ocupacion y Empleo (ETOE), anos de 2020, INEGI. Taken from: www.inegi.gob.mx.

Esquivel, G. (2020). Los impactos economicos de la pandemia en Mexico. *Economia UNAM, 17*(51), 28–44. https://doi.org/10.22201/fe.24488143e.2020.51.543

Felix-Verduzco, G., & Inzunza-Mejia, P. (2019). Persistencia de los roles de género en la participación laboral de las mujeres con estudios profesionales en México. *Papeles de población, 25*(99), 209–248. http://dx.doi.org/10.22185/24487147.2019.99.09

Fernandez, A., & Lugo, D. (2017). Desigualdad laboral por género en México: Análisis de las áreas urbanas. *Revista De Economía Laboral, 14*(2), 169–199.

Garcia, K., Rodriguez, R., & Azpilcueta, E. (2018). Determinantes de la segregación ocupacional por sexo en México en el año 2016. Capítulo Digital en: De la Vega Estrada, Sergio y Ken Rodríguez, Crucita (Coords). DESIGUALDAD REGIONAL, POBREZA Y MIGRACIÓN. Universidad Nacional Autónoma de México y Asociación Mexicana de Ciencias para el Desarrollo Regional A.C, Coeditores, México (pp. 828–852). ISBN UNAM: 978-607-30-0001-7, AMECIDER: 978-607-96649-8-5. http://ru.iiec.unam.mx/id/eprint/3726

Gasca, J. (2021). Diferencias sectoriales y regionales de la recesión económica motivadas por la pandemia de la COVID-19 en México y medidas de política pública para enfrentarla. *Investigaciones geográficas* (105).

Gomez, L. (2021). *Impactos diferenciados. Efectos de la Pandemia de COVID-19 en la situación laboral de las mujeres en México.* COPRED 2021, primera edición.

Instituto Nacional de estadistica y Geografia, INEGI. (2020). *Indicadores de ocupacion y empleo.* Cifras oportunas durante marzo de 2022.

International Labour Organization. (2020). ILO Monitor: COVID-19 and the World of Work. *Updated Estimates and Analysis*. Int Labour Organ.

International Monetary Fund, I.M.F. (2020). World economic outlook: The great lockdown. *International Monetary Fund.*

Ivanov, V., & Kilian, L. (2005). A practitioner's guide to lag order selection for VAR impulse response analysis. *Studies in Nonlinear Dynamics & Econometrics, 9*(1). http://dx.doi.org/10.2202/1558-3708.1219

Jimenez-Bandala, C., Peralta, J., Sanchez, E., Olvera, I., & Aceves, D. (2020). La situacion del mercado laboral en Mexico antes y durante la COVID-19. *Revista Internacional De Salarios Dignos, 2*(2), 1–14.

Mancini, F. (2016). Cambios y continuidades en la movilidad laboral de la fuerza de trabajo femenina en México. *Notas de Población, 43*(102), 229–248. https://doi.org/10.18356/22376cc5-es

Moreno, J., & Cuellar, C. (2021). Informality, gender employment gap, and COVID-19 in Mexico: Identifying persistence and dynamic structural effects. *Revista Mexicana de Economía y Finanzas Nueva Época REMEF, 16*(3), 636. https://doi.org/10.21919/remef.v16i3.636

Paz, J. (2019). La brecha salarial por género en Argentina: un análisis acerca de la segmentación laboral. *Sociedade e Cultura, 22*(1), 157–178. ISSN: 1415-8566. https://doi.org/10.5216/sec.v22i1.57894

Peláez González, C., & Rodríguez, S. A. (2020). Género, trabajo y educación: Diferencias entre hombres y mujeres en la entrada al primer empleo. *Revista Interdisciplinaria de Estudios de Género de El Colegio de México, 6*, 1–37. https://doi.org/10.24201/reg.v6i0.494

Ripani, L., & Azuara, O. (2021). *La pandemia acentuó brechas laborales*. Es tiempo de cerrarlas; División de Mercados Laborales del BID, blog Factor Trabajo, Banco Interamericano de Desarrollo.

Salce, F. (2021). Evolución y análisis de la discriminación salarial por género en Chile. *El Trimestre Económico, LXXXVIII*(1)(349), 39–75.ISSN: 0041-3011. https://doi.org/10.20430/ete.v88i349.984.

Siddiqui, K. (2020). *The impact of COVID-19 on the Global economy*. World.

Sims, C. A. (1980). Macroeconomics and reality. *Econometrica, 48*(1), 1. https://doi.org/10.2307/1912017

CHAPTER 8

Access to Microfinance for Social Mobility in Mexico

Lorena DelaTorre-Díaz

Introduction

In many countries, the effects of the confinement imposed as the initial response to the COVID-19 pandemic included reduction in household income derived from economic activity slowdown and job losses (Bundervoet et al., 2022). These effects have worsened the economic inequality already present particularly in developing countries and have generated worries about the impacts on social mobility.

In Mexico, economic social mobility is threatened by the contraction of economic activity that produced important reductions in household income. According to the 2020 National Household Income and Expen diture Survey, the average reduction in household income was −3% compared to the accounted on the 2018 survey, and the household current expenses reported a compounded annual growth rate of −6.66% in the same period (Instituo Nacional de Estadística y Geografía [INEGI],

L. DelaTorre-Díaz (✉)
Facultad de Ciencias Económicas y Empresariales, Universidad Panamericana, Mexico City, Mexico
e-mail: lotorre@up.edu.mx

E. Murillo et al. (eds.), *Creating Economic Stability Amid Global Uncertainty*, https://doi.org/10.1007/978-3-031-41386-5_8

2020). This scenario along with the low expected GDP rates in the following months is likely to increase inequality and set obstacles for families to climb up in the socioeconomic ladder.

The reduction of inequality is one of the Sustainable Development Goals established by the United Nations toward 2030, as inequalities in human development damage social cohesion and economies get hurt when people are prevented from reaching their full potential (United Nations Development Programme, 2019). It has been stated that while inequality captures a static image of the distribution of a certain variable at a specific point in time, social mobility is related to a more dynamic evolution of the same variable (Yang & Zhou, 2022). Social mobility refers to the ability of an individual or a family to change their socioeconomic status either during a single person's lifetime or compared to previous generation's conditions.

International organizations such as the Organization for Economic Co-operation and Development (2018), the World Bank (Nayaran et al., 2018) and the World Economic Forum (2020) have recognized social mobility as a key element in the effort to reduce inequality and have therefore highlighted the importance of identifying aspects that can promote it.

Different public policies attempt to increase social mobility by reducing the gap in the access to education or health services, but access to financial services is a less explored path to promote social mobility and particularly through microcredits, which are credit schemes originally developed to help in poverty alleviation. An inclusive financial system has positive impacts on social mobility facilitating investment in human capital development for the future generations (López, 2020), and some studies have shown significant relationship between microfinance programs and social mobility (Ferdous et al., 2020; Khan et al., 2019).

The assessment of the level of inequality, welfare or poverty in different regions has often used household income or expenditure as indicators (Harttgen & Vollmer, 2013). However, there are limitations to the use of these information, including the lack of sufficient intertemporal data or weaknesses in data collection derived from changes in the survey instruments (Sahn & Stifel, 2000). An alternative measure of economic welfare in different studies evaluating social mobility has used asset indexes (Behrman & Vélez-Grajales, 2015; Vélez-Grajales et al., 2015b; Vélez-Grajales et al., 2018; Torche, 2020), assuming they can be a valid predictor of the manifestation of poverty, as well as an approximation of long-term wealth with a lower degree of error than the measurement of expenses (Sahn & Stifel, 2003). The present study uses this approach to assess the changes in socioeconomic status.

Derived from social mobility studies, relationships between household assets possession and changes in socioeconomic status of individuals and families have been established. The relation between microfinance and social mobility has been proven as well. However, the association between the household assets possession ***obtained through microcredits*** and social mobility has not been explored, and it may open new perspectives on the use of microcredits in the reduction of inequality.

The purpose of this paper is to analyze this relation, proposing that the use of microcredits destined to the acquisition of a home furnishing kit of assets would favor social mobility, particularly after periods of income and expenses shocks. The main contribution of this study is a novel approach considering that upward mobility may be threatened if it is based on income or educational attainment as a result of the effects of the pandemic. The focus on asset accumulation obtained through microcredits can, therefore, represent a plausible alternative to improve socioeconomic conditions.

The structure of the document is as follows: section "The Income and Expenditure of Households in Mexico in the Face of Covid-19" contains a description of the impact observed on income and expenses in Mexico in 2020. In section "Measuring Social Mobility Using Household Assets" the concept of social mobility and its relationship with inequality is addressed along with how household assets are used in social mobility evaluation. Section "Microfinance and Household Assets" describes the main characteristics of microcredits, the use of this credit schemes in Mexico and how are they related to asset accumulation. The final sections present a discussion of how microcredits and social mobility can be linked if they are used to help families increase their asset possessions and the conclusions obtained.

The Income and Expenditure of Households in Mexico in the Face of Covid-19

As of January 2022, the Mexican Ministry of Health had recorded more than 4.9 million confirmed cases of COVID-19 in Mexico and more than 305 thousand deaths (Secretaría de Salud, 2022). Although the measures taken to contain the spread of the disease were different in each state, in March 2020 the federal government implemented a series of confinement measures that included the cancelation of non-essential economic activities, the prohibition of events with more than 50 people, and the suspension of in-person classes at all educational levels.

The restrictions on economic activities derived from the lockdowns had significant impacts on households' income in Mexico. The results of the 2020 National Household Income and Expenditure Survey (Encuesta Nacional de Ingreso y Gasto de los Hogares, ENIGH by its acronym in Spanish) prepared by INEGI (Instituto Nacional de Estadística e Informática) reported an average annual reduction in household monthly income of −3.0% compared to the income reported on the 2018 survey. When disaggregated by decile, the only segment that showed a positive growth in income, although a low growth, was the first decile (Table 8.1).

Household expenses also reported important changes from 2018 to 2020. Mexican families reduced their expenses in almost all items except for health-related, where the compounded annual growth rate was above 18%. This increase is explained by the COVID-19 effect (see Table 8.2).

The overall distribution of expenses in the average Mexican population changed facing the new challenges derived from the income reduction and the adjustment of priorities. Of considerable importance is the decrease in the percentage destined to education that fell from 12 to 8% (see Fig. 8.1).

Table 8.1 Average monthly income by decile in Mexico and compounded annual growth rate from 2018 to 2020 (in Mexican pesos)

Decile	*ENIGH 2018*	*ENIGH 2020*	*CAGR*
National	17,806.00	16,769.67	−3.0%
I	3,269.00	3,312.67	0.7%
II	5,774.67	5,620.67	−1.3%
III	7,684.33	7,424.67	−1.7%
IV	9,571.33	9,186.00	−2.0%
V	11,587.33	11,122.33	−2.0%
VI	13,965.67	13,369.33	−2.2%
VII	16,948.00	16,223.33	−2.2%
VIII	21,116.00	20,199.33	−2.2%
IX	28,191.67	26,812.33	−2.5%
X	59,954.33	54,427.33	−4.7%

Note CAGR is the Compounded Annual Growth Rate
Source INEGI (2020)

Table 8.2 Distribution of average monthly expenses and compounded annual growth rate in Mexico from 2018 to 2020 (in Mexican pesos)

Expense concept	*ENIGH 2018*	*ENIGH 2020*	*CAGR*
Current monetary expenses	11,443	9,970	−6.66%
Food, beverages and tobacco	4,030	3,793	−2.98%
Transport and communications	2,283	1,851	−9.97%
Housing and services	1,091	1,095	0.17%
Personal care	847	798	−2.93%
Education and recreation	1,386	766	−25.67%
Cleaning and house care	672	653	−1.42%
Health	300	422	18.54%
Clothing and footwear	513	298	−23.83%

Source INEGI (2020)

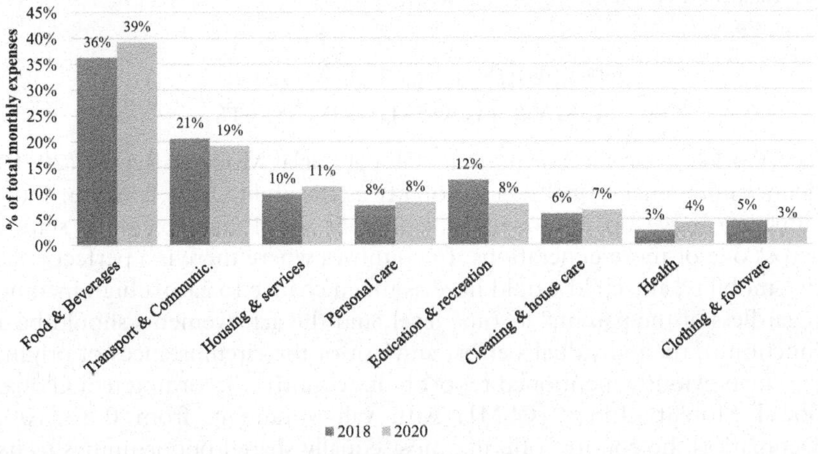

Fig. 8.1 Changes in expenses distribution of Mexican families from 2018 to 2020 (*Source* Author elaboration based on data from INEGI [2020])

The reduction of income may be compensated in some families with the disposal of assets as a source of cash flow when employment sources were restricted. Under these circumstances, access to credit becomes even more relevant to allow households to acquire (or in some cases recover) durable household assets. In this way, microcredits can be an inequality-reducing tool for all levels of the income distribution and not only in households with higher levels of poverty.

Even before the appearance of COVID-19, social mobility in Mexico was low compared to other countries. The Global Social Mobility Index published by the World Economic Forum in 2020 placed Mexico in the 58th place out of a list of 82 countries evaluated (World Economic Forum, 2020), and the results of the 2017 Social Mobility Survey showed high persistence of Mexican households on the upper and lower extremes of the socioeconomic status distribution (Orozco-Corona et al., 2019). There are no studies yet that evaluate the level of social mobility in Mexico in its economic dimension after the confinement, and however, after the considerable impact on household income it is expected to see a reduction on the number of families climbing up to upper quintiles unless policies are designed to promote the opposite.

Measuring Social Mobility Using Household Assets

The World Economic Forum in its Global Social Mobility Report (2020) defines intergenerational social mobility as the ability for a family or individual to move up or down the ladder of social and economic status, across one or more generations. In countries where there is a perfect relative mobility, any child would have as much chance to earn a high income regardless of the parents' income level, and the achievements should be a function of the individual's effort and not of the circumstances of origin.

The previously mentioned report ranks countries according to a Global Social Mobility Index (GSMI) with values ranging from 0 to 100; Denmark is the country offering most equally shared opportunities to its population with an index value of 85.2, followed by Norway with 83.6. In this first edition of the report, 82 countries were evaluated and the lowest index values correspond to African and Asian countries (World Economic Forum, 2020).

Social mobility is considered as an element of study in the broader concept of inequality of opportunities, analyzing the effect that certain ascriptive factors (such as family socioeconomic origin, gender, social conditions of the place of birth) and the circumstances (for which individuals cannot be held responsible) have on the destiny of the individuals (Solís, 2018). When economic advantages and disadvantages pass from parents to children, countries with greater inequality experience less mobility between generations (Corak, 2013).

The absence of upward social mobility in a society produces loss of potential talents that remain hidden, decrease in productivity levels, lack of investment opportunities, hoarding of educational, economic or financial opportunities by higher socioeconomic classes, waste in the allocation of human resources, and finally a breakdown of the social cohesion when citizens perceive barriers that prevent them from accessing better conditions (OCDE, 2018; Vélez-Grajales et al., 2015a, 2015b).

Low social mobility is at the same time a cause and a consequence of inequalities. A vicious cycle can be created when less equality of opportunities produces less social mobility, hence producing more inequalities inherited (World Economic Forum, 2020). The relationships between social mobility and the concepts of capabilities of freedom of agency developed by Sen (1985a, 1985b) are clearly synthetized by Roche (2013) and are illustrated in Fig. 8.2.

People use individual, social, or environmental conversion factors to change their initial resources (or endowments) into functionings. Capabilities are sets of vectors of functionings (real opportunities available) from which a person chooses the combination that better leads to one type of life or another. Thus, according to Sen, "a person's freedom to convert commodities into functioning is dependent upon the social and political opportunities that are available" (Nambiar, 2013, p. 222).

Upward social mobility is possible when people receive better opportunities to create the capabilities necessary to reach their desired lifestyle. Institutions play an important role in this process, defining the social, political, and economic opportunities that are available.

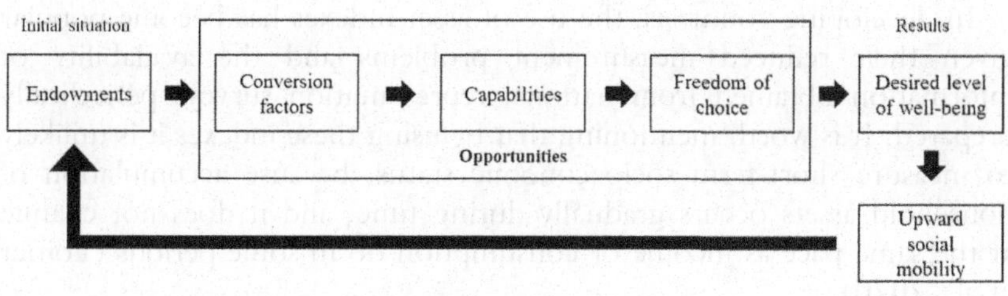

Fig. 8.2 Relationship between capabilities and conversion factors and social mobility (*Source* Adapted from Roche [2013])

According to the GSMI, the level of social mobility in a country is based on ten pillars:

- health,
- education access,
- education quality and equity,
- lifelong learning,
- social protection,
- technology access,
- work opportunities,
- fair wages,
- working conditions,
- efficient and inclusive institutions.

The conceptual framework on which this index is built is the concept of *conversion factors* and enablers of social mobility (World Economic Forum, 2020).

The variable traditionally used to estimate the population's social mobility in economic terms is income. This variable may include not only income from wages and salaries, but also other factors such as financial assets and public and private transfers (Torche, 2020). The drawback of using this approach is the need to have intergenerational reliable income data, which is not always available in all countries or regions. Therefore, a growing trend in the literature is the development of asset indexes allowing the estimation of household wealth and then evaluating its mobility. These indexes can be considered approximations of permanent household income (Behrman & Vélez-Grajales, 2015; Torche, 2020; Vélez-Grajales et al., 2018).

In developing countries, the use of asset indexes has become popular given their reduced measurement problems and the availability of information obtained from national representation surveys periodically prepared. It is worth mentioning that by using these indexes it is unlikely to measure short-term socioeconomic status, because accumulation of household assets occurs gradually during time, and it does not change at the same pace as income or consumption do in some periods (Poirier et al., 2020).

According to Wolff (2005), family wealth is an indicator of well-being in many ways: first, the assets can be a source of consumption since, if needed, they can be sold to become cash; second, the availability of financial assets can provide liquidity in times of economic stress; and finally, in a representative democracy, the distribution of power is related to the distribution of wealth.

Wealth can have a large effect on absolute and relative mobility between generations as there is a possible causal relationship between net worth (wealth) and the parent-child association of income, through education, employment, and choice of the neighborhood (Grawe, 2008). For economically disadvantaged population, different types of durable goods (not necessarily financial assets) are relevant in their well-being because they allow families to engage in productive activities or save time and money on activities like transfers or transportation (Edin, 2005).

Similarly, Cotler and Rodríguez-Oreggia (2010) highlight that although a combination of human, physical, social, and financial assets is required to improve the socioeconomic situation; the accumulation of physical assets can generate greater wealth, and "to that extent they are a possible indicator of their potential to improve their socioeconomic conditions" (p. 65).

Contrasting the appropriateness of wealth indexes versus income and consumption as variables for measuring socioeconomic status, Poirier et al. (2020) estimated a Spearman's correlation coefficient mean of 0.42 and 0.55 among 11 wealth indexes evaluated compared to income and consumption, respectively. According to their findings, wealth indexes are valid measures of household socioeconomic status, and they can be used to study this condition across national boundaries.

Filmer and Pritchett (1998) developed an index of household assets and characteristics based on the principal component analysis methodology to assess the impact of wealth on the educational level of households in Brazil, India, and Kenya, and subsequently to assess the relationship between such wealth and school enrollment in India (2001). A different approach is the one of Sahn and Stifel's (2001, 2003) who used factor analysis to estimate a single common factor that explains the variances in the possession of a set of assets, and that factor is considered as the metric of economic status or well-being.

Numerous studies have followed the mentioned methodologies in the construction of asset indexes, and however, little has been published regarding the importance of specific assets in social mobility. Assets are combined to create an indicator of wealth, but the relative importance of each individual asset has not been analyzed. Nor has the contribution to social mobility of a minimum home furnishing group of assets has been analyzed.

Social Mobility in Mexico

In Mexico, inequality has set obstacles for the ascendant social mobility as can be seen in the Gini coefficient on income. This metric is a popular indicator of income inequality, comparing the cumulative proportion of the population and the cumulative proportion of income they receive. The values range from zero (perfect equality) to one (indicating that one individual accumulates all). In 2018, from a list of 36 countries calculated by the OECD, Mexico was the second highest with 0.418 in the Gini coefficient, only after Costa Rica (Fig. 8.3).

Three Social Mobility Surveys with national representation were conducted in Mexico between 2006 and 2017, including retrospective questions to compare the respondents' current condition to that of their parents. The results of the 2017 survey show that 49% of the population was born in the lowest quintile according to a welfare index and remain in the same level their entire life. On the other hand, 57% of the individuals born in the wealthiest households remain in the highest quintile (Orozco-Corona et al., 2019). The persistence in the extreme sides of the distribution is strong and imposes challenges to upward social mobility.

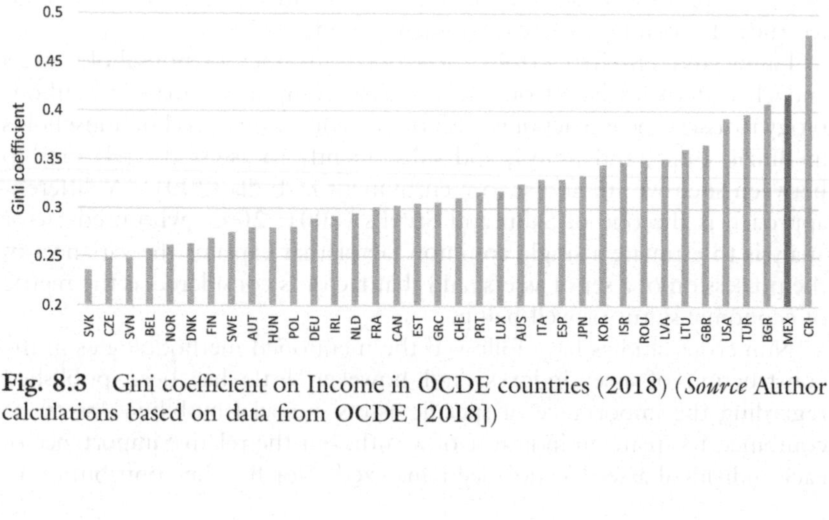

Fig. 8.3 Gini coefficient on Income in OCDE countries (2018) (*Source* Author calculations based on data from OCDE [2018])

Several studies analyzing social mobility in Mexico take as a reference the models developed by Filmer and Pritchett. These references include Behrman and Vélez-Grajales (2015) who, in order to measure Intergenerational Social Mobility by schooling, occupation and household wealth, developed an index based on three types of goods: consumer durables, household characteristics, and financial assets. They include possession of a bank account, credit card, vacuum cleaner, toaster, housekeeping, telephone, savings account, water heater, washing machine, refrigerator, car, indoor bathroom, stove, electricity service, running water, own home, and the rate of household overcrowding. An asset index was also developed by Vélez-Grajales et al. (2018) with the purpose of evaluating social mobility at the state level.

Similarly, Torche (2020) used the information from the 2006, 2011, and 2017 Social Mobility Surveys and created asset indexes including personal computer, cell phone, landline phone, Internet access, cable television, store or business, land or farm, second home, animals, farm equipment, stove, washing machine, refrigerator, indoor bathroom, electricity, housekeeping, savings account, checking account, credit cards, and cars. In a previous study, Torche (2010) had also included the employment status of parents and respondents as variables for the index.

Although principal components analysis is widely use in the development of asset indexes, an alternative method was used by Vélez-Grajales et al. (2015a, 2015b) considering multiple correspondence analysis to adjust better when the variables included are primarily categorical (more specifically, binary). They included additional variables such as vacation home, apartment for rent, and investment in stocks.

Microfinance and Household Assets

Access to financial services represents an important mechanism in reducing income and wealth inequality. Access to credit provides parents with resources to open new opportunities for their children; families can start new businesses or invest in education, health, or household equipment. The financial system contributes to social mobility in two concrete ways: first, allowing the investment in human capital through savings, financing, and capital accumulation. Second, through entrepreneurship and capital formation (López, 2020).

However, access to formal credit through multiple banking institutions is not always easy. The main reason why certain segments of the population cannot access bank credits is the lack of guarantees or the absence of steady verifiable income inflows (Delajara et al., 2018), which has favored the growth of microcredit as a funding option.

Microcredits are a financing scheme whose initial objective was to contribute to poverty alleviation. Muhammad Yunus (2007), founder of the Grameen Bank in Bangladesh, believed that to bring people out of poverty it was required to create an enabling environment, and once they could unleash their energy and creativity, poverty would quickly be over. This idea promoted the microcredit model that later evolved to microfinance; a concept that covers the entire provision of financial services to economically poor families (Beisland et al., 2019).

Microfinance refers to small-scale financial services, mainly credit and savings, offered to individuals or groups of people at the local level in developing countries, both rural and urban (Robinson, 2001). The institutions providing these services are named Microfinance Institutions (MFIs hereafter).

The main difference between a credit granted by commercial banks and microcredits relies on the size of the credit, but another innovative type of microcredit is the group loan, based on the concept of joint liability. In this scheme, loans are granted individually to a person who is part of a group of 3 to 10 people (depending on the institution), but the entire group is responsible for paying the loan. If one individual defaults, it may jeopardize someone else in the group receiving their loan, which motivates the entire group to meet their payments obligations. The first results of these credits showed loan recovery levels of 99.6%, and there were even reports with default rates below 10% (Armendáriz & Morduch, 2011; Banerjee, 2013; Cull et al., 2009).

There are additional distinctive characteristics in microcredits, namely the absence of a collateral guarantee, and credits designed specifically for women. Following Yunus' (2007) proposal, microcredit loans would be traditionally granted to micro-and small-entrepreneurs or individuals needing funding to their productive activities who are unlikely to receive those funds through traditional banking.

As stated by Zeller and Meyer (2002), the performance of MFIs should be based on three fundamental pillars: outreach to the poorest, financial sustainability, and the impact they have on the well-being of the population. The first pillar seeks to reach those sectors that have traditionally been excluded from formal financial systems; financial sustainability refers to the ability of financial institutions to generate economic profits that allow them to grow sustainably (Cull et al., 2009). Finally, the third pillar refers to "the impact associated with the access of the poorest to financial services. That is, to what extent the level of well-being of the target population has increased, or its degree of vulnerability has decreased, as a consequence of greater access to credit" (Minzer, 2009, p. 15). The last pillar is the hardest to measure because rigorous measurement of the impact of microcredit policies on the different dimensions of poverty is technically complicated and costly (Copestake, 2007).

It could be said that the greatest achievements generated with the development of microcredits are access to financial services in poor communities, the creation of viable business models providing access of women to these schemes, and even serving as inspiration for other growth efforts for social benefit.

Microcredits have had an important growth over the years. According to the Microcredit Summit Campaign (Reed, 2011), the number of microcredit clients worldwide increased from 13 million in 1997 to 211 million in 2013, attracting various institutions to participate in this market. This growth at the same time has raised questions about whether the entry of numerous companies is motivated by a truly interest in improving people's living conditions, or if there are merely economic interests derived from a large market of potential customers.

Nonetheless, the evidence of economic benefits produced by microcredits is still not entirely conclusive. According to Cotler and Rodríguez-Oreggia (2010), there is a consensus that financial development contributes to economic growth, however, in microeconomic terms the evidence is not very clear. The growth in the number of microfinance institutions and the consequent demand for their products could be interpreted as proof of the favorable impact that microcredits have, but more supporting evidence is required.

A constant question among those who have dedicated to the study of the effects of microcredits is whether these programs have actually generated growth and economic development among the population. Critics have remarked the problem of addiction to microcredits as one of the negative consequences, which far from contributing to the objective of reducing poverty, prevents them from achieving social mobility. Factors leading to the addiction include high interest rates, multiple loans, or even the satisfaction of the clients with the products offered by the MFIs (Peprah & Koomson, 2014).

Different approaches are used to assess the impact of microcredits on people's living conditions, one being the effect on household welfare. As mentioned previously, asset accumulation serves as an indicator of wealth, and studies have shown positive effects of microcredits in this matter. Salia (2014) found that borrowers' households are more likely to own living houses and more household assets than non-borrowers, and so microcredits contribute to welfare enabling the possession of long-term assets. Another study showed marginal increases in housing conditions and household appliances among borrowers, even though the accumulation of other assets (such as farm, land or livestock) had remained the same (Ahamad et al., 2021).

Other studies remark that the difference between borrowers and non-borrowers is found in productive assets like refrigerators and sewing machines (Adjei et al., 2009). It is worth highlighting that the traditional design of microcredits seeks to improve entrepreneurship and especially among women, thus the type of assets that could be acquired using this funding would be productive assets. However, an unexplored use of microcredits promoting improvements in socioeconomic conditions could come from the acquisition of a minimum set of household assets (mainly appliances) not directly related to a family business, but to the improvement of the family living conditions.

Microcredits in Mexico

Access to credit in Mexico is still lagging compared to similar-developed countries. According to data from the National Banking and Securities Commission (Comisión Nacional Bancaria y de Valores), in 2020 there were only 486 thousand credits granted to small and medium companies (SMEs), which account for around 12.5% of the number of SMEs in the same period. In terms of consumer credit, the International Monetary Fund reported that in Mexico in 2019 there were 5,899 loans to households from commercial banks for every 10,000 adults, compared to 28,087 loans for every 10,000 adults in Brazil or 8,081 in Chile (Comisión Nacional Bancaria y de Valores, 2021).

In terms of microfinance, between 2000 and 2006 there was a growth and evolution in this sector, from a small group to a greater number of companies, including not only non-governmental organizations (NGOs), but also for-profit institutions (Banco Interamericano de Desarrollo, 2011). The National Microentrepreneur Financing Program (Programa Nacional de Financiamiento al Microempresario, PRONAFIM by its acronym in Spanish) destined 13,663 million pesos to projects financed with microcredits between December 2012 and October 2018, benefiting more than 4.2 million people of which 92% were women.

The largest MFI in Mexico is Compartamos Banco, founded in 1990 as a non-profit organization but converted to commercial bank in 2006. This institution offers loan-size as small as $6,000 Mexican pesos (around 300 USD), and they reported that in 2021 the average credit size granted was $14,394 MXN (around 700 USD). This sole organization allocated more than 26 billion pesos in loans in 2021 representing 68.5% of the women-directed, group-loans market and 26% of the mixed-group-loans market (Gentera, SAB de CV, 2022).

Considering the importance of private MFIs in the development of microfinance markets, an aspect worth to analyze is the combination of private and public resources in the design and implementation of micro-credit programs. In Mexico, indirect channels would send funds from specific government programs to microcredit borrowers, using an MFI as the intermediary. However, it has not been explored the creation of microcredit schemes combining the expertise of MFIs in the administration of these credits with public policies and funding focused on reduction of inequality or promotion of social mobility.

A Proposal for Promoting Social Mobility Through Microcredits for Household Assets

Access to credit is a mechanism that favors social mobility increasing productivity and growth in companies and allowing individuals the access to goods or assets that may not be affordable with regular income. As pointed out by Khan et al. (2019), microcredits have changed the level of income for the low-income segments, increasing their economic power by investing in productive activities that help them acquire assets.

Even though there are studies that highlight the importance of assets in the social mobility of families, little has been said about the benefits that the use of a financing scheme such as microcredits would bring to this effect. It has been established that microcredits contribute to the well-being of households and to the accumulation of assets, but this analysis has been mainly focused on the productive assets necessary to carry out the business activities that microcredit lenders have.

A novel scheme is proposed to explore the design of microcredits targeting low- and medium-income families to acquire a basic set of household assets such as appliances or technological items (like computers) benefiting the socioeconomic conditions of subsequent generations. This proposal does not impose the restriction of self-employment to become a microcredit borrower, as long as the borrower's family income is enough to meet the credit payments. Figure 8.4 shows this relationship.

It is common to use percentile ranking to distribute households according to their income level, thus the parents' situation places a family at a certain quintile (condition of origin). Access to the microcredit scheme permits the acquisition of a set of assets. The effect of asset accumulation could place the next generations in a better (higher) quintile, implying an effect of upward social mobility.

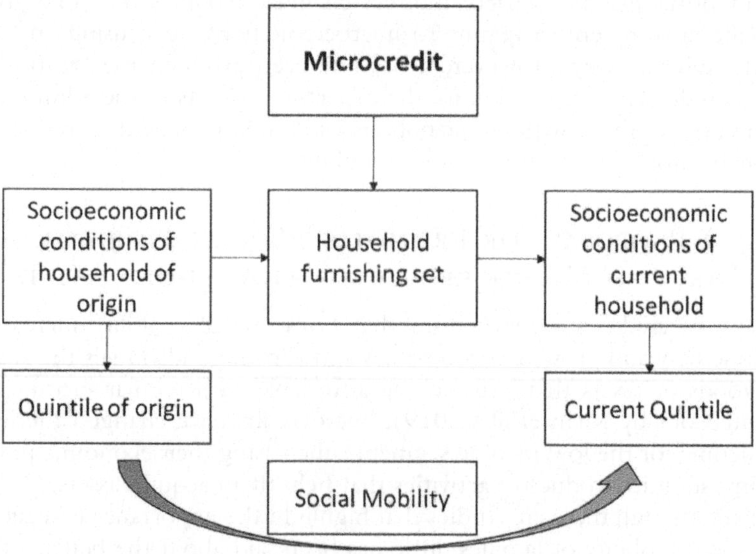

Fig. 8.4 Conceptual model of association of Microcredit and Social Mobility (*Source* Author's elaboration)

Studies that use household assets as part of an index to evaluate the socioeconomic status and further determination of the existence or not of social mobility, use the value of a large combination of assets, and therefore, a household possessing more assets would be in a better situation because the value of that index would be higher. It can be expected that if the acquisition of certain assets is promoted for the lower quintiles; they could eventually climb to a higher level in this distribution.

An asset index created applying the mixed principal components analysis was elaborated by DelaTorre-Diaz and Rodríguez-Aguilar (2021) using the information from the 2018 National Income and Expenses Survey in Mexico. A total of 49 variables were used to build the index including a wide range of assets, from physical household appliances like stove, refrigerator or microwave, health-related items like medical affiliation, education aspects such as the maximum educational level of the house head, financial inclusion aspects like possession of savings account, and even average monthly expenses in certain activities.

The results of this study showed high levels of inequality in assets possession among Mexican households. Considering a 1 to 100 range in the value of the asset index, the mean was 6.93 for the total sample of households contained in the survey, a value that exemplifies the high concentration of assets in the households allocated in the highest quintiles.

Following the same methodology but using the information of the 2020 income and expenses survey, the asset index was calculated again and the distribution obtained is very similar. This asset index was useful to determine the relative importance that each of the individual assets included has on the allocation of a family in a particular quintile through a logistic regression, using the correspondent household's quintile as the dependent variable and the 49 assets as the explanatory variables (DelaTorre-Diaz & Rivas-Aceves, 2022).

The results show that the assets with the highest impact in the probability of a household to belong to a higher quintile are vacuum cleaner, toaster, microwave, house, vehicle, washing machine, refrigerator, computer, DVD, stove, and digital TV.

The acquisition of durable goods such as the ones detected as most relevant implies an important disbursement of resources for households, who do not always have these amounts available. Microcredits represent an opportunity for families to take the step toward a better life condition.

It is true that there is no absolute consensus on the positive effects of microcredits on the borrowers' well-being, due to conditions such as the high interest rates charged or the presence of MFIs that have drifted their mission from the original objective of poverty alleviation toward achieving financial profits. However, there are regions where the use of microcredits has positively impacted social mobility, particularly among women entrepreneurs. It is expected then that microcredits can promote social mobility by facilitating household equipment.

Conclusion

The persistence of inequality of opportunities faced by individuals and families in many countries and particularly in developing countries sets obstacles for upward social mobility, thus forcing generations to persist in the same socioeconomic status. The negative effects of economic activity slowdown after the pandemic-derived confinement have worsened inequality and made social mobility even harder. Promoting strategies to foster social mobility is beneficial for society, but for these strategies to produce the best results, they should be focused on key drivers of mobility.

The accumulation of household assets is a promoter of social mobility since the combination of assets (measured by an asset index) is a valid measure of household wealth. It can also help families in rebuilding their economic conditions after shock periods. Among the assets usually owned by families, some of them increase the likeliness of belonging to higher socioeconomic levels. However, in many cases the available economic resources are not sufficient to afford the acquisition of those long-term assets, and thus, access to credit becomes an important element in the pursuit of better socioeconomic status. A credit scheme with an intrinsic orientation toward inequality reduction and poverty alleviation is the microcredits.

A potential collaboration between public and private institutions in the design, funding, and implementation of microcredit programs is plausible, with the purpose of helping low- and medium-income families to acquire a set of assets to furnish their homes, selecting those assets for their relevance in belonging to higher socioeconomic levels and therefore increase the possibilities of upward social mobility for the next generations. Of great importance is the regulation of this novel scheme to guarantee that the main objective of seeking social mobility is placed in the center.

Among the limitations of the proposed model, it can be mentioned the lack of empirical evidence since there are no similar models found yet. The results on social mobility will vary depending on the selection of the durable goods and the microcredit conditions set. Additionally, even though the asset index aims to evaluate different dimensions of family welfare, the methodology proposed to evaluate social mobility focuses more on the economic dimension rather than educational or occupational as other social mobility studies do.

Of great importance is the design of the microcredit and the conditions defined for this type of credits, since the financial solvency of the families might have been affected by the economic slowdown as well, reducing the number of prospective borrowers. The principal amount, the size of the installments, the term of the loan, and the interest rate charged should be carefully determined to become affordable to lower-income families avoiding a debt trap and becoming a social mobility driver.

Further empirical studies can deep into the implications that these microcredits scheme have for the borrower households, that is, the impact that payments of these credits would have on their income, the risks derived from over-indebtedness, and the need to renew the acquired assets to avoid obsolescence. The use of microsimulation models is recommended for this type of analysis since they allow the evaluation of the effects of a policy or the application of changes in specific aspects of the economic environment over the welfare of a sample of households or individuals. In this particular case, the policy evaluated would be the acquisition of assets through the use of microcredits.

References

Adjei, J., Arun, T., & Hossain, F. (2009). *The role of microfinance in asset building and poverty reduction: The case of Sinapi Aba Trust of Ghana*. Brooks World Poverty Institute.

Ahamad, S., Bhuiyan, A., Solaiman, M., & Joarder, M. (2021). The impact of microfinance programs on borrowers' asset accumulation: An empirical study in Bangladesh. *Journal of Asian Finance, Economics and Business, 8*(5), 1147–1154.

Armendáriz, B., & Morduch, J. (2011). *Economía de las microfinanzas*. FCE, CIDE.

Banco Interamericano de Desarrollo. (2011). *Microfinanzas en México*. México.

Banerjee, A. V. (2013). Microcredit under the microscope: What have we learned in the past two decades, and what do we need to know? *Annual Review of Economics, 5*(1), 487–519.

Behrman, J., & Vélez-Grajales, V. (2015). Patrones de movilidad intergeneracional para escolaridad, ocupación y riqueza en el hogar: el caso de México. In H. W. Vélez-Grajales, *México, ¿el motor inmóvil?* (pp. 299–346). CEEY Centro de Estudios Espinosa Yglesias, A.C.

Beisland, L. A., D'Espallier, B., & Mersland, R. (2019). The commercialization of the microfinance industry: Is there a "personal mission drift" among credit officers? *Journal of Business Ethics, 158*(1), 119–134.

Bundervoet, T., Dávalos, M. E., & Garcia, N. (2022). The short-term impacts of COVID-19 on households in developing countries: An overview based on a harmonized dataset of high-frequency surveys. *World Development, 153*, 105844.

Comisión Nacional Bancaria y de Valores. (2021). *Panorama anual de inclusión financiera.*

Copestake, J. (2007). Mainstreaming microfinance: Social performance management or mission drift? *World development, 35*(10), 1721–1738.

Corak, M. (2013). Income inequality, equality of opportunity, and intergenerational mobility. *Journal of Economic Perspectives, 27*(3), 79–102.

Cotler, P., & Rodríguez-Oreggia, E. (2010). Microfinanzas y la tenencia de activos no financieros en México. *Investigación económica, 69*(274), 63–86.

Cull, R., Demirgüc¸-Kunt, A., & Morduch, J. (2009). Microfinance meets the market. *Journal of Economic Perspectives, 23*(1), 167–192.

Delajara, M., De la Torre, R., & Díaz-Infante, E. (2018). *El México del 2018: Movilidad social para el bienestar.* Centro de Estudios Espinosa Yglesias.

DelaTorre-Diaz, L., & Rivas-Aceves, S. (2022). *Impact of health-care and social-protection related assets on the quintile distribution of mexican households between 2016 and 2020* (Working Paper).

DelaTorre-Diaz, L., & Rodriguez-Aguilar, R. (2021). An Asset Index proposal for households in Mexico applying the Mixed Principal Components Analysis methodology. In *International Conference on Computer Science and Health Engineering* (pp. 88–106). Springer Nature Switzerland.

Edin, K. (2005). More than money: The role of assets in the survival strategies and material well-being of the poor. In T. A. Shapiro & E. N. Wolff, *Assets for the poor* (pp. 206–231). Russell Sage Foundation.

Ferdous, A., Begum, S., & Akter, J. (2020). Microcredit in Bangladesh: Impact on borrowers' social mobility revisited. *Open Journal of Social Sciences, 8*, 163–180.

Filmer, D., & Pritchett, L. (1998). *The effect of household wealth on educational attainment: Demographic and health survey evidence.* The World Bank

Gentera, SAB de CV. (2022). *Informe anual y de sostenibilidad 2021*. Ciudad de México.

Grawe, N. (2008). Wealth and economic mobiltiy. *Economic mobility project: An initiative of the pew charitable trusts*.

Harttgen, K., & Vollmer, S. (2013). Using an asset index to simulate household income. *Economics Letters, 121*, 257–262.

Instituo Nacional de Estadística y Geografía (INEGI). (2020, 11). *INEGI*. Retrieved from Banco de Indicadores: https://inegi.org.mx/app/buscador/default.html?q=gini#tabMCcollapse-Indicadores

Khan, A., Hafeez Siddiqui, S., Saeed, S., & Azam, A. (2019). Impact of microfinance on social mobility and women empowerment: The case of South Punjab. *Review of Economics and Development Studies, 5*(4), 685–694.

López, P. (2020). *Políticas públicas para la inclusión financiera de las mujeres*. Centro de Estudios Espinosa Yglesias, A.C.

Minzer, R. (2009). *La industria microfinanciera en el Istmo Centroamericano y México: la evolución del mercado microcrediticio, el alcance y el desempeño de sus instituciones microfinancieras*. CEPAL.

Nambiar, S. (2013). Capabilities, conversion factors and institutions. *Progress in Development Studies, 13*(3), 221–230.

Nayaran, A., Van der Weide, R., Cojocaru, A., Lakner, C., Redaelli, S., Gerszon Mahler, D., Ramasubbaiah, R., & Thewissen, S. H. (2018). *Fair progress?: Economic mobility across generations around the world*. World Bank Publications.

OCDE. (2018). *A broken social elevator? How to promote social mobility*. OECD Publishing.

Orozco-Corona, M. E., Espinosa-Montiel, R., Fonseca-Godínez, C., & Vélez-Grajales, R. (2019). *Informe Movilidad Social En México 2019: Hacia La Igualdad Regional de Oportunidades*. Centro de Estudios Espinosa Yglesias.

Peprah, J. A., & Koomson, I. (2014). *Addiction to microcredit: An obstacle to social and financial mobility* (MPRA Paper No. 57894).

Poirier, M. J., Grépin, K. A., & Grignon, M. (2020). Approaches and alternatives to the wealth index to measure socioeconomic status using survey data: A critical interpretive synthesis. *Social Indicators Research, 148*(1), 1–46.

Programa Nacional de Financiamiento al Microempresario y a la Mujer Rural. (2018). *Acciones y resultados PRONAFIM*. México.

Reed, L. R. (2011). *State of the Microcredit Summit Campaign Report 2011*. Microcredit Summit Campaign.

Robinson, M. S. (2001). *The microfinance revolution: Sustainable finance for the poor*. The World Bank.

Roche, J. M. (2013). Estratificación social en Venezuela: revelando la estructura latente a la desigualdad en "capacidades". In M. Parra de Niño & V. Zubillaga, *Hacer sociología en Venezuela juntos con Alberto Gruson*. Universidad Católica Andrés Bello.
Sahn, D. E., & Stifel, D. C. (2000). Poverty comparisons over time and across countries in Africa. *World Development, 28*(12), 2123–2155.
Sahn, D. E., & Stifel, D. C. (2003). Exploring alternative measures of welfare in the absence of expenditure data. *Review of Income and Wealth*, *49*(4), 463–489. https://doi.org/10.1111/j.0034-6586.2003.00100.x
Salia, P. J. (2014). The effect of microcredit on the household welfare (Empirical evidences from women micro-entrepreneurs in Tanzania). *International Journal of Academic Research in Business and Social Sciences, 4*, 5.
Secretaría de Salud. (2022). *Informe Técnico Diario COVID-19 MÉXICO.* Ciudad de México.
Sen, A. (1985a). *Commodities and capabilities*. North Holland.
Sen, A. (1985b). Well-being, agency and freedom: The Dewey lectures1984. *The Journal of Philosophy, 82*(4), 169–221.
Solís, P. (2018). *Barreras estructurales a la movilidad social intergeneracional en México*. CEPAL.
Torche, F. (2010). Cambio y persistencia de la movilidad intergeneracional en México. In J. Serrano Espinosa & F. Torche, *Movilidad social en México, Población, desarrollo y crecimiento*(pp. 71–134). Centro de Estudio Espinosa Yglesias, A.C.
Torche, F. (2020). *Changes in intergenerational mobility in Mexico: A cohort analysis*. Centro de Estudios Espinosa Yglesias Documento de trabajo.
United Nations Development Programme. (2019). *Beyond income, beyond averages, beyond today: Inequalities in human development in the 21st century*. UNDP.
Vélez-Grajales, R., Campos-Vázquez, R., & Fonseca, C. E. (2015a). *El concepto de movilidad social: dimensiones, medidas y estudios en México*. Documento de trabajo.
Vélez-Grajales, R., Stabridis Arana, O., & Minor Campa, E. (2018). Still looking for the land of opportunity: Regional differences in social mobility in Mexico. *Sobre México. Temas de Economía, 1*, 54–69.
Vélez-Grajales, R., Vélez-Grajales, V., & Stabridis, O. (2015b). *Construcción de un índice de riqueza intergeneracional a partir de la encuesta ESRU de movilidad social en México*. Retrieved from Centro de Estudios Espinosa Yglesias: http://www.ceey.org.mx/sites/default/files/adjuntos/dt-002-2015_si.pdf
Wolff, E. N. (2005). Recent trends in wealth ownership, 1983–1998. In T. Shapiro & E. Wolff, *Assets for the poor* (pp. 34–73). Russell Sage Foundation.
World Economic Forum. (2020). *The global social mobility report 2020*. Suiza.

Yang, X., & Zhou, P. (2022). *Wealth inequality and social mobility: A simulation-based modelling approach* (Cardiff Economics Working Papers E2022/3). Cardiff University, Cardiff Business School, Economics Section.

Yunus, M. (2007). *Banker to the poor: Micro-lending and the battle against world poverty*. PublicAffairs.

Zeller, M., & Meyer, R. L. (2002). *The triangle of microfinance: Financial sustainability, outreach, and impact*. International Food Policy Research Institute.

CHAPTER 9

Leveraging Strategic Planning to Navigate Volatile Environments

Enrique Murillo and Connie Atristain-Suárez

Introduction

Strategic Planning is arguably the most critical means of fostering the success of an organization and the achievement of its vision, mission, and strategic objectives (Achampong, 2010). Strategic Planning should be understood as a process of preparing business decisions and the means to carry them out (Butuner, 2016; Mintzberg, 1994). Planning within an organization must have marketing, financial, and human resource strategies, among others, with a long-term duration that directs the scope of the companies' activities to obtain advantages over competitors, considering the change in the corporate environment, and fully respecting the values of the organization and the expectations of stakeholders (Johnson et al., 2011).

E. Murillo (✉) · C. Atristain-Suárez
Facultad de Ciencias Económicas y Empresariales, Universidad Panamericana, Mexico City, Mexico
e-mail: emurillo@up.edu.mx

C. Atristain-Suárez
e-mail: connie.atristain@up.edu.mx

E. Murillo et al. (eds.), *Creating Economic Stability Amid Global Uncertainty*, https://doi.org/10.1007/978-3-031-41386-5_9

Within the overall strategic plan of an organization, the marketing function plays a key role. Marketing is tasked with knowing and understanding "the customer so well that the product or service fits him and sells itself" (Drucker, 1976, p. 65). Marketing functional strategies consist of both adapting marketing elements to the needs and characteristics of the market, and centralizing strategic decisions to maintain overall coherence (Cantoni et al., 2019). Among those marketing elements, the brand plays an essential role in the relationship with customers and is, therefore, one of the strategic decisions that must be included in all planning. The emotional connection of the customer to the brand greatly facilitates the sale of branded products and services (Grisaffe & Nguyen, 2011). In the aftermath of the COVID-19 pandemic, and facing unprecedented economic and societal uncertainty, the brand can be used as a tool to signal to customers and other stakeholders how the organization will continue to create value and deliver on its promises (Wilson & Elliot, 2016).

The main objective of this chapter is to illustrate how Strategic Planning can function as a versatile lever that can help organizations trying to navigate the volatile market environment brought about by the pandemic. As of this writing, the events of 2022, including the war in Ukraine, accelerating inflation from supply chain disruptions and food shortages, and the rapid global spread of the Omicron BA.5 variant have only added to the volatility. Accordingly, the chapter examines the process of Strategic Planning at a higher education institution (HEI). Given that the higher education industry was one of the most affected by the Great Confinement, it provides a strong example of the utility of Strategic Planning in periods of high volatility. Specifically, the research question guiding this study is: How does the implementation of functional strategies influence the strategic planning process of HEIs, while facing a rapidly changing environment? Beyond showing the positive impact of the deployed marketing tools, the chapter aims to provide a better understanding of the integration of marketing strategies within the general Strategic Planning of an organization, and of the cyclical nature of the planning process.

Since their origins, HEIs have proven to be the most important venues for the intellectual, economic, cultural, and social life of a country (Castells, 2001). They are counted among the oldest institutions in the world (Sanz & Bergan, 2007), and are considered pillars in economic, social, and cultural development, locally, regionally, and in the world in general (Castells, 2001; Kwiek, 2003; Newman & Couturier, 2001; Sadlak, 2000). They contribute to scientific and technological advances and to the specialization of human resources (Castells, 2001).

A modern HEI assumes, in addition to the traditional functions of education and research, the function of analyzing the services it offers, since, through these, it contributes to the social and economic development of a country or a region (Albulescu & Albulescu, 2014). In recent years, HEIs around the world have faced drastic changes, moving from stability to uncertainty, with rapid technological advances, changes in demand and the obsolescence of academic programs. Therefore, many HEIs have adopted Strategic Planning as a means to make beneficial strategic changes, meet these daunting challenges, and ensure their sustainability (Bosire & Amimo, 2017; Hassanien, 2017).

The higher education industry faced an unprecedented emergency in the Spring of 2020 when the World Health Organization declared COVID-19 a pandemic and governments around the world decreed campus closures to limit the spread of the disease (Morganti et al., 2021). What looked initially like a transitory emergency compromise (Abel Jr, 2020; Kulikowski et al., 2021) eventually morphed into a long period of online instruction (Stracke et al., 2022), disrupting a $600 billion global industry (Hechinger & Lorin, 2020). The experience of confinement led many to question established higher education practices, such as the requirement of in-person instruction or the high cost of a residential four-year degree (Dennis, 2021; Galloway, 2020).

However, the pandemic has also presented an opportunity for HEIs to rethink their strategies and teaching schemes (Ashour et al., 2021; Jandrić et al., 2020; Peters et al., 2020). Academic Management and Strategic Planning have thus become relevant for HEIs, due to the urgent need to achieve quality, identity, sustainability, and resilience within a competitive context in which both public and private universities have developed (Inga et al., 2021). To this point, Watson (2005) has warned about the need to understand and manage the strategic directions and decisions of HEIs from a new institutional perspective, which seeks to mobilize various social institutions, including the market, the community, and the state, to promote the well-being of people. There are domains of value that are particular to HEIs, such as "tell the truth", "be fair", and "respect others", that, in broader contexts, constitute the contributions of higher education to civil society in all its efforts (Watson, 2005). This is because the contributions of HEIs are an important part of a community's social construction, and define how people interact within society. They are determined by the cultures and values of that society, and provide order and stability within it. Hence, HEIs not only satisfy essential needs of society, but also help to build society itself.

This study examined the impact of two marketing strategies implemented by a large HEI, which reflect only part of the Strategic Planning adopted to respond effectively to the COVID-19 crisis. Specifically, the investigated HEI launched an updated corporate visual identity (CVI), and reinforced its commitment to fulfill its personalized education brand promise, notwithstanding the obstacle of operating for nearly two years with a closed campus. Using a student survey ($n = 288$), the study revealed a positive impact of these two marketing strategies on the mediating variables of brand image and student satisfaction, and on the outcome variables of university reputation and intention to recommend. These results contribute to the HEI management literature, specifically the recent focus on the effect of HEI brands on reputation. Furthermore, the study contributes to the Strategic Planning literature, which offers few examples of empirical measurement of the impact of strategic decisions and their intended benefits. In addition, the measurement of students' perceptions of brand promise delivery, and its positive effect on brand reputation and brand advocacy makes a contribution to the internal branding literature.

The chapter is organized as follows: section "Literature Review" provides a literature review of Strategic Planning and marketing strategy in the context of HEIs, with a detailed discussion of the marketing tools deployed by the investigated HEI, and a theoretical justification of the tested hypotheses. Section "Research Methodology" provides the background of the examined HEI, and the methodology used for data collection. Section "Model Estimation and Results" presents model estimation and results, and sections "Discussion" and "Limitations and Managerial Applications" provide the discussion, study limitations, and managerial applications.

Literature Review

Strategic Planning as a Cyclical Process

Strategic planning is a dynamic process that requires a high level of future-focused thinking on the part of those involved in the planning process. Among the keys to the success of strategic planning at the institutional level are, for example, the breadth and depth of the analysis involved; commitment of the institution's management to the plan; communication of the vision with the members of the institution; care with the development and implementation of the plan (Porter, 1980; Steiner, 1979).

For an organization to be more competitive, it must concentrate its efforts on improving its efficiency through the implementation of sound management practices, based on internal control, strategic planning, human resources, and organizational innovation (Atristain-Suárez, 2016). In addition, changes in the outside environment, and internal changes in the organization, require from planners a commitment to continual review, evaluation, and adjustment of the strategic plan (Bryson, 2016; Porter, 1980; Steiner, 1979). Thus, through recurring cycles of strategic planning, institutions of all types (public and private; for-profit and non-profit; small, medium, and large) define or refine their visions and missions, establish strategic goals and objectives, identify strategies to achieve them, and determine how they will measure the success of their efforts and implement improvements (Achampong, 2010).

The effectiveness of strategic planning poses many challenges for an HEI, since, as in any other type of organization, it occurs in a complex, dynamic, and real-world environment (Dooris et al., 2002). Furthermore, HEIs faced an unprecedented crisis when the COVID-19 pandemic led to campus closures in March 2020, and institutions migrated to online instruction practically overnight (Morganti et al., 2021; Rodriguez-Abitia, 2021). As weeks turned into months, with no prospect of reopening, and the economic crisis deepened, impacting students' ability to finance their studies, HEIs were forced to make significant changes to their pre-pandemic market assumptions and strategic plans (Galloway, 2020; Whatley & Castiello-Gutiérrez, 2021). In particular, as part of those revised strategic plans, new marketing strategies were required, for it was clear that the higher education market and competitive environment had changed (Dennis, 2021; Kelchen, 2022; Liu & Gao, 2022).

In any organization, the aim of the marketing strategy is to generate the profitable sale of goods and/or services in target markets in order to achieve company goals and be consistent with grand strategy and other functional plans (Butuner, 2016). Likewise, in the context of HEIs, marketing serves to contribute to a better understanding of the mostly intangible services the institution provides, defines the core value proposition, and creates a brand image and a memorable experience (Wilson & Elliot, 2016). One of the most efficient marketing tools in HEIs is the university brand and, nowadays, it has become a strategic imperative due to the growing competition in the market. Marketing strategy seeks to develop significantly differentiated brands with which to communicate their strengths with the aim of attracting, engaging, and retaining students, as well as positioning HEIs (Perera et al., 2022). However, the marketing strategy is but one part, albeit a critical one, of the broader strategic plan of the institution. This subordinate quality of marketing strategy to the overall HEI strategic plan is reflected in Fig. 9.1, which presents a model for the scope of this research.

The model highlights two important characteristics of the Strategic Planning process: First, it coherently integrates strategic plans from multiple functional areas (Finance, Operations, HR, Marketing, etc.). Second, it is a cyclical process open to continuous reviews, evaluations, and adjustments, after the strategies have been implemented and the objectives achieved, thus allowing organizations to strategically plan and measure their performance (Atristain-Suárez, 2016). In Fig. 9.1, the thin arrows represent this cyclical dynamic. By contrast, the thick arrows connect the findings of the present empirical study, focused on the impact of discrete marketing strategies, and the subsequent cycles of Strategic Marketing Planning, which will have the advantage of validated or revised assumptions.

Marketing Strategy Responses to the Pandemic

In the Fall of 2021, as COVID-19 vaccination campaigns reached the young adult demographic, and HEIs prepared to reopen their campuses, they realized they faced a changed education market and competitive environment (Dennis, 2021; Kelchen, 2022; Liu & Gao, 2022). This required a thorough revision of their strategic plans, with special attention to the marketing strategy. One of the most important resources that organizations are deploying during the post-COVID-19 stage is their corporate

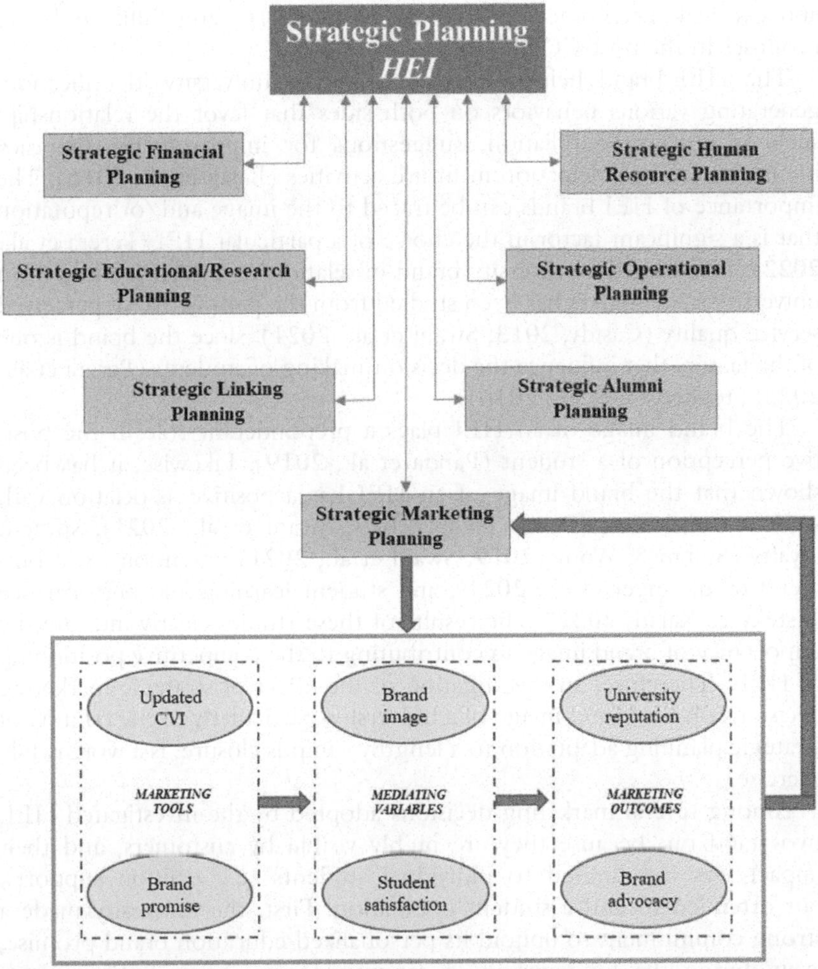

Fig. 9.1 Strategic planning process and the scope of this research (*Source* Authors' elaboration)

brand. Brands are powerful marketing tools that can convey meaningful messages to both company employees and target consumers. In charting a course to transition to the new normal, the brand can be used to signal how the organization will continue to create value for internal and external stakeholders (Wilson & Elliot, 2016) and fulfill its brand promises in the post-COVID-19 era.

The HEI brand helps to create a student-university identification, generating various behaviors on both sides that favor the relationship, such as university affiliation, suggestions for improvement, advocacy intentions, and participation in future activities (Balaji et al., 2016). The importance of HEI brands can be traced to the image and/or reputation that is a significant factor in the choice of a particular HEI (Perera et al., 2022). Likewise, the university brand in relation to students as the main university stakeholders has been studied from the perspective of perceived service quality (Casidy, 2013; Swani et al., 2021), since the brand is one of the factors that influence the decision-making of students (Perera et al., 2022; Stephenson et al., 2016).

The brand image of an HEI plays a preponderant role in the positive perception of a student (Panda et al., 2019). Likewise, it has been shown that the brand image of an HEI has a positive association with student satisfaction (Panda et al., 2019; Swani et al., 2021), student loyalty (Sultan & Wong, 2019; Swani et al., 2021), intention to recommend (Schlesinger et al., 2021), and student learning and performance (Esteky & Kalati, 2021). The results of these studies clearly indicate the importance of brand image in contributing to the competitive positioning of HEIs. Therefore, an investigation of the effect of strategic marketing decisions on the brand image of a university, particularly in the context of strategic planning adaptation to a lengthy campus closure, is a worthwhile exercise.

Among several marketing decisions adopted by the investigated HEI, two stand out because they are highly visible by customers, and their impact was not limited to individual students (e.g. tuition support), but extended to entire student population. First, the university made a strong commitment to uphold its personalized education brand promise, even during the long period of campus closure. Second, the university launched an updated CVI and brand logo (Müller et al., 2013). The following sections describe each marketing decision, and provide theoretical background.

Brand Promise Delivery Marketing Strategy

The proposition that brands, and particularly service brands, make explicit or implicit brand promises to customers, and that fulfillment of those promises, especially during service encounters, enhances customers' favorable evaluations and loyalty to the brand has been advanced by several marketing theorists (e.g. Brodie et al., 2009; Grönroos, 2016; Sirianni et al., 2013). More specifically, the issue of brand promise delivery has been a focal concern of the internal branding literature, which has systematically examined the antecedents of service employees' brand attitudes and the marketing outcomes that follow from employees' brand supportive behavior (King & Murillo, 2022; King et al., 2013; Terglav et al., 2016). Furthermore, the strategic impacts of brand promise delivery have been researched in various types of service organizations, including restaurants (Murillo, 2019), hotels (Terglav et al., 2016; Xiong, 2023), airlines (Erkmen & Hancer, 2015; Murillo, 2022), banks (Garas et al., 2018), ridesharing services (Murillo & Terán-Bustamante, 2020), retail commerce (Du Preez et al., 2017; Murillo, 2020), and universities (Clark et al., 2020).

In the context of higher education, a modern university brand comprises a wide set of promises for the market it serves (Pringle & Fritz, 2019). These promises include, first, the reputation of the HEI, employability and possibilities for professional development, as well as socialization during the period of study. Second, they represent a set of distinctive characteristics that create the brand of an HEI, such as its position in the higher education market and its scientific and educational orientation. Finally, the HEI brand maintains efficient external communication through its name, logo, and slogan (Bennett & Ali-Choudhury, 2009).

Given the strategic importance of brand promise delivery in HEIs, the investigated university was particularly challenged by the campus closure brought upon by the pandemic, because personal attention is understood and conceived as an important element of the brand promise of the institution among academics, administrators, and students. As a consequence, the lengthy period of confinement and online instruction constituted an unprecedented stress test of brand promise fulfillment. As part of their strategic plan to adapt to the changed environment, the university authorities made a strategic decision from the start of the pandemic to uphold the brand promise, by repeatedly stressing to academics and administrators to remain in close contact with students through electronic means during the period of campus closure. This emphasis of brand promise delivery is an important tool in the new marketing strategy, and furthermore, a highly visible one that customers can evaluate.

Accordingly, the current study measured student perceptions of brand promise delivery, and their impact on other brand-related variables. To operationalize brand promise delivery, the Empathy dimension of the SERVQUAL instrument was deemed appropriate given its original intent to measure caring and individualized attention the firm provides to its customers (Parasuraman et al., 1988).

Updated Corporate Visual Identity (CVI) Marketing Strategy
Corporate rebranding is defined as "a change of a corporate brand's attributes such as its name, logo, color and values, singularly or in combination" (Joseph et al., 2021, p. 710). One frequent type of rebranding, commonly undertaken to revitalize aging brands, is updating the CVI, usually by adopting a new brand logo (Müller et al., 2013). Logo update is implemented from time to time at most companies in order to maintain a fresh, modern look (Henderson & Cote, 1998). Universities are no strangers to this strategy, as they operate in an increasingly crowded industry where they need to effectively differentiate their offerings from those of competitors.

A recent review of the logo literature (Kim & Lim, 2019) shows that research on university CVI is relatively sparse compared to research on commercial company logos. Using a survey among undergraduate students, Watkins and Gonzenbach (2013) found that academic logos were mostly associated with the competence brand personality dimension, while athletic logos were mostly associated with excitement. Idris and Whitfield (2014) used an experimental design to evaluate ads showing male and female lecturers with traditional/modern HEI logos; their conclusion is that a traditional logo is positively associated with HEI reputation but only in the case of the male lecturer. The study is limited by a lack of theory to justify this result, and the fact that respondents evaluated lecturers rather than the HEI itself. The study by Japutra et al. (2016) focused on the construct of brand logo benefit, i.e. the value the consumer associates with the brand logo. This value comprises benefits along three dimensions including functional, aesthetic, and self-expressive. The study used a survey of 478 undergraduate students and found a significant positive relationship between brand logo benefit and brand commitment.

Although studies of the positive impacts of the university brand are not lacking (e.g. Esteky & Kalati, 2021; Panda et al., 2019; Sultan & Wong, 2019), similar studies for the effect of HEI logos are less common. Given the strategic importance of the brand in an HEI, a rejuvenation of the visual identity is considered an important marketing tool (Müller et al., 2013).

At the investigated HEI, the need for an updated visual identity was detected years before the pandemic, and a high-end brand consultancy was commissioned to develop a modern brand architecture for the university and its various programs. The project was finished after the onset of the pandemic, in late 2020, and university authorities felt that the launch of the new visual identity would be a useful marketing strategy to support the resumption of campus activities. Hence, the public unveiling took place in August 2021, followed by a gradual rollout in the following months, thus signaling the importance attributed to the rebranding in the "back-to-campus" strategic plan.

Accordingly, the new brand logo was used as a proxy of the updated CVI, and the current study measured student evaluations of the logo and its impact on other brand-related variables. The following section presents the justification for the hypotheses tested in this research.

Hypotheses Justification

Studies from the internal branding literature have shown that when service employees successfully deliver the brand promise, customers' brand evaluations and their satisfaction with the service encounter are enhanced (Erkmen & Hancer, 2015; Sirianni et al., 2013). Therefore, two hypotheses capture these relationships:

H1 There is a positive impact of brand promise delivery on brand image.

H2 There is a positive impact of brand promise delivery on student satisfaction.

Moreover, studies from the services literature report a positive impact of brand image on customer satisfaction (Dam & Dam, 2021; Hosseini & Behboudi, 2017). Within the context of HEIs, recent studies have reported a positive relationship between brand image and student satisfaction (Panda et al., 2019; Schlesinger et al., 2021). Accordingly, the following hypothesis is advanced:

H3 There is a positive impact of brand image on student satisfaction.

Also within the context of HEIs, recent studies have documented a positive relationship between university brand image and university reputation (Kaushal et al., 2021; Panda et al., 2019). Brand image has also been associated with intention to recommend, or brand advocacy (Chen, 2016; Schlesinger et al., 2021; Sultan & Wong, 2019). On the basis of these studies, the following hypotheses are proposed:

H_{4a} There is a positive impact of brand image on university reputation.

H_{4b} There is a positive impact of brand image on brand advocacy.

In the HEI context, recent studies have reported a positive relationship between student satisfaction and university reputation (Kaushal et al., 2021; Moslehpour et al., 2020). Other studies have found a similar positive relationship between student satisfaction and brand advocacy (Abdelmaaboud et al., 2021; Casidy & Wymer, 2015). Accordingly, the following hypotheses are advanced:

H_{5a} There is a positive impact of student satisfaction on university reputation.

H_{5b} There is a positive impact of student satisfaction on brand advocacy.

Lastly, the study posits a positive relationship between brand promise delivery and evaluations of the brand image (H_1). This relationship is expected to be contingent on student evaluations of the updated CVI of the university. In other words, it is proposed that there is a positive interaction between brand promise delivery and the updated brand logo, such that they act as complements, rather than substitutes, in their combined impact on brand image. The hypothesized positive sign of the moderation effect reflects the positive impact on brand image that is expected from each of these marketing tools. Formally, this translates into the following hypothesis:

H_6 The updated CVI positively moderates the relationship between brand promise delivery and brand image, such that favorable evaluations of the new CVI strengthen this relationship.

Research Methodology

The research took place in January of 2022, which in Mexico City coincided with the peak of the Omicron BA.1 wave. The investigated HEI had planned to return to in-person instruction from the start of the

Spring term, but decided to postpone this and start the semester with online classes. Thus, data collection for this research had to rely on a non-probabilistic sample of students attending online classes, similar to many other survey-based studies undertaken since the beginning of the pandemic (e.g. Alzoubi et al., 2020; Morganti et al., 2021). Furthermore, currently enrolled undergraduate students were deemed valid informants for the substantive constructs considered in the hypothesized models.

Accordingly, a survey instrument was designed, using previously published scales, to measure student perceptions of the two marketing tools described above. The support of marketing instructors from the school of business studies was obtained, and the first author visited their online classes through the Zoom platform, explained the research to students, and shared the link to the survey, which was hosted on a professional survey platform (Alchemer.com). The instructors encouraged all attending students to participate, and controlled survey completion by asking for raised hands after finishing, thus ensuring a response rate of nearly 100%. Thirteen different sections were visited in this fashion, spanning from first to last year courses in the five-year programs. A total of 289 surveys were collected, with just one survey discarded due to missing answers. Hence, the valid sample size is 288.

Measurement Scales

To measure student evaluations of the new brand logo, a seven-point semantic differential scale with five dimensions (bad/good, uninteresting/interesting, not distinctive/distinctive, low quality/high quality, dislike/like) was used. This measure was developed by Henderson and Cote (1998), and has been used in other studies of brand logo impacts (e.g. Harmon-Kizer, 2019). The remaining measures used a seven-point Likert scale with "Strongly disagree" and "Strongly agree" as the anchor points (scales are provided in the Appendix). Brand promise delivery was measured with the four-item scale for Empathy in the HEI context, adapted from the studies by Tsiligiris et al. (2021) and Mageto et al. (2020). Brand image was measured with the four-item scale used by Schlesinger et al. (2021). Student satisfaction was measured with three items from the scale used by Abdelmaaboud et al. (2021). University reputation was measured with four items from the scale by Swani et al. (2021). Finally, brand advocacy was measured with the three-item scale for positive word-of-mouth by Schlesinger et al. (2021).

Data Analysis

Sample demographic descriptives, shown in Table 9.1, are consistent with the undergraduate school of business age and gender profile. Older students and students with more than five years of tenure in the university typically changed to a business major from another school and had to start from year one.

Because survey data was collected with a single instrument and self-report measures, common method bias was assessed using the Harman test. To this end, an exploratory factor analysis of the six scales was calculated in SPSS, with principal axis factor extraction restricted to a single factor and a non-rotated solution. The single factor explained 38.8% of the covariance of the items, indicating common method bias is not a concern in this sample.

Table 9.1 Descriptive statistics of the sample

	Number	*Percentage*
Age		
18	27	9.4%
19	61	21.2%
20	62	21.5%
21	49	17.0%
22	55	19.1%
23	19	6.6%
24	8	2.8%
25	3	1.0%
26	2	0.7%
Missing	2	0.7%
Total	288	100%
Gender		
Female	164	56.9%
Male	123	42.7%
Missing	1	0.3%
Total	288	100%
Tenure in years		
1	93	32.3%
2	76	26.4%
3	38	13.2%
4	69	24.0%
5	9	3.1%
6	3	1.0%
Total	288	100%

To estimate the hypothesized mediation and moderation models, the PROCESS macro version 3.5 for SPSS (Hayes, 2018) was used. This requires averaged or summated scales, unlike structural equation models which use latent variables (Hayes et al., 2017). However, good research practice requires that prior to averaging multi-item scales, reliability, convergent validity, and discriminant validity should be assessed through confirmatory factor analysis (del Barrio-García & Prados-Peña, 2019). This was estimated using Mplus version 8.3; results are shown in Table 9.2.

The model displayed good fit, with 0.95 CFI, 0.050 RMSEA, and 0.051 SRMR (Bagozzi & Yi, 2012). Practically, all the indicator loadings exceeded the recommended threshold of 0.70. The Cronbach alpha and composite reliabilities of the scales, as well as the average variance extracted (AVE) all exceeded the recommended thresholds of 0.8 and 0.5 respectively (Martínez-López et al., 2013), which indicates adequate scale reliability and convergent validity. Furthermore, the correlation between the latent variables (not shown) was below the square root of the respective AVE's, complying with the Fornell-Larcker criterion, which indicates adequate discriminant validity (Martínez-López et al., 2013).

Model Estimation and Results

Having thus confirmed scale reliability and validity, the items for the scales were averaged to obtain observed variables as required by PROCESS. Because this macro only accepts one dependent variable at a time, two identical models were estimated with university reputation (Fig. 9.2a) and brand advocacy (Fig. 9.2b) as outcomes and using the Model 83 template within PROCESS (Hayes, 2018). The results of the moderated mediation regressions for the two models are displayed in the four panels of Table 9.3.

At first sight, the results for the BRIMG regression, on the first panel, would seem to indicate a lack of support for H_1, as the coefficient of BRPROM is not statistically significant. However, because the regression includes an interaction term, the impact of BRPROM on BRIMG depends on the value of the moderator CVI. Thus, the slope of the linear function between BRPROM and BRIMG, conditional on a value for the moderator CVI, is given by the formula (Hayes, 2018, p. 227):

$$\Theta_{X \to Y} = b_1 + b_3 W = 0.0496 + 0.0649 \times \text{CVI}.$$

Table 9.2 Standardized factor loadings for the measurement model

Indicator	*Loading*
CVI (Alpha = 0.920, CR = 0.919, AVE = 0.704)	
CVI1	0.911
CVI2	0.859
CVI3	0.716
CVI4	0.780
CVI5	0.913
EMPATH (Alpha = 0.812, CR = 0.819, AVE = 0.528)	
EMP1	0.628
EMP2	0.769
EMP3	0.799
EMP4	0.699
REPUT (Alpha = 0.841, CR = 0.851, AVE = 0.588)	
REP1	0.797
REP2	0.704
REP3	0.755
REP4	0.807
SATISF (Alpha = 0.812, CR = 0.807, AVE = 0.591)	
SAT1	0.703
SAT2	0.792
SAT3	0.807
BRIMG (Alpha = 0.829, CR = 0.824, AVE = 0.555)	
BRIM1	0.758
BRIM2	0.712
BRIM3	0.666
BRIM4	0.833
BRADVOC (Alpha = 0.906, CR = 0.911, AVE = 0.768)	
BRAD1	0.888
BRAD2	0.844
BRAD3	0.896

Note Model Fit: χ^2(df = 215) = 370.543, p = 0.000, CFI = 0.950, RMSEA = 0.050, SRMR = 0.051

At most sample values of the moderator, these slopes are in fact statistically significant, which can be more easily visualized using the plotting function of PROCESS as shown in Fig. 9.3. The graph shows that for representative values of the CVI moderator (the PROCESS defaults of 16th, 50th, and 84th percentiles), the different slopes between BRPROM and BRIMG are all positive and statistically significant ($p < 0.01$). Furthermore, these slopes become steeper as CVI increases. Therefore, regression results reveal a significant positive relationship between BRPROM and

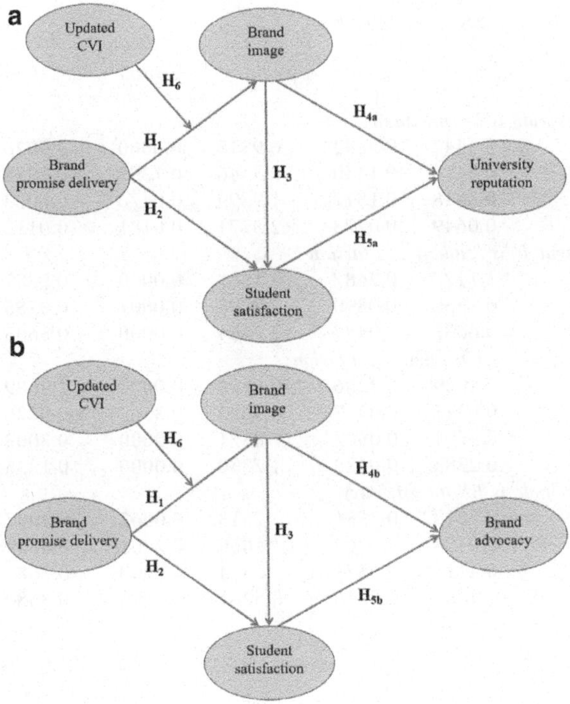

Fig. 9.2 **a** Hypothesized model with University reputation as outcome. **b** Hypothesized model with Brand advocacy as outcome

BRIMG, which supports H_1, and how the strength (slope) of this relationship increases when CVI increases, which supports H_6.

The results for the Student satisfaction regression are more straightforward: the estimated coefficients of BRPROM and BRIMG are both positive and statistically significant, which provides support for H_2 and H_3.

For the outcome variable of University reputation, the results of the regression reveal that the direct path between BRPROM and REPUT is not significant ($p = 0.3362$), but the paths between BRIMG and SATISF and REPUT are both positive and statistically significant, which provides support for H_{4a} and H_{5a}. The substantive interpretation is that the effect

Table 9.3 PROCESS models output

Effect	*Coeff.*	*SE*	t-*value*	p-*value*	*95% Conf.*	*Interval*
Dependent variable is Brand image						
Constant	5.4442	0.7832	6.9515	0.0000	3.9026	6.9857
BRPROM	0.0496	0.1440	0.3446	0.7307	−0.2338	0.3330
CVI	−0.3018	0.1517	−1.9899	0.0476	−0.6003	−0.0033
BRPROMxCVI	0.0649	0.0273	2.3771	0.0181	0.0112	0.1186
Dependent variable is Student satisfaction						
Constant	1.1177	0.2687	4.1588	0.0000	0.5887	1.6467
BRPROM	0.1552	0.0390	3.9798	0.0001	0.0785	0.2320
BRIMG	0.6635	0.0483	13.7464	0.0000	0.5685	0.7586
Dependent variable is University reputation						
Constant	2.4029	0.2256	10.6526	0.0000	1.9589	2.8470
BRPROM	0.0315	0.0327	0.9633	0.3362	−0.0328	0.0958
BRIMG	0.4001	0.0507	7.8871	0.0000	0.3003	0.5000
SATISF	0.2285	0.0483	4.7330	0.0000	0.1335	0.3235
Dependent variable is Brand advocacy						
Constant	0.7018	0.2551	2.7513	0.0063	0.1997	1.2039
BRPROM	0.0408	0.0369	1.1050	0.2701	−0.0319	0.1135
BRIMG	0.4217	0.0574	7.3514	0.0000	0.3088	0.5347
SATISF	0.4655	0.0546	8.5261	0.0000	0.3580	0.5729

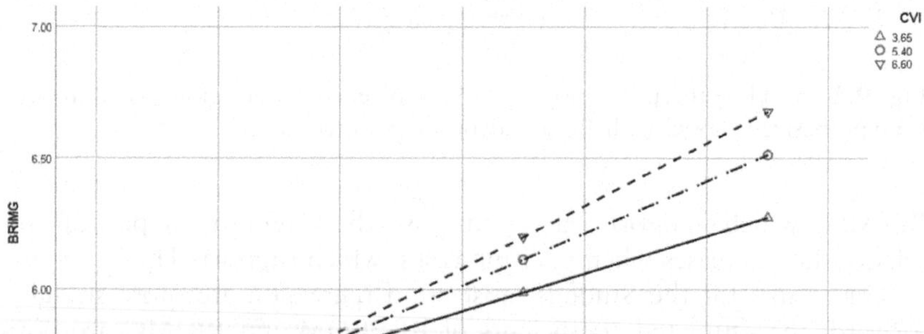

Fig. 9.3 Effect (slope) of BRPROM on BRIMG moderated by CVI

of Brand promise delivery on University reputation is statistically significant and fully mediated by Brand image and Student satisfaction, with 53% of the variance of University reputation explained. In addition, the Change in the visual image moderates the effect of Brand promise on the Brand image.

Finally, the results of the identical model with Brand advocacy as the outcome variable again yield no significant direct path between BRPROM and BRADV but a significant fully mediated impact through the coefficients of BRIMG and SATISF, both strongly significant. The R^2 of the regression is 0.637, indicating that 64% of the variance of Brand advocacy is explained by the model. Therefore, both H_{4b} and H_{5b} are supported.

In summary, model results show statistical support for all the hypothesized relationships.

Discussion

This research highlights the importance of strategic marketing planning in the academic field, as one part of the strategic planning process of the HEI. Through this deliberate process, the HEI can assess its current state and the possible future condition of its environment, identify possible future states, and develop strategies, policies, and organized procedures to select and arrive at one or more of them. Strategic decisions in HEIs not only have an impact on their historical image and prosperity, but also make a vital contribution to society and the economy of countries (Watson, 2005).

The study set out to empirically investigate the impact of strategic marketing decisions implemented by a private HEI in Mexico City as one of the dimensions of its revised strategic plan in the post-pandemic period. The study measured student perceptions of the two deployed marketing tools and their impact on mediating marketing variables, and from there to the two important outcomes of brand reputation and brand advocacy. The results show significant positive effects of these marketing strategies on the outcome variables, which provide empirical validation to the decisions adopted within the strategic planning in the critical marketing dimension. In this regard, the study makes a contribution to the Strategic Planning literature, which provides very few instances of empirical measurement of the impact of decisions and their intended benefits (e.g. Hu et al., 2018; Tapinos et al., 2005).

The present study also makes an incremental contribution to the HEI management and marketing literature, specifically the nascent research stream that examines the effects of HEI brands on university reputation (e.g. Kaushal et al., 2021; Moslehpour et al., 2020; Panda et al., 2019). In particular, the moderating effect of HEI brand logo evaluation on the relationship between brand promise delivery and brand image has not been examined before within this literature.

The study also contributes to the literature on internal branding which has been characterized by a permanent interest on the topic of brand promise delivery (e.g. Clark et al., 2020; King et al., 2013; Terglav et al., 2016) and the essential role played by employees in making this possible. More specifically, the measurement of customer (i.e. students) perceptions of brand promise delivery by university employees, and the positive impact this has on the important outcomes of brand reputation and brand advocacy have not been examined before within internal branding research.

Limitations and Managerial Applications

It may be rightly pointed out that the study only examines the impact of marketing decisions, without considering the systemic effects of these changes, or indeed of other strategic tools that the investigated HEI deployed in response to the COVID-19 crisis, such as operational strategies (e.g. the launching and management of technological platforms to provide online instruction), human resource management strategies (e.g. the monitoring and support of employee health and welfare during the confinement), and financial strategies (e.g. the budgetary rationalization to overcome the tuition shortfall). This exclusive focus on the marketing strategies, and only two of the available marketing tools, is indeed a limitation of the study, as advanced in the model for the scope of this research (Fig. 9.1). However, the model hints at future research opportunities, given the lack of empirical studies of the effects of functional strategic decisions adopted after the advent of disruptive environmental change, a topic of clear relevance at this historical moment.

The measurable positive impact of the emphasis on brand promise delivery and the updated CVI provide empirical validation to HEI planners with respect to the marketing dimension of the plan, at least within the current planning cycle. Because of high environmental volatility, planners need to continually review, evaluate, and adjust the strategic plan. For instance, the recovery stage after the most serious days of the pandemic has now been marred by the unexpected war between Russia and Ukraine, and its worldwide economic impact. Therefore, the possibility of running limited-scope empirical studies to evaluate the impact of strategic planning decisions can generate relevant and timely feedback to planners to improve the next cycle of planning.

The results of this study have limited generalizability because the sample comes from a single organization, and moreover from the specific sector of HEIs. However, the model for the scope of this study (Fig. 9.1), while specific to the HEI industry, is broadly similar to that used at other large organizations. Accordingly, the research approach used in this study serves to illustrate a flexible evidence-based exercise of validating strategy assumptions, and expected functional impacts, that are usually taken for granted in each strategic planning cycle. The research approach of hypothesis testing can be extended to other dimensions of the strategic plan (Operations, Human Resources, Finance, etc.), provided sound theory is used in each case and is applied to the actual strategic tools deployed in each case. For a research-based HEI, the disciplinary expertise is probably available in-house, as academics are very familiar with the research process. For their part, business organizations can approach HEIs to seek this research expertise, resulting in more numerous and more impactful university-industry collaborations.

In conclusion, conducting an agile research study with survey data from key stakeholders (e.g. employees, customers) can strengthen the foundations of the Strategic Planning process, and enhance the strategic learning of the planning team. In times of accelerated social and economic change, such as the rebuilding stage after the COVID-19 pandemic, short cycles of strategic planning and disciplined validation of assumptions and key relationships, can enhance the effectiveness of the Strategic Planning process and the confidence of stakeholders in its validity.

Appendix: Survey Scales

Empathy (Brand promise delivery)

The university has academics/mentors who monitor and care about the performance of their students.
The university has administrative and academic staff who provide individual attention to each student.

The university understands and responds to the specific personal issues and circumstances of each student.
Teaching staff are approachable to assist with coursework queries.

Brand image

I have always had a good impression of this university.
In my opinion, this university has a good image in the minds of consumers.
I believe that the university has a better image than its competitors.
In general, I have a positive image of this university.

Student satisfaction

My university has helped me to fulfill my aspirations.
My university has met my expectations.
My decision to choose this university was correct.

University reputation

The [university name] has a reputation of performing well.
People have told me that the [university name] is a reliable college.
The university has high academic standards.
The university has a well-known academic reputation.

Brand advocacy

If somebody asks me, surely I'll recommend my university.
If the opportunity arose, I would make positive comments to family and friends.
I would encourage others to study at this university.

References

Abdelmaaboud, A. K., Peña, A. I. P., & Mahrous, A. A. (2021). The influence of student-university identification on student's advocacy intentions: The role of student satisfaction and student trust. *Journal of Marketing for Higher Education, 31*(2), 197–219.

Abel, A., Jr. (2020). The phenomenon of learning at a distance through emergency remote teaching amidst the pandemic crisis. *Asian Journal of Distance Education, 15*(1), 127–143.

Achampong, F. K. (2010). Integrating risk management and strategic planning. *Planning for Higher Education, 38*(2), 22–27.

Albulescu, I., & Albulescu, M. (2014). The University in the community. The university's contribution to local and regional development by providing educational services for adults. *Procedia—Social and Behavioral Sciences, 142*, 5–11.

Alzoubi, H., Alnawaiseh, N., Al-Mnayyis, A., Abu-Lubad, M., Aqel, A., & Al-Shagahin, H. (2020). COVID-19-knowledge, attitude and practice among medical and non-medical University Students in Jordan. *Journal of Pure and Applied Microbiology, 14*(1), 17–24. https://doi.org/10.22207/JPAM.14.1.04

Ashour, S., El-Refae, G. A., & Zaitoun, E. A. (2021). Post-pandemic higher education: Perspectives from university leaders and educational experts in the United Arab Emirates. *Higher Education for the Future, 8*(2), 716–742.

Atristain-Suárez, C. (2016). Best management practices: SMEs' organizational performance management based on internal controls in Mexico. *Journal of International Business and Economics, 4*(2), 41–58.

Bagozzi, R., & Yi, Y. (2012). Specification, evaluation, and interpretation of structural equation models. *Journal of the Academy of Marketing Science, 40*(1), 8–34.

Balaji, M. S., Roy, S. K., & Sadeque, S. (2016). Antecedents and consequences of university brand identification. *Journal of Business Research, 69*(8), 3023–3032.

Bennett, R., & Ali-Choudhury, R. (2009). Prospective students' perceptions of university brands. *Journal of Marketing for Higher Education, 19*(1), 85–107.

Bosire, J., & Amimo, C. (2017). Emerging issues and future prospects in the management of transnational education. *International Journal of Higher Education, 6*(5), 143–154.

Brodie, R. J., Whittome, J. R., & Brush, G. J. (2009). Investigating the service brand: A customer value perspective. *Journal of Business Research, 62*(3), 345–355.

Bryson, J. M. (2016). Strategic planning and the strategy change cycle. In D. O. Renz & R. D. Herman (Eds.), *The Jossey-Bass handbook of nonprofit leadership and management*. Wiley.

Butuner, H. (2016). Before and after phases of strategic planning. *Universal Journal of Management, 4*(3), 120–129.

Cantoni, A. D., Rocha, T. V., Galhanone, R. F., & Righetti, M. L. (2019). International marketing strategies adopted in the franchise internationalization process: A multiple case study in the apparel industry. *Brazilian Journal of Marketing, 18*(2), 19–53.

Casidy, R. (2013). The role of brand orientation in the higher education sector: A student-perceived paradigm. *Asia Pacific Journal of Marketing and Logistics, 25*, 803–820.

Casidy, R., & Wymer, W. (2015). The impact of brand strength on satisfaction, loyalty and WOM: An empirical examination in the higher education sector. *Journal of Brand Management, 22*(2), 117–135.

Castells, M. (2001). The new global economy. In J. Muller, N. Cloete, & S. Badat (Eds.), *Challenges of globalisation: South African debates with Manuel Castells* (pp. 2–21). Maskew Miller Longman.

Chen, C. T. (2016). The investigation on brand image of university education and students' word-of-mouth behavior. *Higher Education Studies, 6*(4), 23–33.

Clark, P., Chapleo, C., & Suomi, K. (2020). Branding higher education: An exploration of the role of internal branding on middle management in a university rebrand. *Tertiary Education and Management, 26*(2), 131–149.

Dam, S. M., & Dam, T. C. (2021). Relationships between service quality, brand image, customer satisfaction, and customer loyalty. *The Journal of Asian Finance, Economics and Business, 8*(3), 585–593.

Dennis, M. J. (2021). Pandemic magnifies pre-COVID-19 US higher education challenges. *Enrollment Management Report, 24*(10), 3–3.

del Barrio-García, S., & Prados-Peña, M. B. (2019). Do brand authenticity and brand credibility facilitate brand equity? The case of heritage destination brand extension. *Journal of Destination Marketing & Management, 13*, 10–23.

Dooris, M. J., Kelley, J. M., & Trainer, J. F. (2002). *Strategic planning in higher education* (New Directions for Higer Education, No. 116, Fall 2002).

Du Preez, R., Bendixen, M., & Abratt, R. (2017). The behavioral consequences of internal brand management among frontline employees. *Journal of Product & Brand Management, 26*(3), 251–261.

Drucker, P. (1976). *Management: Tasks, responsibility and practices.* Harper and Row.

Esteky, S., & Kalati, S. H. (2021). The educational placebo effect: Branding higher education benefits student learning. *Journal of Marketing for Higher Education*, 1–16.

Erkmen, E., & Hancer, M. (2015). Do your internal branding efforts measure up? *International Journal of Contemporary Hospitality Management, 27*(5), 878–895.

Galloway, S. (2020). *Post corona: From crisis to opportunity*. Penguin.

Garas, S. R. R., Mahran, A. F. A., & Mohamed, H. M. H. (2018). Internal corporate branding impact on employees' brand supporting behaviour. *Journal of Product & Brand Management, 27*(1), 79–95.

Grisaffe, D. B., & Nguyen, H. P. (2011). Antecedents of emotional attachment to brands. *Journal of Business Research, 64*(10), 1052–1059.

Grönroos, C. (2016). *Service management and marketing: Managing the service profit logic*. Wiley.

Harmon-Kizer, T. (2019). The role of logo recoloring on perceptual fluency in cause-related marketing campaigns. *Journal of Promotion Management, 25*(7), 959–982.

Hassanien, M. A. (2017). Strategic planning in higher education, a need for innovative model. *Journal of Education, Society and Behavioural Science, 23*(2), 1–11.

Hayes, A. F. (2018). *Introduction to mediation, moderation, and conditional process analysis: A regression-based approach* (2nd ed.). Guilford.

Hayes, A. F., Montoya, A. K., & Rockwood, N. J. (2017). The analysis of mechanisms and their contingencies: PROCESS versus structural equation modeling. *Australasian Marketing Journal (AMJ), 25*(1), 76–81.

Hechinger, J., & Lorin, J. (2020). *Coronavirus forces $600 billion higher education industry online*. http://www.bloomberg.com/news/articles/2020-03-19/colleges-are-going-online-because-of-the-coronavirus

Henderson, P. W., & Cote, J. A. (1998). Guidelines for selecting or modifying logos. *Journal of Marketing, 62*(2), 14–30.

Hosseini, S. H. K., & Behboudi, L. (2017). Brand trust and image: Effects on customer satisfaction. *International Journal of Health Care Quality Assurance, 30*(7), 580–590.

Hu, J., Liu, H., Chen, Y., & Qin, J. (2018). Strategic planning and the stratification of Chinese higher education institutions. *International Journal of Educational Development, 63*(1), 36–43.

Idris, M. Z., & Whitfield, T. A. (2014). Swayed by the logo and name: Does university branding work? *Journal of Marketing for Higher Education, 24*(1), 41–58.

Inga, E., Inga, J., Cárdenas, J., & Cárdenas, J. (2021). Planning and strategic management of higher education considering the vision of Latin America. *Education Sciences, 11*(4), 188.

Jandrić, P., Hayes, D., Truelove, I., Levinson, P., Mayo, P., Ryberg, T., & Hayes, S. (2020). Teaching in the age of Covid-19. *Postdigital Science and Education, 2*(3), 1069–1230.

Japutra, A., Keni, K., & Nguyen, B. (2016). What's in a university logo? Building commitment in higher education. *Journal of Brand Management, 23*(2), 137–152.

Johnson, G., Whittington, R., & Scholes, K. (2011). *Exploring strategy: Text and cases* (9th ed.). Pearson Education.
Joseph, A., Gupta, S., Wang, Y., & Schoefer, K. (2021). Corporate rebranding: An internal perspective. *Journal of Business Research, 130*, 709–723.
Kaushal, V., Jaiswal, D., Kant, R., & Ali, N. (2021). Determinants of university reputation: Conceptual model and empirical investigation in an emerging higher education market. *International Journal of Emerging Markets*. https://doi.org/10.1108/IJOEM-12-2020-1494
Kelchen, R. (2022). The lasting effects of the pandemic on graduate and professional education. *Journal of Student Financial Aid, 51*(1), 5.
Kim, M. J., & Lim, J. H. (2019). A comprehensive review on logo literature: Research topics, findings, and future directions. *Journal of Marketing Management, 35*(13–14), 1291–1365.
King, C., & Murillo, E. (2022). Hire dirtbags: Three tools to help employees become brand champions with a purpose. *Fox Business Review, 1*(4), 15–21.
King, C., So, K. K. F., & Grace, D. (2013). The influence of service brand orientation on hotel employees' attitude and behaviors in China. *International Journal of Hospitality Management, 34*, 172–180.
Kulikowski, K., Przytula, S., & Sulkowski, L. (2021). Emergency forced pandemic E-learning—Feedback from students for HEI management. *Open Learning, 36*(3), 245–262.
Kwiek, M. (2003). *The state, the market and higher education: Challenges for the new century*. In M. Kwiek (Ed.), *The university, globalization, Central Europe*. Peter Lange.
Liu, J., & Gao, Y. (2022). Higher education internationalisation at the crossroads: Effects of the coronavirus pandemic. *Tertiary Education and Management, 28*(1), 1–15. https://doi.org/10.1007/s11233-021-09082-4
Mageto, J., Luke, R., & Heyns, G. (2020). Investigating the quality of university education: A focus on supply chain management. *International Journal of Learning, Teaching and Educational Research, 19*(8), 424–446.
Martínez-López, F. J., Gázquez-Abad, J. C., & Sousa, C. M. (2013). Structural equation modelling in marketing and business research. *European Journal of Marketing, 47*(1/2), 115–152.
Mintzberg, H. (1994). The fall and rise of strategic planning. *Harvard Business Review, 72*(1), 107–114.
Morganti, P., Terán-Bustamante, A., & Murillo, E. (2021). Finally back to campus? Motivations for facemask adoption in the higher education sector. In A. M. López-Fernández & A. Terán-Bustamante (Eds.), *Business recovery in emerging markets: Global perspectives from various sectors*. Palgrave Macmillan.
Moslehpour, M., Chau, K. Y., Zheng, J., Hanjani, A. N., & Hoang, M. (2020). The mediating role of international student satisfaction in the influence of

higher education service quality on institutional reputation in Taiwan. *International Journal of Engineering Business Management*. https://doi.org/10.1177/1847979020971955

Müller, B., Kocher, B., & Crettaz, A. (2013). The effects of visual rejuvenation through brand logos. *Journal of Business Research, 66*(1), 82–88.

Murillo, E. (2019). El branding interno como antecedente de la autoestima basada en la organización: Un estudio en una cadena de restaurantes. *Entreciencias: diálogos en la sociedad del conocimiento, 7*(21), 37–52.

Murillo, E. (2020). Branding interno en organizaciones de comercio minorista: un estudio en una cadena de farmacias. *Mercados y Negocios, 21*(42), 85–109. https://www.redalyc.org/journal/5718/571864273002/

Murillo, E. (2022). Enhancing brand understanding through brand training: A conditional process analysis of recent hires at an airline. *Revista Brasileira de Gestão de Negócios, 24*(2), 312–331. https://doi.org/10.7819/rbgn.v24i2.4170

Murillo, E., & Terán-Bustamante, A. (2020). El branding interno en la economía colaborativa: un estudio exploratorio de Uber. *Revista ESPACIOS, 41*(22), 268–282. https://www.revistaespacios.com/a20v41n22/20412218.html

Newman, F., & Couturier, L. K. (2001). The new competitive arena market forces invade the academy. *Change: The Magazine of Higher Learning, 33*(5), 10–17.

Panda, S., Pandey, S. C., Bennett, A., & Tian, X. (2019). University brand image as competitive advantage: A two-country study. *International Journal of Educational Management, 33*(2), 234–251.

Parasuraman, A., Zeithaml, V. A., & Berry, L. L. (1988). Servqual: A multiple-item scale for measuring consumer perc. *Journal of Retailing, 64*(1), 12.

Perera, C. H., Nayak, R., & Nguyen, L. T. V. (2022). The impact of social media marketing and brand credibility on higher education institutes' brand equity in emerging countries. *Journal of Marketing Communications*, 1–26. https://doi.org/10.1080/13527266.2022.2086284

Peters, M. A., Rizvi, F., McCulloch, G., Gibbs, P., Gorur, R., Hong, M., & Misiaszek, L. (2020). Reimagining the new pedagogical possibilities for universities post-Covid-19. *Educational Philosophy and Theory*. https://doi.org/10.1080/00131857.2020.1777655

Porter, M. E. (1980). *Competitive strategy; techniques for analyzing industries and competitors*. Free Press.

Pringle, J., & Fritz, S. (2019). The university brand and social media: Using data analytics to assess brand authenticity. *Journal of Marketing for Higher Education, 29*(1), 19–44.

Rodríguez-Abitia, G. (2021). Coping with COVID-19 in Mexico: Actions for educational inclusion. *Communications of the Association for Information Systems, 48*(1), 11.

Sadlak, J. (2000). Globalization versus the universal role of the university. *Higher Education in Europe, 25*, 2.
Sanz, N., & Bergan, S. (Eds.). (2007). *The heritage of European universities* (Council of Europe Higher Education Series No. 7, 2nd ed.).
Schlesinger, W., Cervera-Taulet, A., & Wymer, W. (2021). The influence of university brand image, satisfaction, and university identification on alumni WOM intentions. *Journal of Marketing for Higher Education*, 1–19.
Sirianni, N. J., Bitner, M. J., Brown, S. W., & Mandel, N. (2013). Branded service encounters: Strategically aligning employee behavior with the brand positioning. *Journal of Marketing, 77*(6), 108–123.
Steiner, G. A. (1979). *Strategic planning: What every manager must know*. Free Press.
Stephenson, A. L., Heckert, A., & Yerger, D. B. (2016). College choice and the university brand: Exploring the consumer decision framework. *Higher Education, 71*(4), 489–503.
Stracke, C. M., Burgos, D., Santos-Hermosa, G., Bozkurt, A., Sharma, R. C., Swiatek Cassafieres, C., dos Santos, A. I., Mason, J., Ossiannilsson, E., Shon, J. G., Wan, M., Obiageli Agbu, J.-F., Farrow, R., Karakaya, Ö., Nerantzi, C., Ramírez-Montoya, M. S., Conole, G., Cox, G., & Truong, V. (2022). Responding to the initial challenge of the COVID-19 pandemic: Analysis of international responses and impact in school and higher education. *Sustainability, 14*(3), 1876. https://doi.org/10.3390/su14031876
Sultan, P., & Wong, H. Y. (2019). How service quality affects university brand performance, university brand image and behavioural intention: The mediating effects of satisfaction and trust and moderating roles of gender and study mode. *Journal of Brand Management, 26*(3), 332–347.
Swani, K., Wamwara, W., Goodrich, K., Schiller, S., & Dinsmore, J. (2021). Understanding business student retention during Covid-19: Roles of service quality, college brand, and academic satisfaction, and stress. *Services Marketing Quarterly*, 1–24.
Tapinos, E., Dyson, R. G., & Meadows, M. (2005). The impact of performance measurement in strategic planning. *International Journal of Productivity and Performance Management, 54*(5/6), 370–384.
Terglav, K., Ruzzier, M. K., & Kaše, R. (2016). Internal branding process: Exploring the role of mediators in top management's leadership–commitment relationship. *International Journal of Hospitality Management, 54*(1), 1–11.
Tsiligiris, V., Kéri, A., & Cheah, J. E. T. (2021). Exploring the relationship between student individual culture and service quality expectations in higher education. *Quality Assurance in Education, 30*(1), 51–72.
Watkins, B. A., & Gonzenbach, W. J. (2013). Assessing university brand personality through logos: An analysis of the use of academics and athletics in university branding. *Journal of Marketing for Higher Education, 23*(1), 15–33.

Watson, D. (2005). The university and its communities. *Higher Education Management and Policy, 19*(2), 14–23.

Whatley, M., & Castiello-Gutiérrez, S. (2021). Balancing finances, politics, and public health: International student enrollment and reopening plans at US higher education institutions amid the COVID-19 pandemic. *Higher Education*, 1–22. https://doi.org/10.1007/s10734-021-00768-7

Wilson, E. J., & Elliot, E. A. (2016). Brand meaning in higher education: Leaving the shallows via deep metaphors. *Journal of Business Research, 69*(1), 3058–3068.

Xiong, L. (2023). It takes a village: Examining how and when brand-specific transformational leadership affects employees in internal brand management. *Journal of Brand Management*, 1–14. https://doi.org/10.1057/s41262-022-00308-3

CHAPTER 10

Knowledge Management and Innovation in the Furniture Industry in Mexico

Víctor Manuel Castillo-Girón, Suhey Ayala-Ramírez, Antonieta Martínez-Velasco, and Antonia Terán-Bustamante

V. M. Castillo-Girón · S. Ayala-Ramírez
Universidad de Guadalajara, Guadalajara, Mexico
e-mail: victor.cgiron@academicos.udg.mx

S. Ayala-Ramírez
e-mail: suhey.ayala@academicos.udg.mx

A. Martínez-Velasco (✉)
Facultad de Ingeniería, Universidad Panamericana, Mexico City, Mexico
e-mail: amartinezv@up.edu.mx

A. Terán-Bustamante
Facultad de Ciencias Económicas y Empresariales, Universidad Panamericana, Mexico City, Mexico
e-mail: ateran@up.edu.mx

E. Murillo et al. (eds.), *Creating Economic Stability Amid Global Uncertainty*, https://doi.org/10.1007/978-3-031-41386-5_10

Introduction

Innovation and knowledge management are critical for productivity, innovation, and competitiveness in the furniture industry (FI). The organizational aptitudes will improve on par with how quickly different factors adapt to processes—enabling them to increase the absorption capacity for new technology.

The first stage of the Covid-19 pandemic (from March to May 2020) affected all sectors nationally and internationally; industrial sectors with high technological dynamism and, therefore, learning and innovation were particularly strained. This situation also hindered sectors reliant on natural resources and labor, such as the furniture sector, due to the shortage of wood and other essential materials like leather and plastic products (Economic Commission for Latin America and the Caribbean, 2021). Once this first stage of the sanitary crisis finally ended, enterprises changed how their logistics managed the flow of information and materials. That was done mainly due to the transformation of the decision-making processes in companies. In a sense, firms were adapting their business model and characteristics to mimic the procedures applied in other international contexts, such as Malaysia, which also has a high furniture production (Ratnasingam et al., 2020). In Mexico, people decided to improve their environment and change the furniture in their homes. As a result, the national demand for furniture increased between 2 and 4%. That is no surprise, as the concept of home as a place to rest drastically changed due to confinement. Work and education became hybrid, and the home became an office, a meeting place, a school, and a space for leisure (AFAMJAL, 2021; Genc & Merdan, 2021). In the same vein as the national increase in demand for furniture, this sector has also benefited from a growing and increasingly renown position in the world market. Thanks to the network of commercial agreements with other countries, the Mexican FI has gained international recognition not only due to the originality of its designs but also because of its diversity, functionality, comfort, and attention to detail while fulfilling the specific demands of consumers (CIMEJAL, 2021a).

Nevertheless, this sector's predominance of micro and small family enterprises stands out. These companies are frequently supported by informal labor, which is dependent on the tacit knowledge of their members. In addition, they often lack financing to incorporate new and better equipment and technology to ensure sufficient production for national or international markets (De la Torre, 2017). Along with these aforementioned not-optimal conditions, which highlight inadequacies and emerging issues of the sectors, new problems arose. To give succinct examples of said issues, these ranged from disruptions in supply chains, inconsistent quality of procured products, poor use of information technology and automation, and financial management problems (Pirc et al., 2021; Ratnasingam et al., 2020).

On the other hand, medium and large companies have expanded their market niches through new organizational structures and incorporated new technologies in their design, production, and marketing processes (CIMEJAL, 2021b). Despite this, such companies also experience difficulties as they all share the same context at the national level, which creates problems for themselves. These sector exports are concentrated almost solely in the United States of America (95%), followed by Canada (4%). In addition, electronic commerce remains very scarce due to the lack of infrastructure and the country population's low level of access to banking services. In addition, the FI suffers from limited industrialization of the wood available in the country. A prime example of this hardship is that wood is often imported. That is due to various local problems associated with land tenure, organizational policies, illegal logging, and increasing deforestation, which afflicts national forests and jungles (De la Torre, 2017).

In times of crisis, having a tool to manage knowledge and innovation is essential. Through this management, employees can improve the quality and speed of decision-making by accessing the knowledge of the entire organization. Furthermore, when making decisions, these tools facilitate access to different people's data, information, opinions, and experiences, providing additional perspectives to their choices (Graziele & de Moura, 2016). Unfortunately, now, there is scarce literature that analyzes the furniture sector and its processes. Consequently, this research proposes a model of the main factors that FI companies must consider in their management.

Considering the context, the research questions that guide this research are: What are the critical factors for optimal knowledge management in the furniture sector? How can a furniture company make better decisions to innovate its products/services, processes, sales, and marketing within the company using a knowledge management model? What are the correlations between the various factors in the knowledge management model in the FI?

Theoretical Framework

Knowledge and Learning Processes for Innovation and Competitively

The manifestations of innovation vary according to the characteristics of the actors, processes, and organizations (Solleiro & Terán-Bustamante, 2012). Organizations can generate or improve their products and processes through innovation, saving capital, reducing costs, and improving quality. Innovation is the ability to manage knowledge creatively in response to market demands. It constitutes the most efficient way for an organization to build competitive advantages and differentiate itself from its competitors (Solleiro & Terán-Bustamante, 2012). Thus, the company, its human capital, and knowledge management are crucial elements of the innovative process.

The analysis of knowledge and its contribution to economic development has gained relevance since the 1980s, as the post-Fordist model gained relevance. It is based on the primacy of knowledge and radical innovation in new information and communication technologies (ICT). As a result, organizational transformations of companies (organizational innovation) and markets (market innovation) were consolidated, as well as forms of regulation based on novelty-oriented behaviors and intellectual property (Dutraive, 2008). In this framework, as a driver of the economic system, knowledge and the learning processes which enable its construction are perceived as essential to achieving a more productive economy and higher rates of societal welfare (Stiglitz & Greenwald, 2016). Learning can be understood as various processes through which individuals and organizations acquire knowledge. Knowledge is a high-value form of information ready to be applied to decisions and actions. Its effectiveness is conditioned by the speed with which new knowledge is constructed, and conditions exist to facilitate access to it (Dutraive, 2008; Hualde, 2005).

Suppose productive activities and the level of effectiveness or competitiveness of an organization reside in the knowledge of the individuals and groups that comprise it (Prévot et al., 2010). In that case, it is assumed that although an individual has access to his knowledge through practice of the activity, its application is conditioned by organizational procedures that put the members of an organization in interaction (Conner & Prahalad, 1996). This social knowledge, derived from the integration of personal knowledge, leads to a portfolio of options, platforms, or developments that enhance the organization's growth and survival possibilities.

Because knowledge is the most important strategic resource of organizations (Grant, 1996a), the primary competitive dimension is the ability to increase this knowledge efficiently. That must be done under organizational principles through which it is possible to transform the experience of people and groups in an organization into economically valuable products and services. However, these cannot be reduced solely to individuals, achieving a competitive advantage over others. This knowledge is easily replicable within the organization, avoiding the risk of being transferred or imitated by the competition with the simple rotation of its employees (Kogut & Zander, 1992).

To explain the integration of knowledge within the organization and how it generates a sustained competitive advantage, there are two dimensions: tacit knowledge and explicit knowledge. The fundamental distinction between the two types of knowledge lies in the transferability and transfer mechanisms between individuals over time and space. On the one hand, tacit knowledge cannot be codified; it is observed through its application, it is acquired through practice, and consequently, its transferability between individuals is slow, costly, and uncertain (Grant, 1996a, 1996b; Kogut & Zander, 1992). On the other hand, the efficiency in transmitting knowledge depends on its potential or aggregation capacity to absorb or add new knowledge to the existing one. This intake improves substantially when knowledge is standardized in a common language, which allows information to be socialized or transmitted in its entirety within the organization (Grant, 1996a).

The strategic nature of knowledge implies that its owner can appropriate the inherent added value. On the other hand, tacit knowledge's appropriability is achieved through its application in productive activities. In the case of explicit knowledge, it can be appropriated through market transactions and generates ambiguity about its ownership. This ambiguity makes it difficult to share its benefits and to make an optimal investment in new one (Grant, 1996a).

The production of organizational knowledge implies greater specialization than is necessary for its strategic use. It cannot be managed effectively from the traditional perspective focused on the management of information flows and is practiced through databases, registries, reports, and systems that capture, store, categorize, and transmit information. Knowledge is contextualized since it depends on a specific time and space, and its dynamic continuous creation requires a series of conditions. An example of this is the role of managers. This is crucial to define the type of knowledge which, in turn, it is expected to be promoted in the workgroups that monitor it to later incorporate it into organizational processes and promote its development and management (Nonaka & Konno, 1998; Nonaka & Takeuchi, 1995; Nonaka et al., 2000).

Although the FI seeks to implement automation technology to improve its processes, it is not considered part of the high-tech sectors. It is intensive in using natural resources and craftsmanship (Economic Commission for Latin America and the Caribbean, 2021). The interruption of markets and commercialization due to the COVID-19 pandemic confronted this industry with a series of disturbances which made it a necessity to enhance its creativity to adapt, survive, and remain sustainable (González & Pérez, 2021). Studies on the specificities of the capability of these businesses in the face of the disruptions caused by the COVID-19 pandemic are usually based not only on European and Anglo-American contexts but also on high-tech sectors (González & Pérez, 2021). These results need to be tested in different contexts. Even more so in an industry with a polarized structure, with many small companies and a small number of large producers. These are important distinctions when analyzing the decision-making process for successful innovation, which can lead to designing best practices in each context.

Characterization of the Furniture Industry in Mexico

The FI in Mexico is integrated by over 30,000 enterprises which generate around 330,000 direct jobs (Arum Journal, 2021; Casado, 2021). Of the various manufacturing activities in the country, the FI is one of the most dynamic sectors, with an annual growth oscillating between 2 and 4% (CIMEJAL, 2021; Ogazón, 2019). Mexico is one of the leading producers and exporters of wooden furniture worldwide. Thus, Mexico is the fourth largest exporter of height-adjustable swivel seats, the eighth of wooden chairs and stools, and the ninth of wooden pieces and parts for furniture (Ogazón, 2019). Mexico is the leading furniture exporter within the American continent, followed by the United States of America.

This relevance is associated with the close relationship and proximity with the American market and the network of 12 trade agreements, active and connected to 52 countries (Ogazón, 2019). Another critical factor is the overturning of design companies' technological transformation and innovation and the production of new products replicated at other levels and latitudes (CIMEJAL, 2021).

This industry is heterogeneous in the geographical distribution of the productive units and the aggregate production and infrastructure composition. Although the companies in the furniture sector are distributed throughout the country, four states (Michoacán, Veracruz, the State of Mexico, and Jalisco) make up about 40% of the economic units. In addition, the urban area of Mexico City and the State of Mexico, together with the Jalisco Metropolitan Area, account for 43% of the country's total furniture production. Likewise, of the 33,600 companies registered in 2014, nearly 90% were micro-enterprises, and only 222 had more than 100 employees (Arum Journal, 2021). In addition, there is a territorial focus in these states, as would be the case of the municipality of Ocotlán and the Guadalajara Metropolitan Area in the state of Jalisco (Lozano, 2007, 2010).

It is observed in the characteristics of its human resources, and the level of the workforce is reflected in modernization. The degree of technology increases as the size of the company increases (Ratnasingam et al., 2020). Thus, while small companies continue to produce based on family work with traditional tools and machinery (Lozano, 2010), large companies in the wood and furniture sector have adopted industry 4.0 information and automation technologies (Ratnasingam et al., 2020). These large companies have built Smart Factories, where organizational and production processes are increasingly supported by custom software in the design of their products and the use of robotics, Big Data, barcodes, and other scanning methods of products, AI, and automated production processes are used in tandem with secure supply for material chains. That leads to keeping its production volumes in line with demand and the quality expected by consumers. That is enhanced using digital marketing through websites, email, social networks, and affiliate marketing (CIMEJAL, 2021b; Ratnasingam et al., 2020).

According to CIMEJAL (2021b), the FI was disruptive despite the unfavorable economic and health conditions associated with the COVID-19 pandemic. In a certain sense, it managed to adapt despite the circumstances because the sales volume decreased in the early stages of the pandemic, at the end of 2020, and throughout 2021. Nevertheless, new companies were incorporated into the sector, and most furniture entrepreneurs managed to keep their sales. In addition, the growing importance of new technologies was taken advantage of since working and studying from home became the norm, as well as the population's interest in spending more time in contact with nature and open spaces or outdoors (Genc & Merdan, 2021). In this context, the FI has become a relevant sector in the global market. It has also focused on both the functionality of its results and the convenience of consumers. Thus, it is essential to use and combine different materials such as wood, metal, ironwork, and upholstery (CIMEJAL, 2021a; Genc & Merdan, 2021). Hence, while Latin America and the Caribbean are significant producers and consumers of conifer wood, such as pines, Mexico leads the wood veneer production, distinctive due to its resistance and fine texture (CIMEJAL, 2021a).

Materials and Methods

This research has a mixed-methods approach: qualitative (descriptive) and quantitative, with a correlational scope and validated by information obtained through questionnaires, semi-structured interviews, and a focus group that took place in the first bimester of the year 2022: four questionnaires and three script-based semi-structured interviews to experts and consultants. The questionnaire was administered to the same number of furniture enterprises. These companies are from a small group of substantial companies participating in the export market. This industry is characterized by the ongoing use of new technologies and a wide production range. In addition, interviews were conducted with managers and key staff who perform essential processes and activities within a company, such as production and administration. Furthermore, three interviews were conducted (one of them collectively) with three furniture sector consultants, plus two with businesspeople with a broad trajectory in the guild of Jalisco's FI. Overall, the interviewees handle strategic information for the generation of knowledge and management of technology and innovation within their respective companies and the sector.

Based on expert opinions, a conceptual model was built to identify the most critical processes necessary for knowledge management and innovation in the FI in Mexico, see Fig. 10.1. The arcs indicate the cause-effect direction between the variables (high-definition versions of this chapter's network diagrams are available at https://tinyurl.com/ch9-Figures). The conceptual model is the basis of the Bayesian network that will be modeled below.

BN is used for modeling to improve the understanding of the system, make modeling participatory, guide knowledge discovery, and synthesize

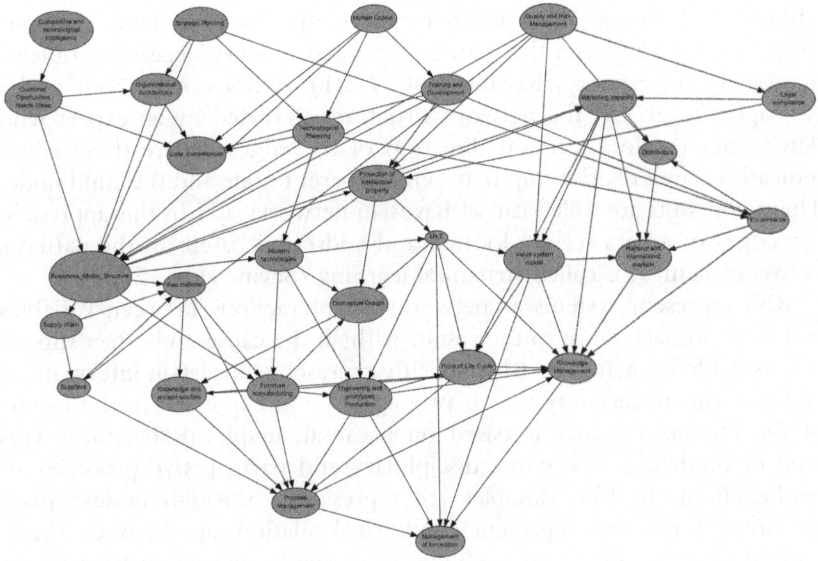

Fig. 10.1 Conceptual model (*Source* Authors)

or codify knowledge and data. Not only that, but also for prediction, exploratory and scenario analysis, informing and supporting management and decision-making, and identifying knowledge and data gaps, among others (Chen & Pollino, 2012). The main objective of Artificial Intelligence (AI) is to generate models that perform intellectual tasks that humans usually perform. Previously, formal logic had been considered adequate for representing knowledge and reasoning in AI. However, problems where logic was not enough and uncertain reasoning was a feature of the problem needed to be tackled with another approach. At this time, the Bayesian approach emerges, which aims to produce a model that performs these tasks as well or better than humans, that can adapt to stochastic and changing environments, recognize its limited knowledge, and deal with uncertainty. Moreover, its ability to parameterize BN models using expert opinion is an advantage quantitative data cannot achieve, which is necessary for statistical approach models (Smith et al., 2007).

A Bayesian network (BN) is a probabilistic model that relates a set of random variables through a directed graph. They are graphic networks without cycles in which random variables and the probability relationships that exist between them are represented to solve decision problems in cases of uncertainty (Kyrimi et al., 2021). A BN can be built under two approaches: (1) the network structure is created by an expert who determines the location and direction of the edges, where these edges indicate a causal relationship between the parent node and the child node. These networks are called causal Bayesian networks. (2) In this approach, the edges of a data set are located and addressed based on the patterns between them. It is called structural learning (Sevinc et al., 2020).

BNs represent systems as networks of interactions between variables from the primary cause to the result, with all the cause-and-effect suppositions made explicit. The BN explicitly represents uncertain information, and it is this uncertainty that is propagated and expressed in the results of the model. The BN is based on a causal, graphical structure. This type of modeling allows interdisciplinary and participative processes to be beneficial. In BN, variables are represented through nodes linked by directed arcs that represent conditional relationships between them. Each node has a set of mutually exclusive states, which can be categorical, Boolean, continuing, or discreet. BN can use experts' judgment to estimate conditional probabilities based on observation, knowledge, and previous experience.

There are several types of algorithms to calculate posterior probabilities, which are applied depending on the type of BN. In this article, we use the Estimated Posterior Importance Sampling (EPIS) algorithm, a stochastic sampling algorithm. The EPIS algorithm uses loop probability propagation to compute an estimate of the posterior probability across all nodes in the network and then uses importance sampling to improve this estimate. It uses Loopy Belief Propagation (LBP), an algorithm originally proposed by Judea Pearl and Russell (2011) for polytrees and later applied by others to multiple connection Bayesian networks (Ogunsanya, 2012).

Nodes connected by an arc are called parent nodes and child nodes, respectively. A child node can have multiple parent nodes; this node can be affected by numerous factors (Rohmer & Gehl, 2020). The strength of these relationships specifies the level of belief that the node will be in a particular state, given the states of the central nodes. Link Strength measures play an essential role among constraint-based structure learning algorithms to derive hypotheses of the main causal pathways of a system from the data. It is calculated from the conditional probabilities of the child node, and it expresses the distance between various conditional probability distributions from the child node to the states of the parent node (Ebert-Uphoff, 2007).

To define the Link Strength used, we use the Conditional Mutual Information (CMI), which compares the uncertainty in Y if we know the state of Z, with the uncertainty in Y if we know the states of Z and X. In the context of Bayesian networks, CMI is used to verify how well a set of variables, Z, shields X from Y. Then, Link Strength is defined as mutual information of condition on the set Z of all other parents of Y:

$$\mathrm{LS}(\mathrm{X} \rightarrow \mathrm{Y}) = \mathrm{MI}(\mathrm{X}, \mathrm{Y}|\mathrm{Z}) \tag{10.1}$$

Based on Eq. 10.1, the Link Strength (LS) is enunciated as:

$$\mathrm{LS} = \sum_{x,z} P(x, z) \sum_{y} P(x|x, z) log_2 \frac{P(y|x, z)}{P(y|z)} \tag{10.2}$$

where x is the state of node X, and z is the state of node Z.

In this way, LS indicates how much the uncertainty in Y is reduced by knowing the state of X if the states of all the other parent nodes are known (averaging over the principal states using their actual joint probability).

The odds are updated through the spread of beliefs in the other nodes thanks to Bayes' Theorem. This spread of beliefs allows BN to be utilized for diagnosis or explicatory ends (Chen & Pollino, 2012). The conditional odds are established for every child node by combining states from its parent nodes. Meaning that the conditional probability and its magnitude rely on the number of parent nodes and the number of their states, which is increased by the number of parent nodes (Eq. 10.3),

$$\mathrm{CP} = S \prod_{i=1}^{n} P_i \tag{10.3}$$

where CP is the conditional probability, S is the number of states, and Π is the number of states in the *i-th* parent node.

To model the problem, we follow these specific steps: (A) Definition of the purpose of the model. (B) Specifying the scope and sources. (C) Conceptualization of the system based on previous knowledge. (D) Selection of the variables. (E) Determination and structure of the model and its metrics. (F) Evaluation of the model (Fig. 10.2).

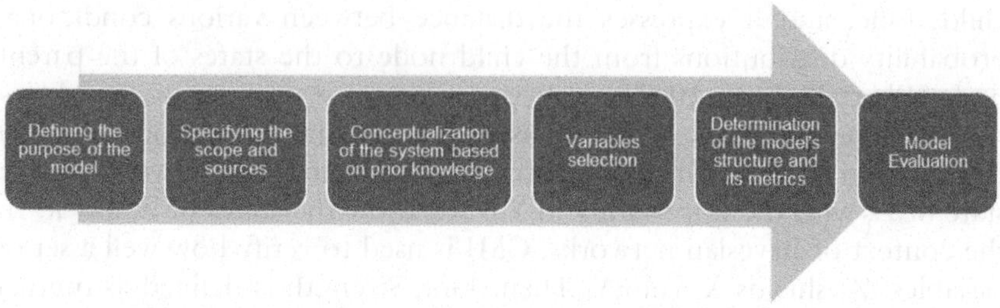

Fig. 10.2 Process to model knowledge management and innovation in the FI in Mexico

The BN developed includes 30 key factors, with six parent nodes: Competitive and technological intelligence, strategic planning, technological planning, human capital, intellectual property protection, quality and risk management, and 26 child nodes (Fig. 10.3 and Table 10.1).

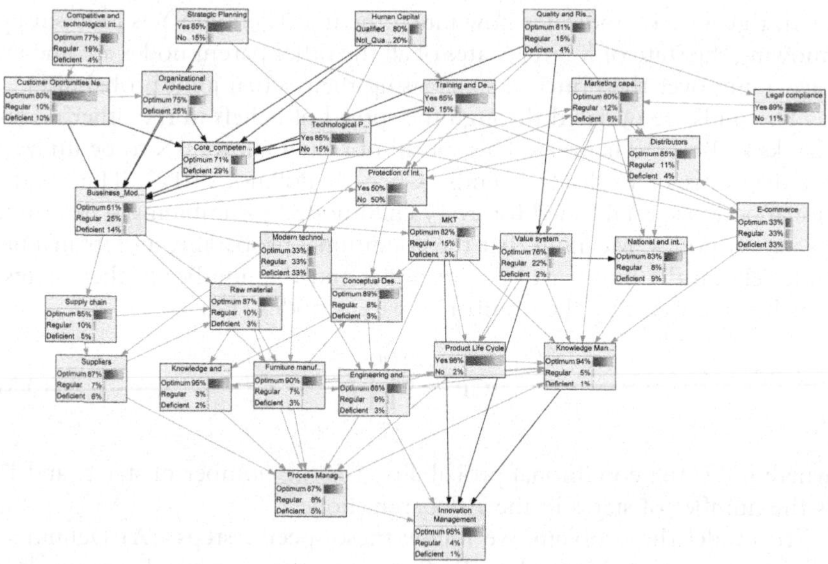

Fig. 10.3 BN for knowledge management and innovation in the FI in Mexico

Table 10.1 Definition of the variables and nodes

#	*Variable*	*Concept*	*Dimension*
1	Competitive and technological intelligence	Activities that are carried out to monitor the technological environment of an organization	Optimum Regular Deficient
2	Strategic planning	The plan presents the strategy planning, defined for the organization, as the guiding thread	Yes/No
3	Human capital	People possess knowledge, attitudes, skills, motivations, and values—technological managers or facilitators with facilitating characteristics that promote innovation	Qualified Not Qualified
4	Quality and risk management	A set of techniques and tools to support and help make the appropriate decisions, considering uncertainty, the possibility of future events, and the effects on the agreed objectives	Optimum Regular Deficient
5	Customers' needs and opportunities	Analysis of customer needs and opportunities in the market. Who? What? How? Analytics	Optimum Regular Deficient
6	Organizational and technological architecture	It explains how an organization works and coordinates its work processes, the management of people, the assignment of authority, the technologies to be developed and used, and decision-making	Optimum Deficient
7	Technological planning	The plan presents the technological strategy, defined for the organization, as the guiding thread. It allows us to identify products/services that a company can offer to satisfy market needs	Yes/No
8	Training and development	Activity focused on continuous training and formation of human talent	Yes/No
9	Compliance in regulatory and legal matters	It is focused on fulfilling the legal aspects and corresponding regulations	Yes/No

(continued)

Table 10.1 (continued)

#	*Variable*	*Concept*	*Dimension*
10	Core competences	It refers to the unique and differential knowledge or skill that a company has that gives it a competitive advantage	Optimum Deficient
11	Business model structure	Design process to create a widely new business model in the market, which is accompanied by a value proposition that generates or ensures a sustainable competitive advantage	Optimum Regular Deficient
12	Intellectual property protection	It recognizes the technological elements they have developed, which represent business possibilities to decide how to protect them legally	Yes/No
13	Supply chain	It is the set of activities, facilities, and means of distribution necessary to carry out the process of selling a product in its entirety	Optimum Regular Deficient
15	Marketing capacity	Search, promote, serve, and adapt to markets	Optimum Regular Deficient
16	Raw material	A natural resource that is transformed during the production process until it becomes a product able to be sold	Optimum Regular Deficient
17	Suppliers	Individual or company which supplies other companies with goods and resources	Optimum Regular Deficient
18	(Furniture) Manufacturing	Process of converting raw materials into an elaborated product	Optimum Regular Deficient
19	Knowledge and ancient wisdom/ Artisans' craft	Techniques applied to furniture production that is based on ancient knowledge	Optimum Regular Deficient
20	Conceptual design	Concept, products with a higher aggregated value Ecological design Multipurpose	Optimum Regular Deficient
21	Engineering/prototypes/ production	Prototyping is an essential part of the product development process. It is a set of techniques used to rapidly fabricate a scale model of a part or set of parts derived from design information	Optimum Regular Deficient

(continued)

Table 10.1 (continued)

#	*Variable*	*Concept*	*Dimension*
22	MKT	Understand and satisfy customer needs. The process by which companies create value for customers and build strong relationships with them to capture their value in return	Optimum Regular Deficient
23	Processes management	It is the management model of all processes of the company value chain	Optimum Regular Deficient
24	Product life cycle	It is the set of stages that marketable products or services of a company must go through from their release until their decay	Yes/No
25	Value system model	Structure of value proposition, value creation, value & delivery, value capture, topology of value chain partners The value propositions. What are we offering to whom? Target Segment(s) Product or Service Offering Revenue Model	Optimum Regular Deficient
26	e-commerce	Sales through the Internet	Optimum Regular Deficient
27	National and international markets	Set of real and potential buyers both nationally and internationally	Optimum Regular Deficient
29	Management of innovation	It is the organization and management of both economic and human resources to increase the creation of new knowledge, and the generation of technical ideas that allow the creation of new products, processes, or services	Optimum Regular Deficient
30	Knowledge management	A systematic process of generation, documentation, dissemination, exchange, use, and enhancement of individual and organizational knowledge	Optimum Regular Deficient

Source Authors' creation, based on Terán-Bustamante et al. (2019, 2021a, 2021b) and Martínez-Velasco and Terán-Bustamante (2022)

Model Evaluation: Sensitivity Analysis

Once the BN for the focus of the study was designed, a SA was conducted. It is a technique that allows the validation of different parameters of a BN as it researches the changes in subsequent probabilities (Chan, 2009). In the validation framework of BN, the SA plays a significant role in studying the outcomes of a model with the variation of conditional probability parameters (Rohmer & Gehl, 2020).

A mathematical function is a relationship between a calculated probability based on a BN and the network parameters. Any prior probability can be expressed as a multilinear function on the network parameters. Consequently, any subsequent probability is a coefficient of these functions. These allow us to give a clear idea of the robustness of a BN. For this, it is necessary to establish the coefficients of the functions. In general, the validation of the relationship between a calculated network-based probability and the network parameter is called sensitivity analysis (Coupe et al., 2000).

The sensitivity function expresses the probability of interest in the parameter under study. In the sequel, we denote the probability of interest by $Pr(a|e)$, where a is a specific value of the variable A of interest and e denotes the available evidence. The network's parameters are denoted by $x = P(b_i|\pi)$, where b_i is a value of a variable B and π is a combination of values for the parents of B. We denote the sensitivity by $f(x)$. It expresses the probability $Pr(a|b)$ in terms of the parameter x. If a parameter $x = p(b_i|\pi)$ is varied in a BN, the other parameters $p(b_j|\pi), j \neq i$, specified for node B must covary. Each parameter can be seen as a function $g_j(x)$ of the parameter x. The parameters $p(b_j|\pi)$ covariance keeps the proportional relationship constant. So, this parameter is as follows:

$$g_j(x) = \begin{cases} x & \text{if} j = i \\ p(b_j|p).\frac{1-x}{1-p(b_i|\pi)} & \text{otherwise} \end{cases} \tag{10.4}$$

$$\text{for} p(b_i|\pi) < 1$$

Thus, a sensitivity function $f(x)$ is a measure of two functions that are linear in the parameter x. The function is defined as:

$$f(x) = \frac{a \cdot x + b}{c \cdot x + d} \tag{10.5}$$

where a, b, c are constants, and d is constructed from the valuation for the parameters that are not varied. The sensitivity is determined in this work by applying the algorithm proposed by Kjaerulff and van der Gaag (2000). The most sensitive parameters influence the model results more significantly. In this way, identifying these parameters allows us to focus our efforts on obtaining more precise results in a BN.

Results and Discussion

This research aims to analyze and build a knowledge management model and innovation in the FI of Mexico. As the foundation of knowledge is derived from experts in the area, 30 variables have been selected as relevant in this industry. Following this, the corresponding probabilities have been assigned, which has allowed us to obtain a 95% conditional probability for the innovation management in its optimal state (Fig. 10.3). This has been the first section of the model's evaluation, where it is possible to visualize the existing interactions among the variables that form it. The evaluation is completed with the strength measurement of the arcs among nodes.

In BN, variables are represented through nodes that are joined by arcs. The arcs that join the nodes represent the dependency relationships between variables. The designation of the parent node and child node is relative to the position one node occupies relative to the other. In this way, we can name the variables Competitive and Technological intelligence, Strategic Planning, Human Capital, and Quality and Risk management as the central parent nodes. Thus, the strength of these relationships is defined by the conditional probability values, which specify the level of belief (probability) that the node will be in a particular state, given the states that the central nodes are in. In Table 10.2, the values in the "strength" column indicate the degree of influence that the primary and secondary variables have.

The arcs of greatest strength for the model generated for this research, which includes the main parent nodes, are Human Capital—Core (0.614286), Quality and Risk Management—Suppliers (0.482113), Quality and Risk Management—Distributors (0.466083), Quality and Risk Management—Legal Compliance (0.4), Human Capital—Business Model Structure (0.397157), Quality and Risk Management—Business

Table 10.2 Strongest nodes relationships among the variables

Variable	*Variable*	*Strength*
Training and Development	Core_competences	0.7
Customer Opportunities Needs Ideas	Core_competences	0.614286
Human Capital	**Core_competences**	**0.614286**
Technological Planning	Core_competences	0.614286
Quality and Risk Management	**Suppliers**	**0.482113**
National and international markets	Knowledge Management	0.474377
Value system model	Knowledge Management	0.474377
Quality and Risk Management	**Distributors**	**0.466083**
Value system model	Innovation Management	0.465009
Organizational Architecture	Core_competences	0.414286
Quality and Risk Management	**Legal compliance**	**0.4**
Customer Opportunities Needs Ideas	Bussiness_Model_Structure	0.397157
Human Capital	**Bussiness_Model_Structure**	**0.397157**
Organizational Architecture	Bussiness_Model_Structure	0.397157
Quality and Risk Management	**Bussiness_Model_Structure**	**0.397157**
Strategic Planning	**Bussiness_Model_Structure**	**0.397157**
Technological Planning	Bussiness_Model_Structure	0.397157
Value system model	Product Life Cycle	0.39
Knowledge Management	Innovation Management	0.278134
MKT	Innovation Management	0.278134
Quality and Risk Management	**Value system model**	**0.217945**
Value system model	National and international markets	0.190788
Training and Development	Bussiness_Model_Structure	0.185203

Model Structure (0.397157), Strategic Planning—Business Model Structure (0.397157), and Quality Risk management—Value System Model (0.397157).

The most relevant variables are the core competencies, impacting in the first place Training and Development, Customer Opportunities Needs Ideas, Technological Planning, and Human Capital. Second, by Quality and Risk Management and Suppliers. Then, innovation is the product of an organizational learning process in which internal and external factors intervene. This learning cannot be done if it is not with the worker's involvement, which will impact both individual and organizational core competencies. It would be ideal to simultaneously consider all the variables highlighted in the decision-making knowledge and innovation management model. However, starting with the most relevant variables would allow companies that decide to adopt them to have better results.

Sensitivity Analysis

As part of the model evaluation, a sensitivity analysis (SA) was performed to verify the importance of the probability changes of the parent nodes toward posterior probabilities. The sensibility analysis is done by researching the effect of small changes in the parent nodes' probabilities on the posterior nodes' probabilities. The results are presented through a graph in shades of red. The nodes colored with a more intense red have parameters that are important to calculate the distribution of posterior probabilities in those nodes that are marked as targets. The greater the intensity of the red color of the nodes, the less influence the child nodes have on them. Light pink nodes do not have any parameters that are used to calculate the posterior probability distribution of the target variables.

Therefore, the nodes in a more intense red are the variables that should be considered to obtain the best results in the modeling process through a BN. These are Competitive and Technological Intelligence, Strategic Planning, Human Capital, Quality and Risk Management, Organizational Architecture, Technology Planning, Training and Development, Legal Compliance, Value System Model, E-commerce, Suppliers, Knowledge, and Ancient Wisdom (Fig. 10.4).

In summary, the SA presents the variables that if small changes occur, it will have repercussions on other variables. The strength of the arches expresses the dependence between the variables it unites. Thus, the result presented by each of them validates the other. In Table 10.2, the arcs with the highest strength join the variables with the highest sensitivity (Fig. 10.4).

Discussion

The analysis of the furniture sector can be separated into two groups of sources. The first group includes bulletins, sectoral files, or brief periodical publications generated by business chambers, government units (IIEG, 2018), or some companies or research centers that concentrate and publish data and information. These secondary sources rely on associated jobs, exports, consumption trends by type of furniture, materials, and inputs, technologies in the sector, sales strategies, and leading manufacturers, among others. Unfortunately, these data are often not sequenced and do not follow an explicit methodology that allows them to be

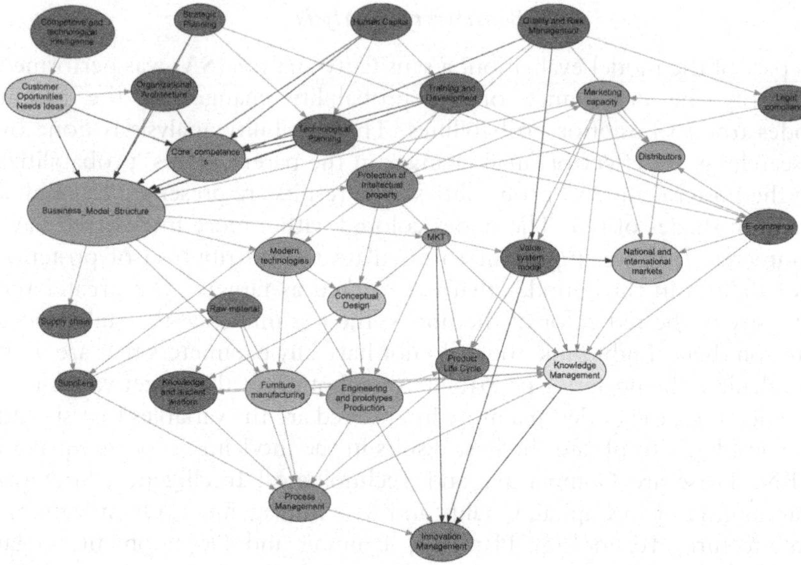

Fig. 10.4 Sensitivity analysis for management of innovation and knowledge model

subjected to a consistent analysis. At the international level, and in Jalisco's case respectively, we can point out the Ficha ICEX (2020) and the Boletín del Observatorio Tecnológico (2022) of the Universidad de Guadalajara, which publishes data and information on the current situation and trends in the sector. Given its nature, companies' absence of global information management systems stands out as a sector's weakness. As a result, there is little interest in identifying, concentrating, generating, and using knowledge as a significant asset for the competitiveness of companies and the sector as a whole.

The second group of sources in academic papers, a review of publications in SCOPUS and WoC, shows that international academic production in the FI is scarce. Only 32 publications are registered, which began to be registered in 2005. Moreover, their most extraordinary production has been from 2020 onward: 6 for that year, 6 in 2021, and 5 so far in 2022. The most cited authors are Abidin, Dyba, Alyazidi, Mattozzi, Lopez, Sopinska, and Glinska-Newes. In thematic areas, the texts mainly address environmental management initiatives, knowledge sharing for decision-making, knowledge management for design innovation, management of production processes, collaborative networks to improve innovation capacity, and knowledge as an added value for furniture production. Two articles refer to intelligent technologies and expert systems for knowledge management; another addresses the low technification of the furniture sector. None refer to Mexico, and only two address the Latin American context, with Brazil and Chile as prime examples.

The texts on knowledge focus on proposing knowledge management systems through expert system technologies for furniture manufacturers, distributors, and consumers (Alyazidi et al., 2020). As well as on commonly available knowledge sources (Internet, professional press, magazines), highlighting that they are more valuable than external sources related to "cluster advantages." Mainly, the most valuable and efficient innovation capacity in the sector is the creativity and ideas of workers, as well as participation in fairs or events (Dyba, 2018). Meanwhile, Sopinska and Glinska-Newes (2021) address knowledge sharing in decision-making and market participation processes by furniture companies in Poland. Finally, the article by López et al. (2020) refers to the current state of Chilean furniture design firms, concluding that, despite government support, the absence of knowledge management skills and production capabilities to reach international markets remains the main export constraints.

Talking about Mexico in particular, research is often outside of high impact databases; the type of study undertaken is usually qualitative with an exploratory or descriptive approach. It is generally focused on a local or regional context with data obtained through surveys, interviews, or direct observation in the field. Such works primarily seek to explain the number of workers, the size of the companies, the type of inputs used, the type and variety of furniture produced and marketed, the machinery used, and the profile of their buyers, among other dimensions that account for the structure of the FI (López & Montes, 2002; Quintero & Martínez, 2012; Venegas & Castañeda, 2013). The cases that assume a broader perspective emphasize such indicators from an aggregated perspective (Espinosa, 2012) or at regional or cluster levels. These also include some strategies for successful business practice in international markets (Lozano, 2016), or specific dimensions of the environment, such as participation in fairs or calls for proposals by government agencies or educational institutions (Gerónimo & Calderón, 2020). In addition to geo-concentration and technological and productive differences, furniture companies in

Mexico are asymmetric in terms of the knowledge they possess, and how they transfer it among their members. While large companies base their competitiveness on technological innovations and industrial production oriented mainly to the international market (Lozano, 2016; Quintero & Martínez, 2012; Venegas & Castañeda, 2013), the vast majority of micro and small companies continue to work wood, iron, textiles, and various components based on traditional knowledge. This knowledge is learned and transferred intergenerational through practice (De la Torre, 2017). These practices give meaning to the so-called trades. Therefore, they are not just a traditional economic activity that goes beyond specialized manual work since they are based on the skills, commitments, judgments, and values of those who practice those (Ayala & Castillo, 2014). Thus, the activities of micro and small furniture companies and the very lives of their members are embedded in the localities. These enterprises are essential for family subsistence and remain in the market thanks to the experience and "affection for this activity" from those who labor in it (Quintero & Martínez, 2012).

Conclusions

This work contributes to the literature by delving into the conditions that lead to decision-making for business innovation in the furniture sector in Mexico, with knowledge management at the center, and by applying Bayesian theory as a methodology. This is a perspective little explored even in other types of industries. We find that this approach has a strong explanatory value of decision-making for innovation based on organizational knowledge.

The results highlight that public and private sector policies and programs linked to the furniture sector in Mexico should not only favor physical assets, labor qualification, acquisition of inputs, furniture design, modification of production processes, and marketing innovation (Espinosa, 2012; López & Montes, 2002; Technological Observatory, 2022), but also the implementation of global information systems (Technological Observatory, 2022) and, above all, favor the creation of organizational capabilities that allow innovation and added value to their products based on both the knowledge possessed by their members and the knowledge that remains in them once they leave their work activities. In a complex and changing context, the effective management of knowledge is the most valuable resource for the competitiveness of the national FI. Therefore, a focal objective of public policy should be to increase the incentives to enhance this knowledge and reduce the asymmetries between the most productive companies in the economy and the rest. As Stiglitz and Greenwald (2016) point out, what separates developed and less prosperous societies are not their resource differential but their knowledge gap.

Knowledge and innovation depend on the context in which they are developed and imply an understanding of all the processes, interrelationships, and behaviors of people. Therefore, knowledge management for innovation is about getting the proper knowledge to the right person at the right time. It implies a strong link between all the internal and external actors of the company. It also requires understanding where and how knowledge exists to create processes that allow it to be properly managed, identified, and exploited to generate value that brings innovations and competitive advantages to the company (Terán-Bustamante et al., 2021a).

This work contributes to a model that allows for better knowledge and innovation management and for better decisions that grant competitive advantages. Currently, innovation and knowledge management are essential factors for the success and continuity of companies. Knowledge is a crucial factor for innovation and a necessary resource for gaining a sustainable competitive advantage. Specifically, it is reflected in more efficient organizational, operational, and commercial processes and quality improvement, as well as in the ability of companies to recognize creative and innovative solutions to meet their customer's needs. However, few organizations have a well-defined process for managing it on an ongoing basis. Instead, most companies have a formal methodology for product innovation and systematically work to reinvent their business processes for speed and efficiency.

Innovation and knowledge management change how people work and what they do and focus on linking, collaborating, and being more competitive (Chen & Fong, 2015; Hamel, 2006; Terán-Bustamante et al., 2021a). The furniture sector is no exception, and there are few companies where adequate knowledge and innovation management predominate—especially since most are small and medium-sized. According to Carrillo and Vázquez (2019), innovation in this sector should be focused on the market's new needs, which demand ecological and environmentally friendly, multifunctional, self-assembly products, and personalized design, among others.

BN provides a logical and flexible environment that applies to various problems. For example, uncertainty in the data can be addressed through expert judgment and vice versa. BNs can be built entirely from expert knowledge and experience or learning from data; applications are more meaningful and valuable when both expert judgment and data are incorporated. Based on the analysis of the patterns generated through the BN, the strength of the arcs that join two nodes indicates that they have a high dependence on each other. The evaluation of the behavior of the variables through SA suggests that a slight change in one of the nodes implies essential changes in the nodes with high sensitivity. In this way, the values obtained for the strength metric and the results of the SA coincide in pointing out that the variables, Human Capital, Basic skills, Technological Planning, Quality and Risk Management, Strategic Planning, Suppliers, Distributors, Legal Compliance, Training and Development, Structure of the Business Model, have a high degree of dependency. Therefore, based on these evaluations, it is essential to ensure that these variables are developed together to achieve the best results in the target variable of this study, knowledge, and innovation management.

It is worth mentioning that the strongest correlations are found in human capital and attention to both national and international markets. The data analysis through the correlation between the variables supports the importance of human capital in managing knowledge and innovation. An aspect related to human capital is the tacit artisanal knowledge that has passed from generation to generation, which occurs in small and medium-sized companies, in contrast to modern technologies where the use of robots and eco-innovation has been adopted by large and medium businesses.

Future work is recommended to collect more data to extend the predictions according to the model generated in this research. Thus, timely interventions will be proposed to improve the performance of companies in terms of innovation management. New studies should delve into the qualitative analysis of the decision-making process and the understanding of why and how companies in the FI implemented their strategies to remain competitive in the face of disruptions in the context of the global market. In addition, the number of companies under study and the participation of other actors, such as consumers and decision-makers of public policies that directly affect the development of this industry, should be expanded.

Without undermining the study of the restructuring of the sector due to bankruptcy or disappearance of the most vulnerable furniture producers in the face of the impact of the COVID-19 pandemic, it should be kept in mind that any public policy and even decision-making affecting the sector require a follow-up study on the scope of the effects and adjustments in the FI in a post-pandemic period. Furthermore, understanding the effects and strategies deployed by the various actors in the face of this type of global disruption will always be an opportunity to integrate, replicate, and share knowledge continuously. Therefore, quickly develop new forms of configuration in rapidly changing contexts.

References

AFAMJAL. (2021). *Retos y oportunidades para el sector del mueble. Análisis sectorial de la industria del mueble* [Challenges and opportunities in the furniture sector]. https://afamjal.com.mx/2021/06/25/retos-y-oportunidades-para-el-sector-del-mueble/

Alyazidi, H. Y., Syaifudin, Santoso, G. B., Murwonugroho, W. (2020). The knowledge management system of furniture production and distribution. *International Journal of Scientific and Technology Research*, *9*(3), 1379–1384.

Arum Journal. (2021, September 7). *¿Cómo funciona la industria del mueble en México?* [How does the furniture industry work in Mexico?]. https://arumjournal.com/como-funciona-la-industria-del-mueble-en-mexico/

Ayala, S., & Castillo, V. (2014). La gestión del conocimiento como factor para el desarrollo de los oficios tradicionales. *Cultura, Tecnología y Patrimonio*, *9*(17), 49–62.

Carrillo, G., & Vázquez, A. (2019). Tendencias y oportunidades para el sector mueblero en México en el campo de la innovación y la sustentabilidad. In H. Estrada (Coord.), *Tendencias de mercado, innovación y aprovechamiento de residuos sólidos del sector muebles en países de Iberoamérica*. Memorias del segundo encuentro de investigadores de la red a RITMMA. ISSN: 2665-606X.

Casado, L. (2021). *Mobiliario en México* [Furnishings in Mexico]. ICEX España Exportación e Inversiones. https://www.icex.es/icex/es/navegacion-principal/todos-nuestros-servicios/informacion-de-mercados/paises/navegacion-principal/el-mercado/estudios-informes/ficha-sector-mobiliario-mexico-2021-doc2021887748.html?idPais=MX

Chan, H. (2009). Of Bayesian networks and its application for service engineering. *2009 International Conference of Soft Computing and Pattern Recognition*, 551–556. https://doi.org/10.1109/SoCPaR.2009.110

Chen, L., & Fong, P. S. (2015). Evaluation of knowledge management performance: An organic approach. *Information & Management, 52*(4), 431–453. https://doi.org/10.1016/j.im.2015.01.005

Chen, S. H., & Pollino, C. A. (2012). Good practice in Bayesian network modeling. *Environmental Modelling and Software, 37*, 134–145. https://doi.org/10.1016/j.envsoft.2012.03.012

CIMEJAL. (2021a, octubre 8). *¿Cómo ha sido la evolución de la industria del mueble?* [How has been the evolution of the furniture industry?]. http://cimejal.com.mx/blog/mexico-lider-en-industria-mueblera/

CIMEJAL. (2021b, diciembre 17). *México un líder en la industria mueblera de América Latina* [Mexico, a leader in the furniture industry in Latin America]. http://cimejal.com.mx/blog/mexico-lider-en-industria-mueblera/

Conner, K., & Prahalad, C. (1996). A resource-based theory of the firm: Knowledge versus opportunism. *Organization Science, 7*(5), 477–501.

Coupe, V. M. H., Jensen, F. v., Kjaerulff, U., & Van der Gaag, L. (2000). *A computational architecture for N-way sensitivity analysis of Bayesian networks.* Retrieved March 23, 2022, from http://citeseerx.ist.psu.edu/viewdoc/summary?doi=10.1.1.34.1434

De la Torre, R. (2017, October 24). Seis claves y una paradoja para entender la industria del mueble en México [Six key aspects and a paradox to understand Mexico's furniture industry]. *Más Madera.* http://masmadera.net/industria-del-mueble-en-mexico/

Dutraive, V. (2008). Économie fondée sur la connaissance et théories récentes de la firme: une lectura Veblenienne [Knowledge-based economy and recent theories of the firm: A Vleblenian reading]. *Revue D'économie Industrielle, 124*, 51–70.

Dyba, W. (2018). Nature and effects of knowledge sourcing in a competing environment. *Proceedings of the European Conference on Knowledge Management, ECKM, 1*, 190–197.

Ebert-Uphoff, I. (2007). *Measuring connections strengths and link strengths in discrete Bayesian Networks* (Georgia Tech Research Report: GT-IIC-07-01). http://www.dataonstage.com/PAPERS/GIT-IIC-07-01.pdf

Economic Commission for Latin America and the Caribbean. (2021). *Building a better future: Actions to strengthen the 2030 Agenda for sustainable development*. CEPAL.

Espinosa, L. (2012). La industria y el comercio del mueble en México. *Revista internacional de investigación en mobiliario y objetos decorativos, 1*(1), 73–87.

Genc, A., & Merdan, R. (2021). Investigating the effect of Covid-19 pandemic process on furniture usage frequency and consumer preferences. *Res Mobilis, 10*(12), 109–126.

Gerónimo, E., & Calderón, R. (2020). La formación de talento humano a través de la vinculación y los modelos de hélice basados en la sociedad del conocimiento. *Revista Iberoamericana para la Investigación y el Desarrollo Educativo, 10*(20). http://ride.org.mx/index.php/RIDE/article/view/641

González, A., & Pérez, M. (2021). Family business resilience under the COVID-19: A comparative study in the furniture industry in the United States of America and Colombia. *Estudios Gerenciales, 37*(158), 138–152.

Grant, R. (1996a). Toward a knowledge-based theory of the firm. *Strategic Management Journal, 17*, 109–122.

Grant, R. (1996b). Prospering in dynamically competitive environments: Organizational capability as knowledge integration. *Organization Science, 7*(4), 375–387.

Graziele, D., & de Moura, G. L. (2016). Organizational performance evaluation in intangible criteria: a model based on knowledge management and innovation management. *RAI,Revista de Administração e Inovação, 13*(3), 211–222. https://doi.org/10.1016/j.rai.2016.06.005

Hamel, G. (2006). The why, what, and how of management innovation. *Harvard Business Review, 84*(2), 72.

Hualde, A. (2005). La educación y la economía el conocimiento: una articulación problemática [Education and knowledge economy: A problematic articulation]. *Revista de la Educación Superior, 4*(136), 107–127.

ICEX. (2020). *Mobiliario en México.* Ministerio de Industria Comercio y Turismo del Gobierno de España.

IIEG. (2018). *Industria mueblera, ficha sectorial.* Gobierno de Jalisco.

Kjaerulff, U., & van der Gaag, L. (2000). Making sensitivity analysis computationally efficient. *Uncertainty in Artificial Intelligence Proceedings*, 317.

Kogut, B., & Zander, U. (1992). Knowledge of the firm, combinative capabilities, and the replication of technology. *Organization Science, 3*(3), 383–397.

Kyrimi, E., McLachlan, S., Dube, K., Neves, M. R., Fahmi, A., & Fenton, N. (2021, May). A comprehensive scoping review of Bayesian networks in healthcare: Past, present, and future. *Artificial Intelligence in Medicine, 117*, 102108. https://doi.org/10.1016/j.artmed.2021.102108

López, D., Cáceres, J., Munõz, F., & Núñez, A. (2020). Internationalization of creative industries: Chilean design. *International Journal of Design in Society, 14*(1), 1–22.

López, G., & Montes, A. (2002, de mayo 24–26). *Estrategias del sector mueblero de Jalisco ante la apertura comercial: investigación, desarrollo, innovación y nuevas formas de comercialización* [Sesión de conferencia]. VI Congreso Nacional y 1er. Internacional de Investigaciones en Ciencias Administrativas, Ciudad de México.

Lozano, K. (2007). Los sistemas productivos locales y la importancia de la innovación en la construcción del territorio: El caso de la industria mueblera en Jalisco, México [Local productive sistems and the importance of innovation in the construction of land: Mexico's furniture case]. *Economía Informa, 345*, 177–201.

Lozano, K. (2010). *Desarrollo local a partir de los sistemas productivos locales: el caso de la industria mueblera en Jalisco* (Tesis de doctorado, UNAM) [Local development through local productive systems: The furniture industry case in Jalisco]. Mexico. http://132.248.9.195/ptb2011/febrero/0666755/0666755_A1.pdf

Lozano, K. (2016, de noviembre 15–18). *Inserción de las empresas globales en las dinámicas productivas locales: identificación y análisis de las estrategias de la cadena de valor de madera-muebles en México* [Sesión de conferencia]. 21° Encuentro Nacional sobre Desarrollo Regional en México. Mérida, México.

Martínez-Velasco, A., & Terán-Bustamante, A. (2022). Business model innovation and decision-making for the productive sector in times of crisis. In A. M. López-Fernández & A. Terán-Bustamante (Eds.), *Business recovery in emerging markets.* Palgrave Studies in Democracy, Innovation, and Entrepreneurship for Growth. Palgrave Macmillan. https://doi.org/10.1007/978-3-030-91532-2_8

Nonaka, I., & Konno, N. (1998). The concept of "Ba": Building a foundation for knowledge creation. *California Management Review, 40*(3), 40–54.

Nonaka, I., & Takeuchi, H. (1995). *The knowledge-creating company.* Oxford University Press Inc.

Nonaka, I., Toyama, R., & Konno, N. (2000). SECI, BA, and leadership: A unified model of dynamic knowledge creation. *Long Range Planning, 33*(1), 5–34.

Observatorio Tecnológico. (2022). *¿Cómo detectar nuevas oportunidades en el sector de muebles?* Universidad de Guadalajara, Cámara de la Industria Mueblera de Jalisco y Asociación de Fabricante de Muebles de Jalisco.

Ogazón, A. (2019). El gran potencial de la industria mueblera en México. *MEM INDUSTRIAL.* https://www.hfmexico.mx/MEMIndustrial/2019/12/el-gran-potencial-de-la-industria-mueblera-en-mexico/

Ogunsanya, O. V. (2012). *Decision support using Bayesian networks for clinical decision making* (Issue February).

Pearl, J., & Russell, S. (2011). *Bayesian networks* (UCLA Department of Statistics Papers). https://escholarship.org/uc/item/53n4f34m

Pirc, A., Kitec, M., Vergot, T., & Grošelj, P. (2021). Monitoring consumer purchasing behavior for wood furniture before and during the COVID-19 pandemic. *Forests, 12*(873), 1–17.

Prévot, F., Brulhart, F., Guieu, G., & Maltese, L. (2010). Perspectives fondées sur les ressources. Proposition de synthèse. *Revue française de gestion, 5*(204), 87–103.

Quintero, L., & Martínez, D. (2012, de julio 11–13). *Experiencias de vinculación Universidad-Industria: desarrollo del cluster mueblero de Jalisco* [Sesión de conferencia]. XVI Congreso Internacional de Ingeniería de Proyectos. Valencia, España.

Ratnasingam, J., Khoo, A., Jegathesan, N., Chee, L., Ab, H., Thanasegaran, G., Choon, L., Yan, L., Othman, K., & Afthar, M. (2020). How are small and medium enterprises in Malaysia's furniture industry coping with COVID-19 pandemic? Early evidences from a survey and recommendations for policymakers. *BioResources, 15*(3), 5951–5964.

Rohmer, J., & Gehl, P. (2020). Sensitivity analysis of Bayesian networks to parameters of the conditional probability model using a Beta regression approach. *Expert Systems with Applications, 145*, 113130. https://doi.org/10.1016/j.eswa.2019.113130

Sevinc, V., Kucuk, O., & Goltas, M. (2020). A Bayesian network model for prediction and analysis of possible forest fire causes. *Forest Ecology and Management, 457*, 117723. https://doi.org/10.1016/j.foreco.2019.117723

Smith, C. S., Howes, A. L., Price, B., & McAlpine, C. A. (2007). Using a Bayesian belief network to predict the suitable habitat of an endangered mammal—The Julia Creek dunnart (Sminthopsis douglasi). *Biological Conservation, 139*(3–4), 333–347.

Solleiro, J., & Terán-Bustamante, A. (2012). *Buenas prácticas de gestión de la innovación en centros de investigación tecnológica* [Best management practices of innovation in technological research centres]. Universidad Autónoma de México e Instituto de Investigaciones Eléctricas.

Sopinska, A., & Glinska-Newes, A. (2021). Knowledge sharing in teams making strategic decisions in companies—The results of research carried out in the furniture industry in Poland. *Problemy Zarzadzania-Management Issues, 19*(2), 24–48. https://doi.org/10.7172/1644-9584.92.2

Stiglitz, J., & Greenwald, B. (2016). *La creación de una sociedad del aprendizaje* [Creation of a learning society]. España, La esfera de los libros.

Terán-Bustamante, A., Davila, G., & Castañon, R. (2019). Management of technology and innovation: A Bayesian network model. *Económia, Teória y Práctica, 50*, 63–100. https://doi.org/10.24275/ETYPUAM/NE/502019/Teran

Terán-Bustamante, A., Martínez-Velasco, A., & Dávila-Aragón, G. (2021a). Knowledge management for open innovation: Bayesian networks through machine learning. *Journal of Open Innovation: Technology, Market, and Complexity, 7*, 40. https://doi.org/10.3390/joitmc7010040

Terán-Bustamante, A., Martínez-Velasco, A., & López-Fernández, A. (2021b). University-industry collaboration: A sustainable technology transfer model. *Administrative Sciences, 11*, 142. https://doi.org/10.3390/admsci11040142

Venegas, M., & Castañeda, P. (2013). *Transformaciones urbanas. Los efectos de la industria en la ciudad de Ocotlán, Jalisco. 1994–2004* [Sesión de conferencia]. 180 Encuentro Nacional sobre Desarrollo Regional en México. Hidalgo, México.

Index

E. Murillo et al. (eds.), *Creating Economic Stability Amid Global Uncertainty*, https://doi.org/10.1007/978-3-031-41386-5

SPRINGER NATURE

GPSR Compliance

The European Union's (EU) General Product Safety Regulation (GPSR) is a set of rules that requires consumer products to be safe and our obligations to ensure this.

If you have any concerns about our products, you can contact us on ProductSafety@springernature.com

In case Publisher is established outside the EU, the EU authorized representative is:

Springer Nature Customer Service Center GmbH
Europaplatz 3
69115 Heidelberg, Germany

The manufacturer's authorised representative in the EU is Springer Nature Customer Service Centre GmbH, Europaplatz 3, 69115 Heidelberg, Germany. If you have any concerns regarding our products, please contact ProductSafety@springernature.com

Printed and bound by CPI Group (UK) Ltd, Croydon, CR0 4YY
28/09/2026
02224072-0006